IMAGES
*of America*

# THE DALLAS MUSIC SCENE 1920s–1960s

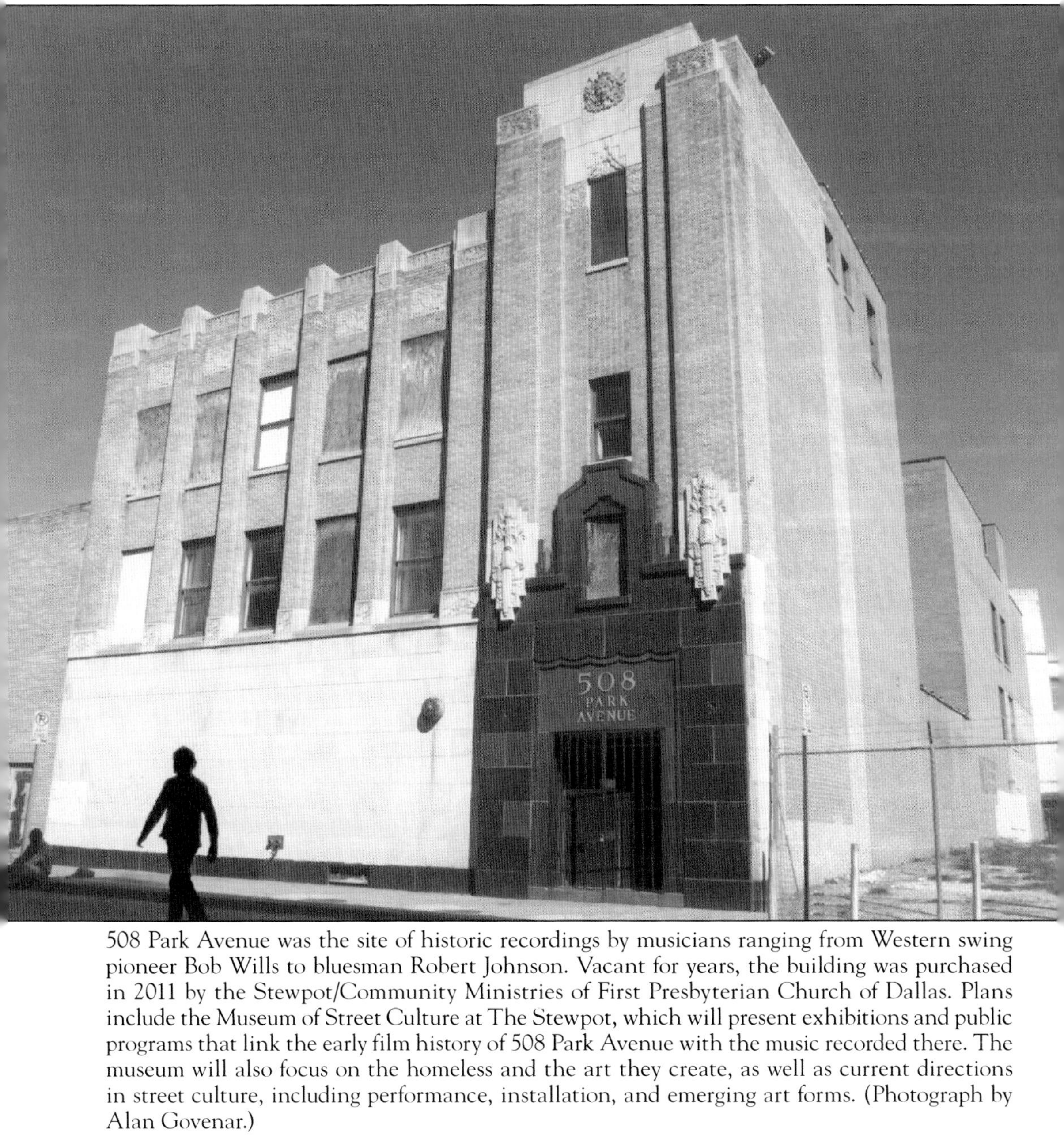


508 Park Avenue was the site of historic recordings by musicians ranging from Western swing pioneer Bob Wills to bluesman Robert Johnson. Vacant for years, the building was purchased in 2011 by the Stewpot/Community Ministries of First Presbyterian Church of Dallas. Plans include the Museum of Street Culture at The Stewpot, which will present exhibitions and public programs that link the early film history of 508 Park Avenue with the music recorded there. The museum will also focus on the homeless and the art they create, as well as current directions in street culture, including performance, installation, and emerging art forms. (Photograph by Alan Govenar.)

**On the Cover:** The Light Crust Doughboys visit Dallas's Fair Park during the 1936 Texas Centennial Exposition. When the popular band traveled to California that year to appear in a Gene Autry Western, the musicians promoted the state's various centennial observances, including one in Fort Worth, where the group was based. (Courtesy of Marvin Montgomery.)

IMAGES
*of America*

# THE DALLAS MUSIC SCENE 1920s–1960s

Alan Govenar and Jay Brakefield

ARCADIA
PUBLISHING

ISBN 978-1-4671-3151-3

Published by Arcadia Publishing
Charleston, South Carolina

Printed in the United States of America

Library of Congress Control Number: 2013955459

For all general information, please contact Arcadia Publishing:
Telephone 843-853-2070
Fax 843-853-0044
E-mail sales@arcadiapublishing.com
For customer service and orders:
Toll-Free 1-888-313-2665

Visit us on the Internet at www.arcadiapublishing.com

# Contents

# Acknowledgments

This book builds on more than three decades of work to document the vast Dallas music scene. The Downtown Dallas Traditional Music Festival, organized by Alan Govenar in 1981, led to the growth of the Dallas Folk Festival, held in different areas of the city in 1983, 1984, 1986, 1988, and 1991, and provided a forum for fieldwork and interviews with countless local musicians.

Over the years, Govenar's and Jay Brakefield's research into Dallas music has been far-reaching and has resulted in the books *Deep Ellum and Central Track: Where the Black and White Worlds of Dallas Converged* and *Deep Ellum: The Other Side of Dallas*. Govenar has authored several other books, including *Everyday Music* and *Texas Blues: The Rise of a Contemporary Sound*. In addition, he has produced through Documentary Arts, the nonprofit organization he founded in 1985, radio series, films, videos, and CDs focused on various areas of Texas music. Brakefield has published numerous articles and coauthored the book-length liner notes for the eight-CD Bear Family box set *Big "D" Jamboree*.

For this book, we have benefited from the assistance of many individuals, including businesspeople and others with ties to Deep Ellum, musicians, librarians, folklorists, and writers. Pat Bywaters, Carol J. Adams, Cary Ginell, Kip Lornell, David Dennard, Kevin Coffey, and Stanley Oberst shared their insights into misunderstood parts of Dallas. Lou Novacheck, Scott D. Wilkinson, and Alex van der Tuuk were very helpful on the subject of Paramount Records. Jason Johnson-Spinos worked with us to prepare the final images for publication.

We are grateful for the support of Documentary Arts, the Texas African American Photography Archive, and the 508 Park Project Committee in bringing this book to fruition. And, of course, we want to acknowledge the love and support of our families, especially our wives, Kaleta Doolin and Shirley Brakefield.

# INTRODUCTION

Dallas's rich history belies stereotypes. Since it was founded in 1841, the city has grappled with its image. It has been celebrated for its cotton, oil, banking, and real estate wealth, reviled as the site of the Kennedy assassination, and mythologized beyond recognition in the *Dallas* television series. But the legacy of Dallas is ultimately more complex than the way it has been represented in the popular media and includes slavery, the Ku Klux Klan, vibrant Jewish, Latino, Asian, and African American communities, a sprawling Arts District, and outstanding contributions to blues, jazz, and Western swing.

In the 1870s, the coming of two railroads created Deep Ellum, where whites and blacks mingled relatively freely despite the looming threat of racism and discrimination. During Deep Ellum's 1920s heyday, it was alive with the sounds of theater orchestras and guitar-playing street singers such as Blind Lemon Jefferson, who influenced countless other musicians and became the first male country blues artist to make commercially successful records. During the 1930s, a makeshift studio at 508 Park Avenue produced more than 800 recordings by artists ranging from Western swing pioneer Bob Wills to Mississippi bluesman Robert Johnson and Mexican *conjunto* performers Lolo Cavazos and José Almeida. From the late 1940s to the mid-1960s, the popular weekly live broadcast *Big "D" Jamboree* featured country artists and rockers such as Elvis Presley, Carl Perkins, and Gene Vincent.

This book focuses on the foundation on which the Dallas Music Scene has been built. Deep Ellum, 508 Park, and the *Big "D" Jamboree* set the stage on which Texas music has flourished. Musicians such as Jimmie and Stevie Ray Vaughan and Doyle Bramhall fused rock and blues in Dallas nightclubs in the 1960s, while blues flourished in black South Dallas. The 1969 Texas International Music Festival, in suburban Lewisville, became known as the Texas Woodstock. Deep Ellum languished, but its 1980s rebirth produced bands such as New Bohemians and the Butthole Surfers. The area continues to wax and wane, and some of the 1980s clubs have been reborn in the 21st century in a city where historic musical forms coexist with new rock and hip-hop.

# One

# Deep Ellum

In the early 1870s, a new business district sprang up at a railroad crossing a mile east of downtown Dallas. The area came to be called Deep Ellum: "Deep" because of its distance from the courthouse square, "Ellum" for the colloquial pronunciation of Elm by rural blacks and Eastern European Jews. Anglo merchants and Jews established businesses along Elm Street, which became the central corridor to downtown. African Americans created a commercial strip along Central Track, the section of the Houston & Texas Central line that stretched north from Elm Street to the black community known as Freedmantown and later as North Dallas. The racial climate in Deep Ellum/Central Track was relatively relaxed, while much of Dallas was rigidly segregated and the city was ruled by the Ku Klux Klan in the 1920s. Blacks bought goods in white-owned stores and hocked them in nearby pawnshops, which served as banks and sold everything from jewelry to clothing.

Black-owned theaters featured vaudeville and showcased the burgeoning African American film industry. The renowned black actor and filmmaker Spencer Williams lived in Dallas for nearly a decade. The best-known blues musician to perform in Deep Ellum was the guitarist and singer Blind Lemon Jefferson, who played on the street and, in March 1925, became one of the first country bluesmen to record. Other musicians included songster Huddie "Lead Belly" Ledbetter, "holy blues" master Blind Willie Johnson, barrelhouse blues pianist Alex Moore, and seminal jazz musician Buster Smith. Deep Ellum was an incubator of blues and jazz that helped to shape the course of American popular music.

The 1930s saw the first of many recordings of "Deep Elm Blues," by the Shelton brothers, and the emergence of hot fiddle bands and Western swing, performed by musicians as varied as the Light Crust Doughboys, Bob Wills, and Roy Newman. Many white musicians were influenced by black music and were eager to cash in on Deep Ellum's notoriety. With the Great Depression, the area went into a long decline. The death of its best-known pawnbroker, Rubin "Honest Joe" Goldstein, in 1972 marked the end of an era.

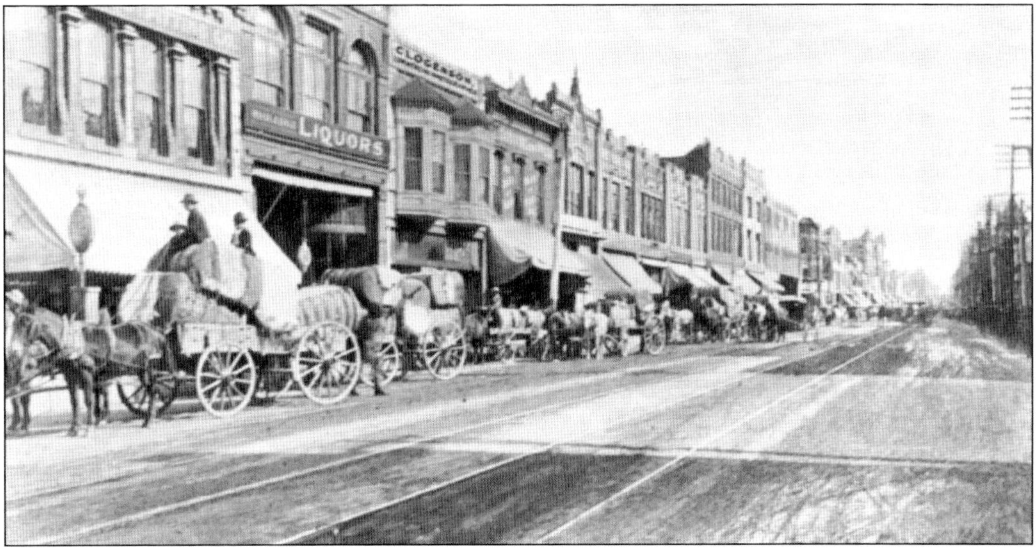


A postcard view looking east from the 1400 block of Elm Street (above), toward Deep Ellum, includes a familiar sight in the late 19th and early 20th centuries: wagons laden with cotton. Dallas at that time was the world's largest inland cotton market. Visible at right in the 1920s postcard view of the 1900 block of Elm (below) is a portion of the sign of the Melba Theatre, part of Dallas's "Theater Row." The Melba was demolished in 1976. The Majestic, a few doors down, is the only remnant of the strip of glittering movie palaces that was once a Dallas landmark.

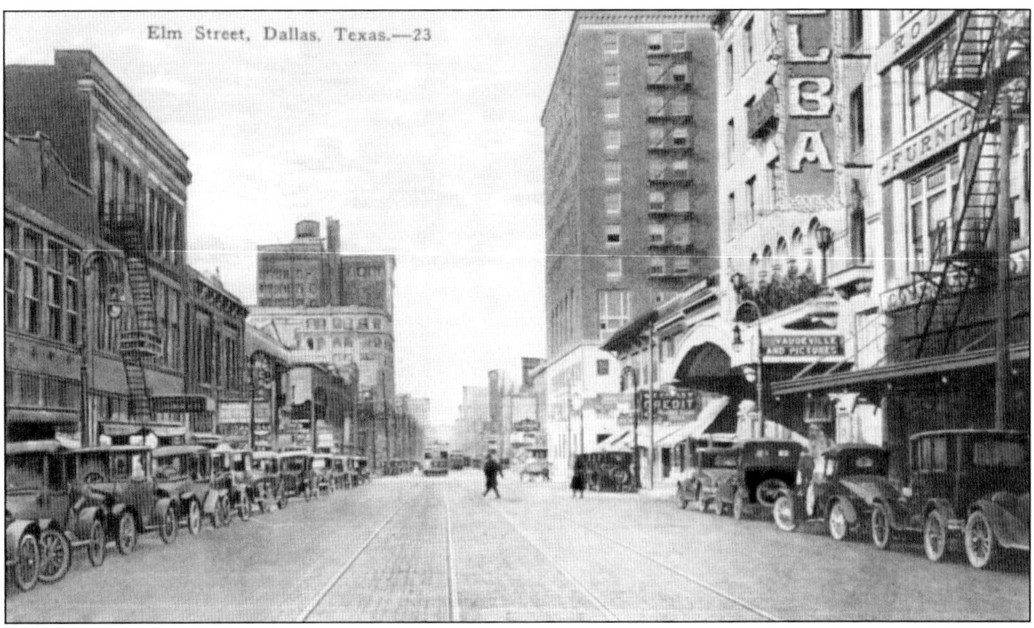

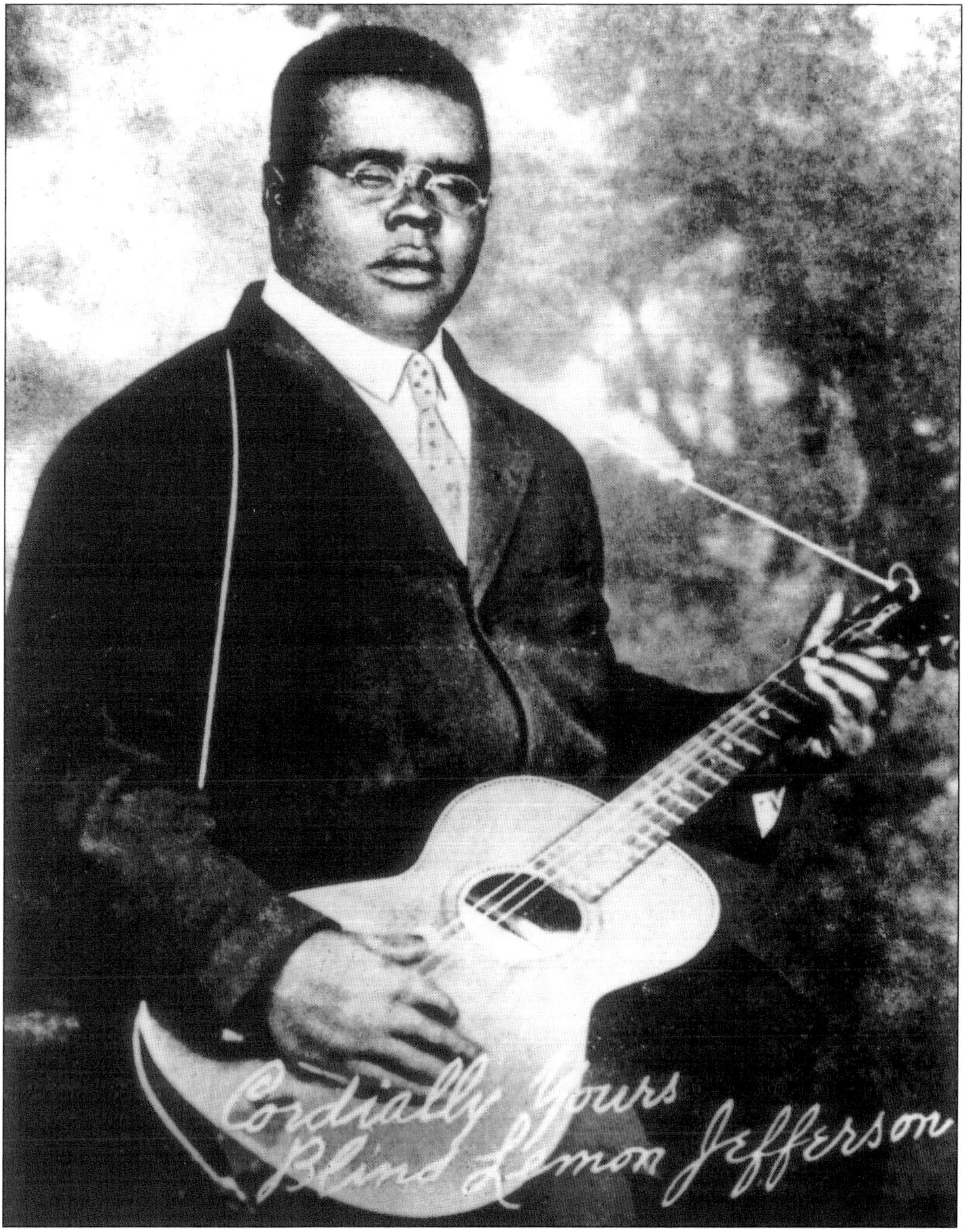


Blind Lemon Jefferson, born in 1893 in the small East Texas farming community of Couchman, became a familiar sight at the corner of Elm Street and Central Track in the 1920s. At the urging of blues pianist Sammy Price, African American record merchant R.T. Ashford got Jefferson a contract with Paramount, a Wisconsin-based record label. Jefferson recorded in Chicago and became the first commercially successful male solo country blues singer in the era of divas such as Bessie Smith and Dallas's Lillian Glinn. This publicity photograph was taken about 1927, two years before Jefferson's mysterious death in Chicago. (Courtesy of Documentary Arts.)

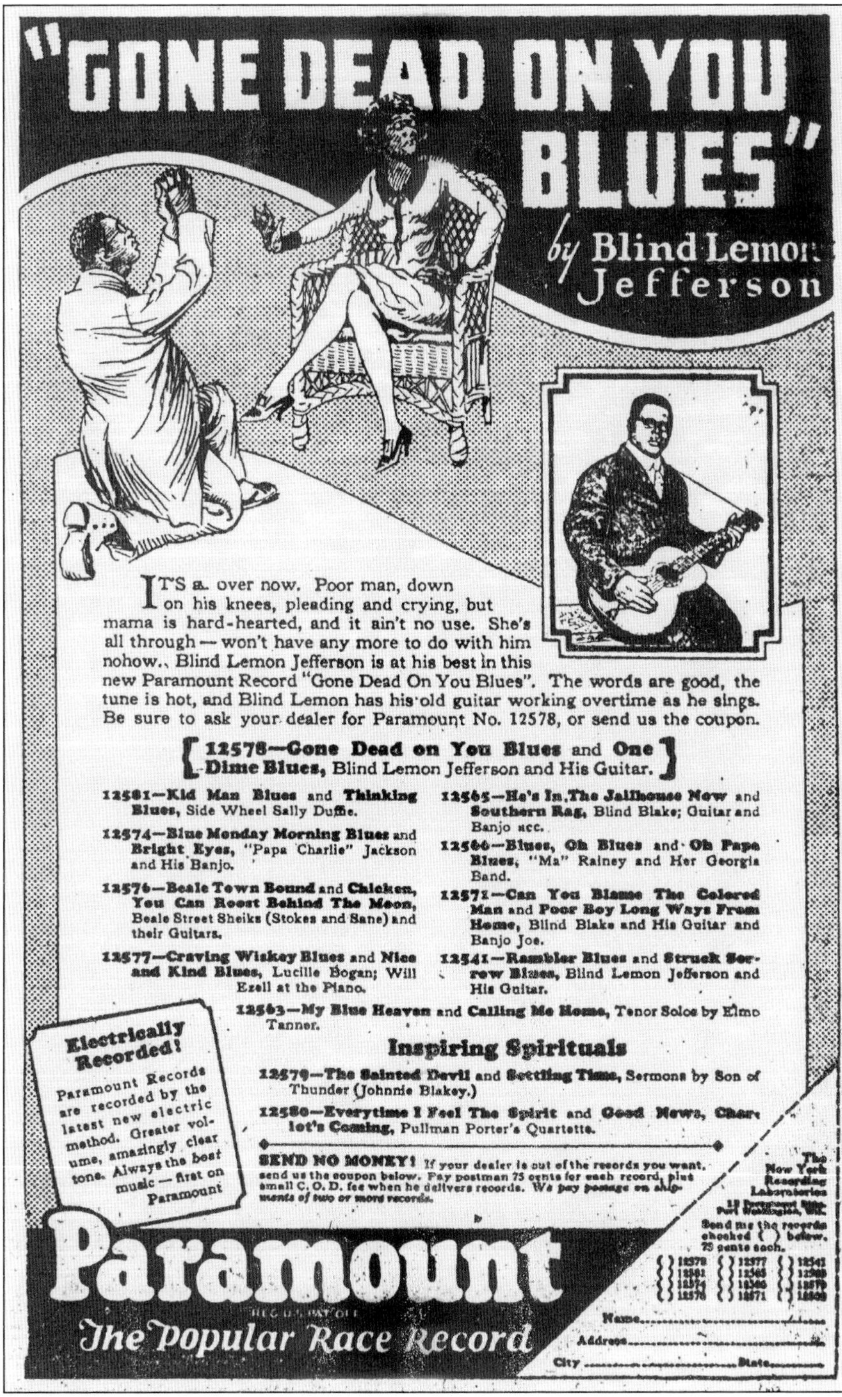


Paramount's race-record advertisements mixed cartoon illustrations with photographs—in this case, the only known one of Blind Lemon Jefferson. The copy aims to emulate African American colloquial speech, using "mama" for the woman in the song and employing double negatives. Paramount did not consult African Americans on the copy, according to Mayo "Ink" Williams, a black man who produced records for the label. (Courtesy of Kip Lornell.)

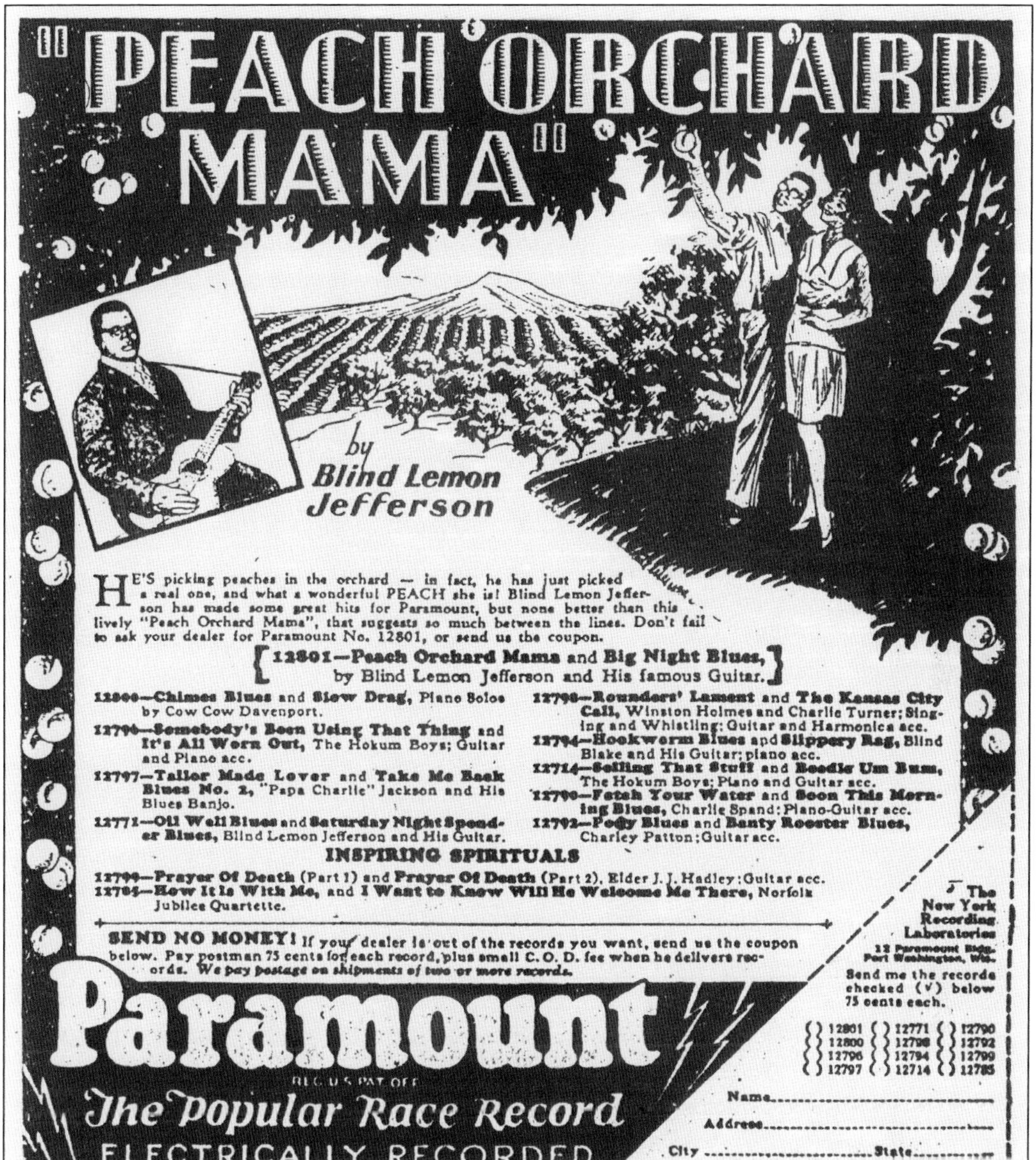


"Peach Orchard Mama," recorded in 1929, employs a familiar food-sex metaphor: "Mama, you swore nobody'd pick your peaches but me / I found three kid-men shaking down your peaches tree." A white listener might not have known that "kid-man" was slang for a surreptitious sex partner, but the song's meaning is clear. Nonetheless, the cartoonist played it straight, leading one to wonder whether he listened to the record. (Courtesy of Kip Lornell.)

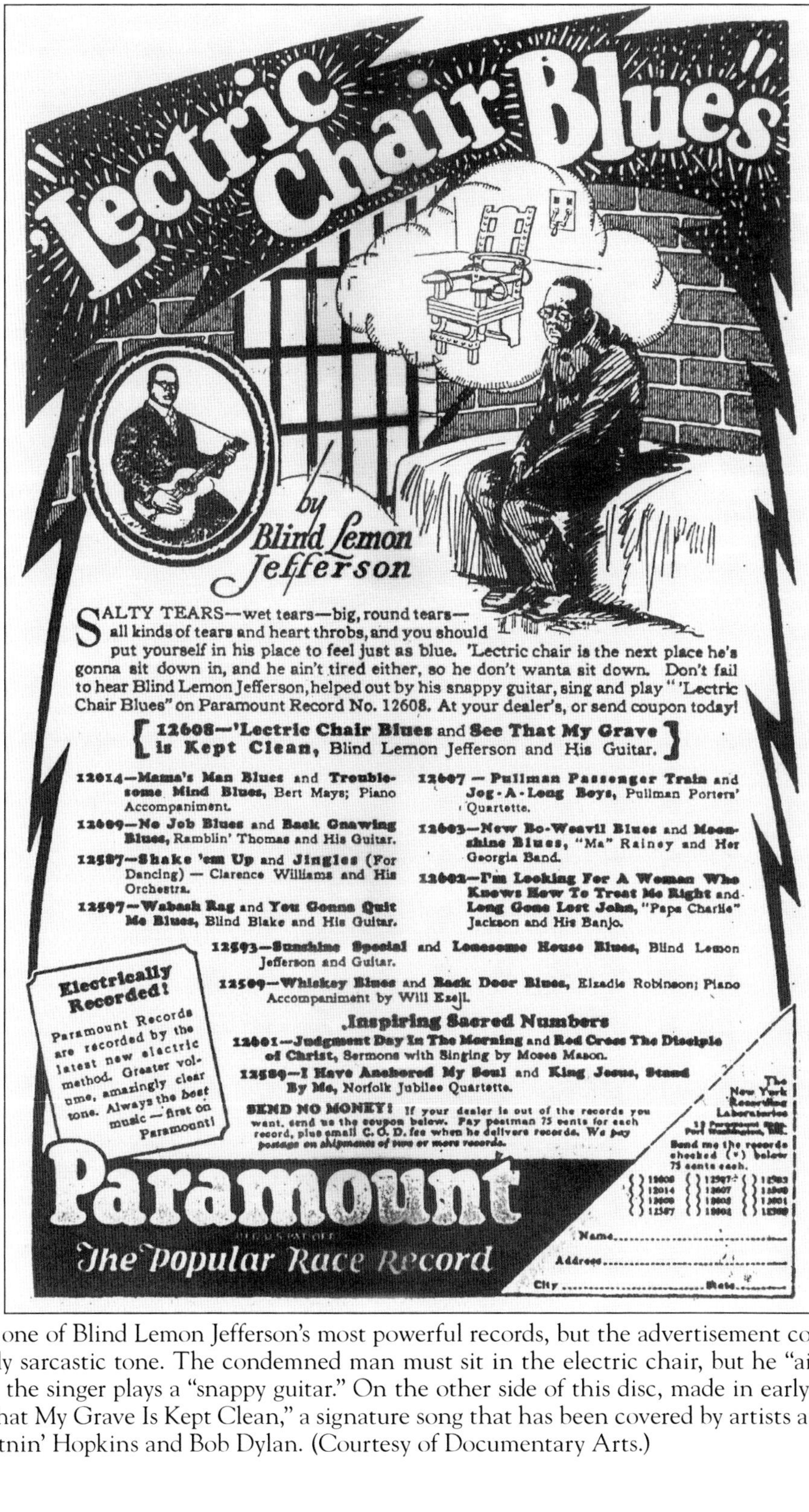


This is one of Blind Lemon Jefferson's most powerful records, but the advertisement copy has a typically sarcastic tone. The condemned man must sit in the electric chair, but he "ain't tired either"; the singer plays a "snappy guitar." On the other side of this disc, made in early 1928, is "See That My Grave Is Kept Clean," a signature song that has been covered by artists as diverse as Lightnin' Hopkins and Bob Dylan. (Courtesy of Documentary Arts.)

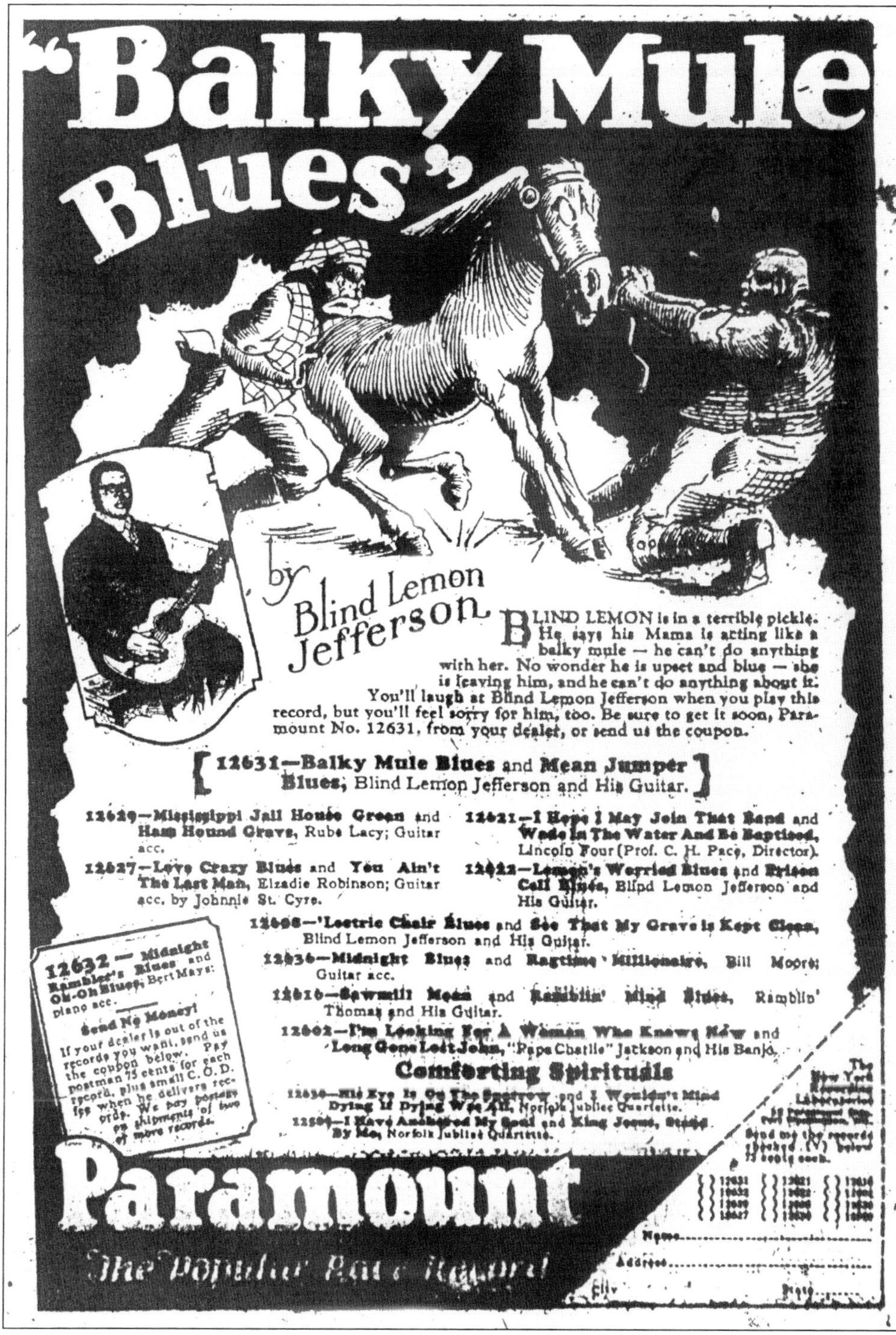


The racism in this 1928 advertisement is overt, with its depiction of the man at left with stereotypically large, white lips. The copy strikes an odd note: "You'll laugh at Blind Lemon Jefferson . . . but you'll feel sorry for him, too." The artwork is literal, though the copy acknowledges that a metaphor is at work: "His Mama is acting like a balky mule." (Courtesy of Kip Lornell.)

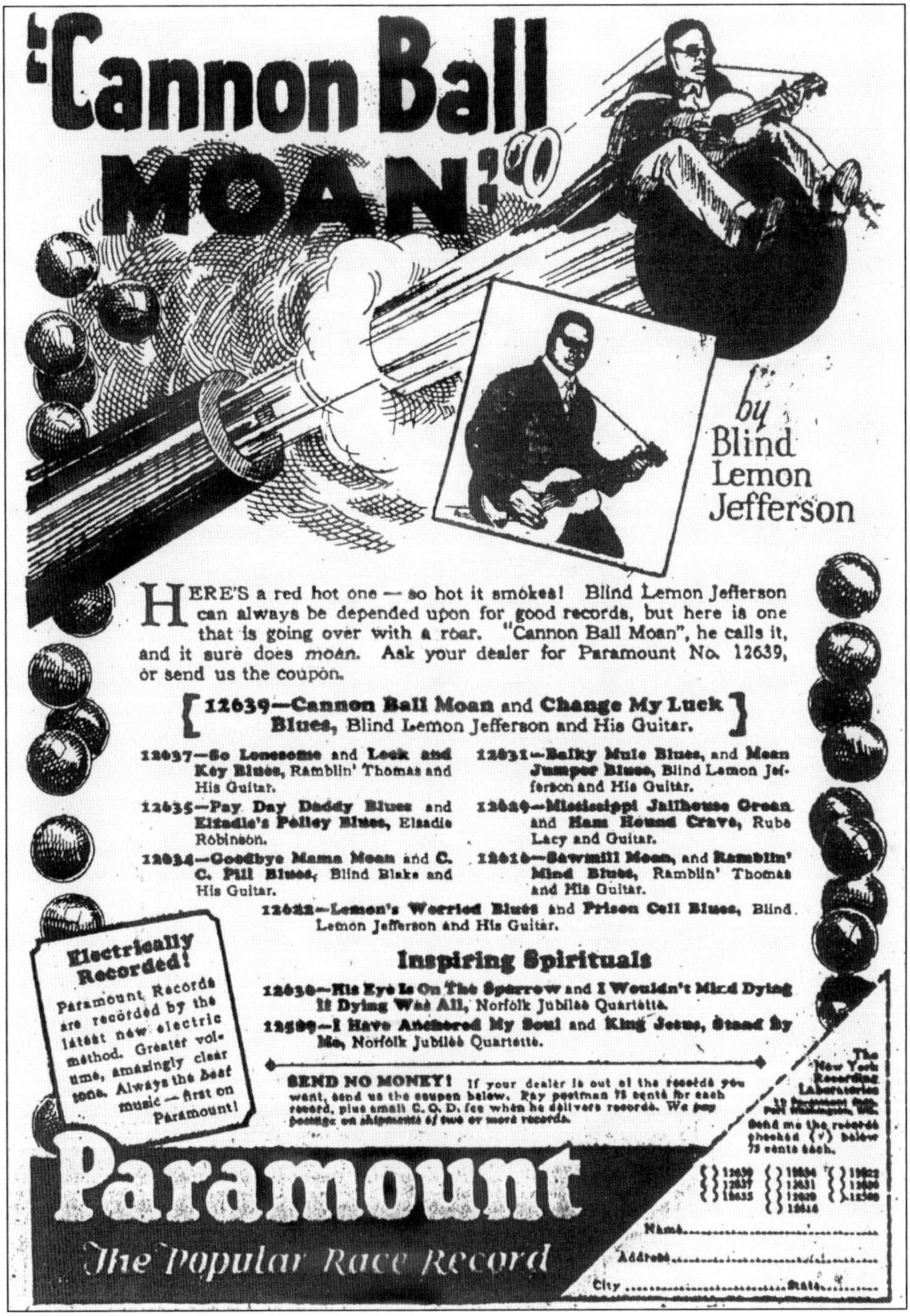


In "Cannon Ball Moan," recorded in early 1928, Jefferson wryly notes, "Competition worrying me, and I don't even know what 'competition' means." His best friend has taken his woman and left town, and the singer may follow suit, so "cannon ball" may refer to a fast train. Perhaps this advertisement's artist interpreted the singer as feeling like he had been shot out of a cannon. (Courtesy of Kip Lornell.)

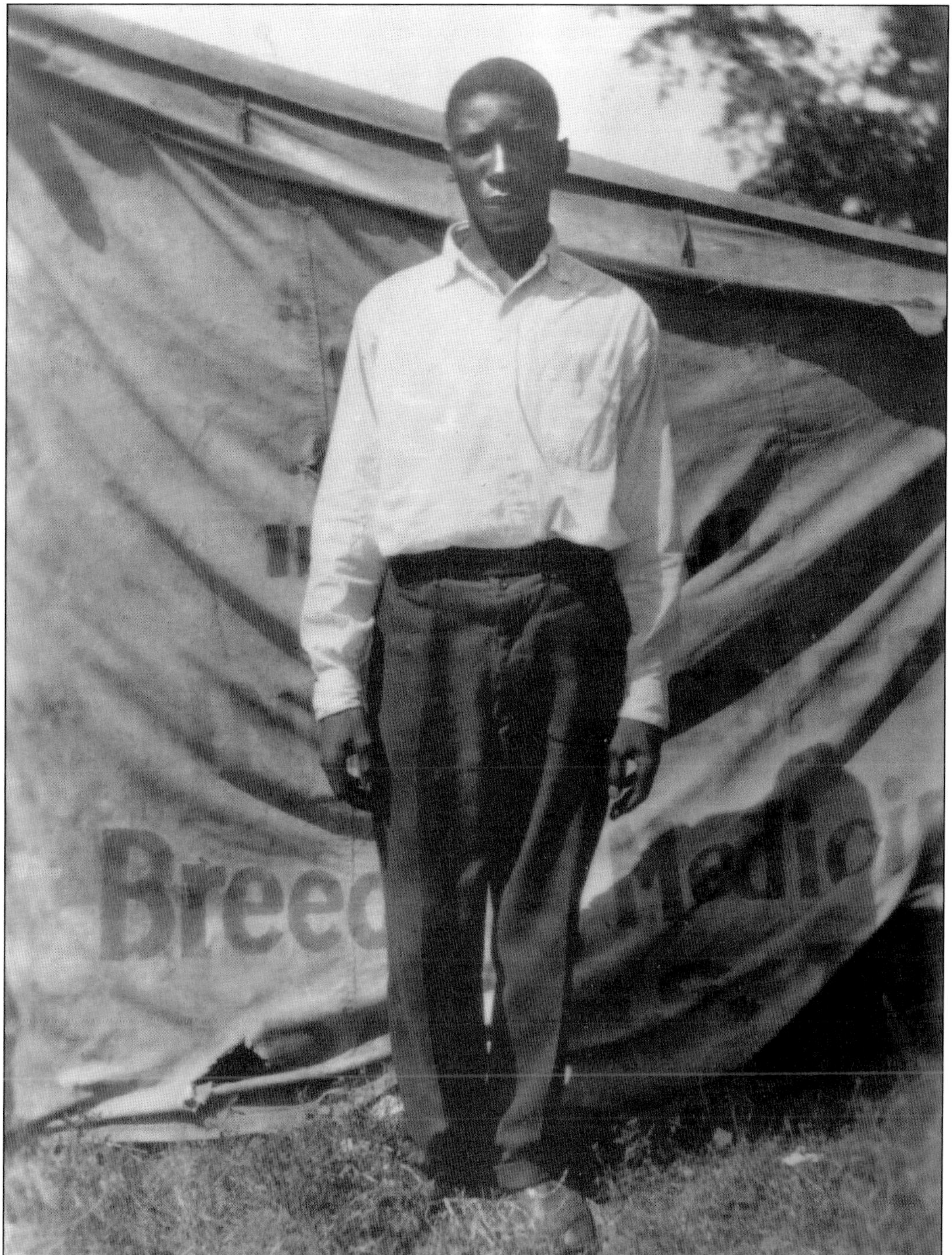

The seminal blues guitarist Aaron "T-Bone" Walker recalled that he led Blind Lemon Jefferson around Dallas and danced on the streets of Deep Ellum for tips. Pictured here in the mid-1920s, when he worked in Dr. Breeding's Medicine Show, Walker was influenced by Blind Lemon's playing. He became a star after moving to Southern California in the 1940s and pioneering big-band electric blues. (Courtesy of Helen Oakley Dance.)

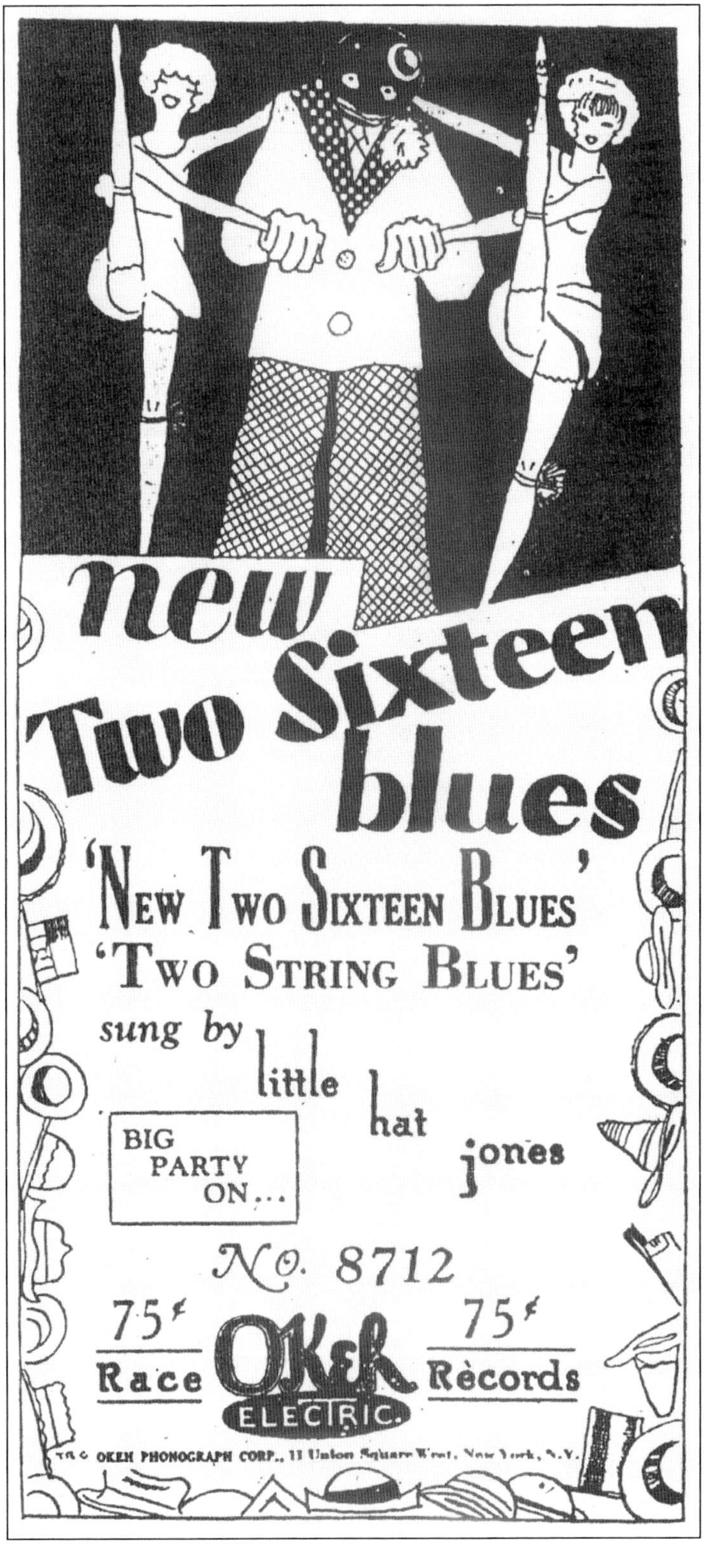


George "Little Hat" Jones made the records listed here in 1929 and 1930 in San Antonio, where he was living at the time. At the June 1929 session, he also backed singer Texas Alexander on several songs. Jones told interviewers in 1964 that he got his nickname from a construction foreman in Garland, Texas, because Jones had cut off part of the brim of his hat. Nonetheless, OKeh chose to take the more obvious approach of depicting a stereotyped black man wearing outlandish clothes and a small hat. In fact, the cartoon hardly resembles Jones: A photograph taken at the time of the interview shows a lean, dark-complected man with large hands, playing a guitar. Jones died in 1981 while living in the area of northeast Texas where he had grown up. (Courtesy of Documentary Arts.)

Blind Willie Johnson was a powerful singer of "holy blues," featuring religious lyrics accompanied by powerful slide blues guitar. He recorded all four of the songs in these advertisements on December 3, 1927, in Dallas. These Columbia advertisements treat him in a relatively dignified way, eschewing the use of cartoons and referring to him as an artist. But the copy displays little knowledge of the songs, referring, for instance, to "Mother's Children" as "a wonderful song of mother love," when in fact it deals with children's struggles after their mother is dead. Johnson's songs have been recorded by other musicians, from Son House to Bob Dylan, and one, "Dark Was the Night—Cold Was the Ground," was included on the golden record launched into space aboard the Voyager 1 in 1977. (Courtesy of Kip Lornell.)

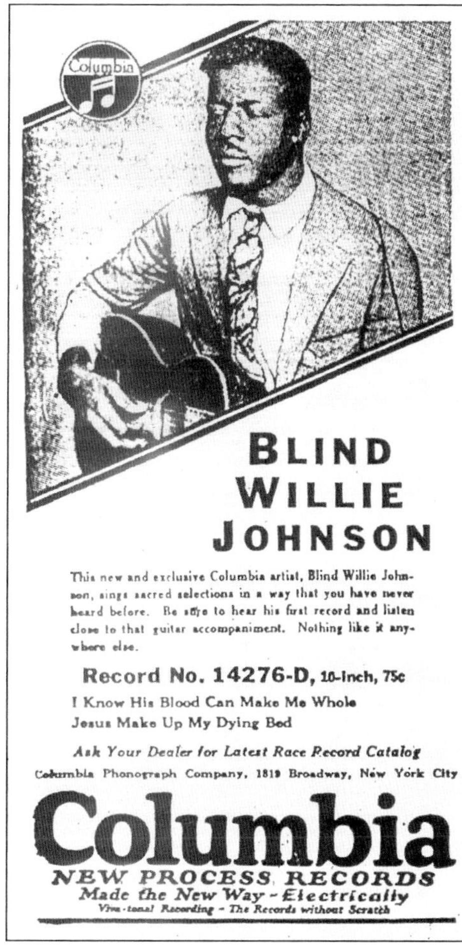


"Mother's Children Have a Hard Time"

*Sung by BLIND WILLIE JOHNSON*

A very popular artist sings a wonderful song of mother love. Everyone who loves mother will love this record. The coupling is a different kind of number. "If I Had My Way I'd Tear the Building Down."

**Record No. 14343-D, 10-inch, 75c**

"Mother's Children Have a Hard Time"
"If I Had My Way I'd Tear the Building Down" *Vocals—Blind Willie Johnson*

**OTHER POPULAR RECORDS**

Record No. 14342-D, 10-inch, 75c
"Jacksonville Blues"
"Midnight Weeping Blues" *Vocals—Nellie Florence*

Record No. 14341-D, 10-inch, 75c
"Farm Hand Papa"
"My Woman Done Me Wrong (As Far As I Am Concerned)" *Vocals—Clarence Williams*

*Ask Your Dealer for Latest Race Record Catalog*
Columbia Phonograph Company, 1819 Broadway, New York City
Columbia Phonograph Company
434 So. Wabash Ave., Chicago, Ill Wholesale Branch
Write or Phone Us for Name of Nearest Dealer

**Columbia NEW PROCESS Records**
*Made the New Way - Electrically*
Viva-tonal Recording - The Records without Scratch

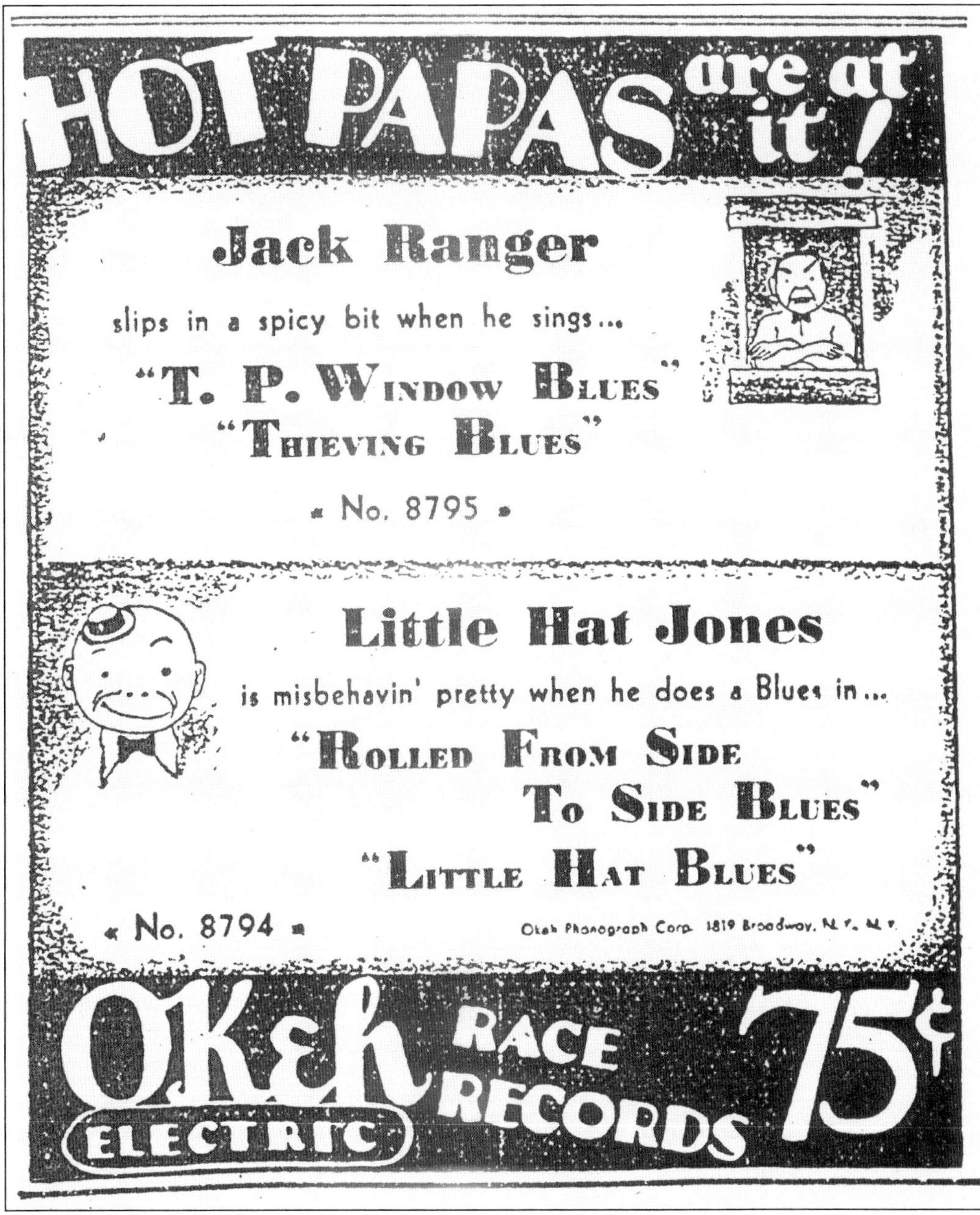


Despite its title, "Little Hat Blues" makes no reference to the singer's hat. In contrast to the advertisement's references to "hot papas" and "misbehavin' pretty," the song admonishes women that "you can't get to heaven triflin'." Little is known of the singer called Jack Ranger. He recorded these two songs and two others in Dallas in June 1929, accompanied by an uncredited guitarist and pianist. (Courtesy of Kip Lornell.)

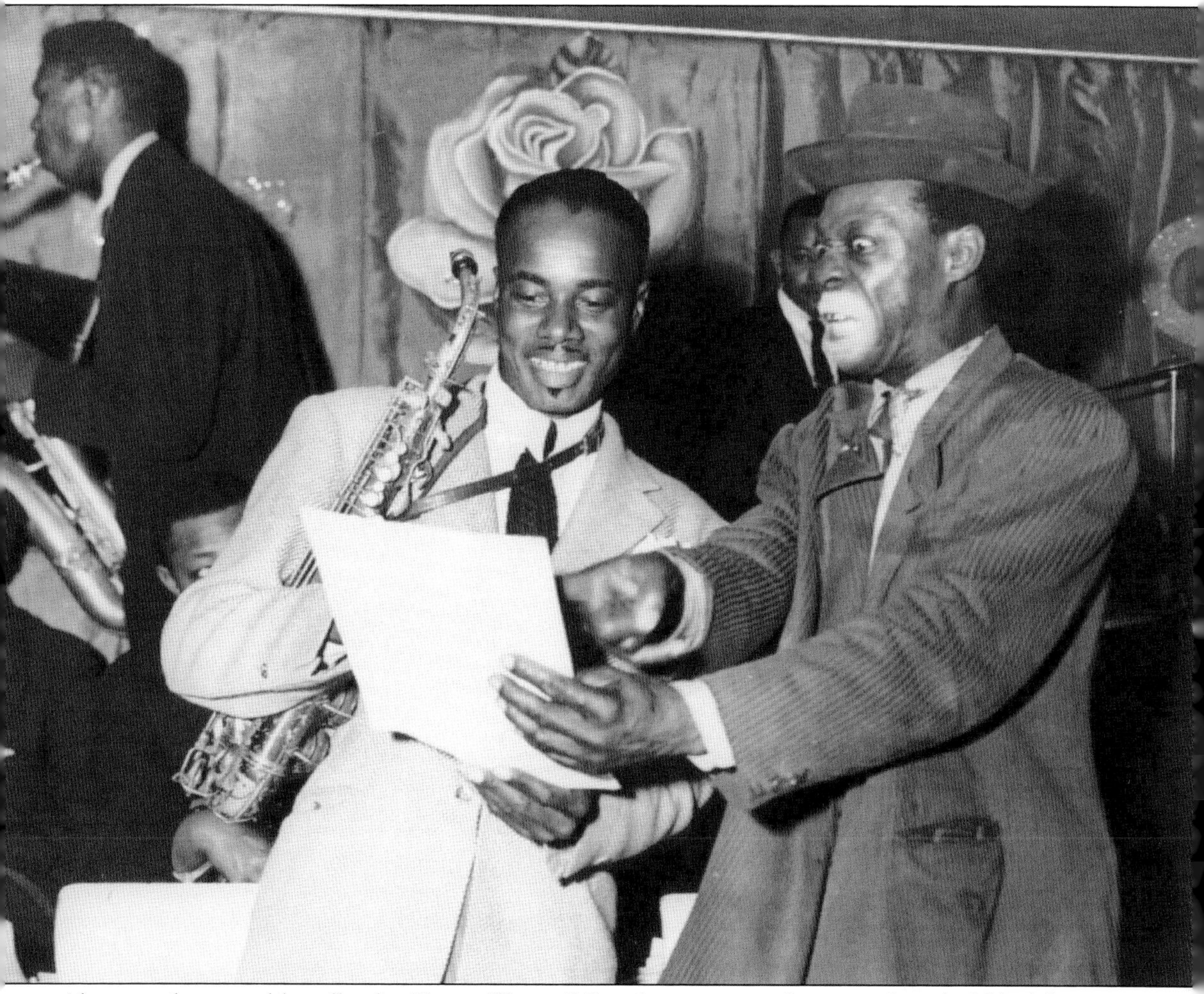

Alto sax player and bandleader Henry "Buster" Smith appears with an unidentified blackface comedian at the Rose Room in North Dallas in the 1940s. Smith left Dallas in 1925 with the Blue Devils, an Oklahoma City–based band that at various times included such top musicians as Bill "Count" Basie, tenor sax player Lester Young, and another former Dallasite, trumpet player and singer Oran "Hot Lips" Page. After the Blue Devils broke up in 1933, Smith formed a band with Basie but left just before the group hit the big time. Smith tired of the road and returned in the early 1940s to Dallas. He remained in the city for the rest of his life and was a mentor to David "Fathead" Newman, among other local musicians. (Photograph by Marion Butts; courtesy of the Texas African American Photography Archive.)

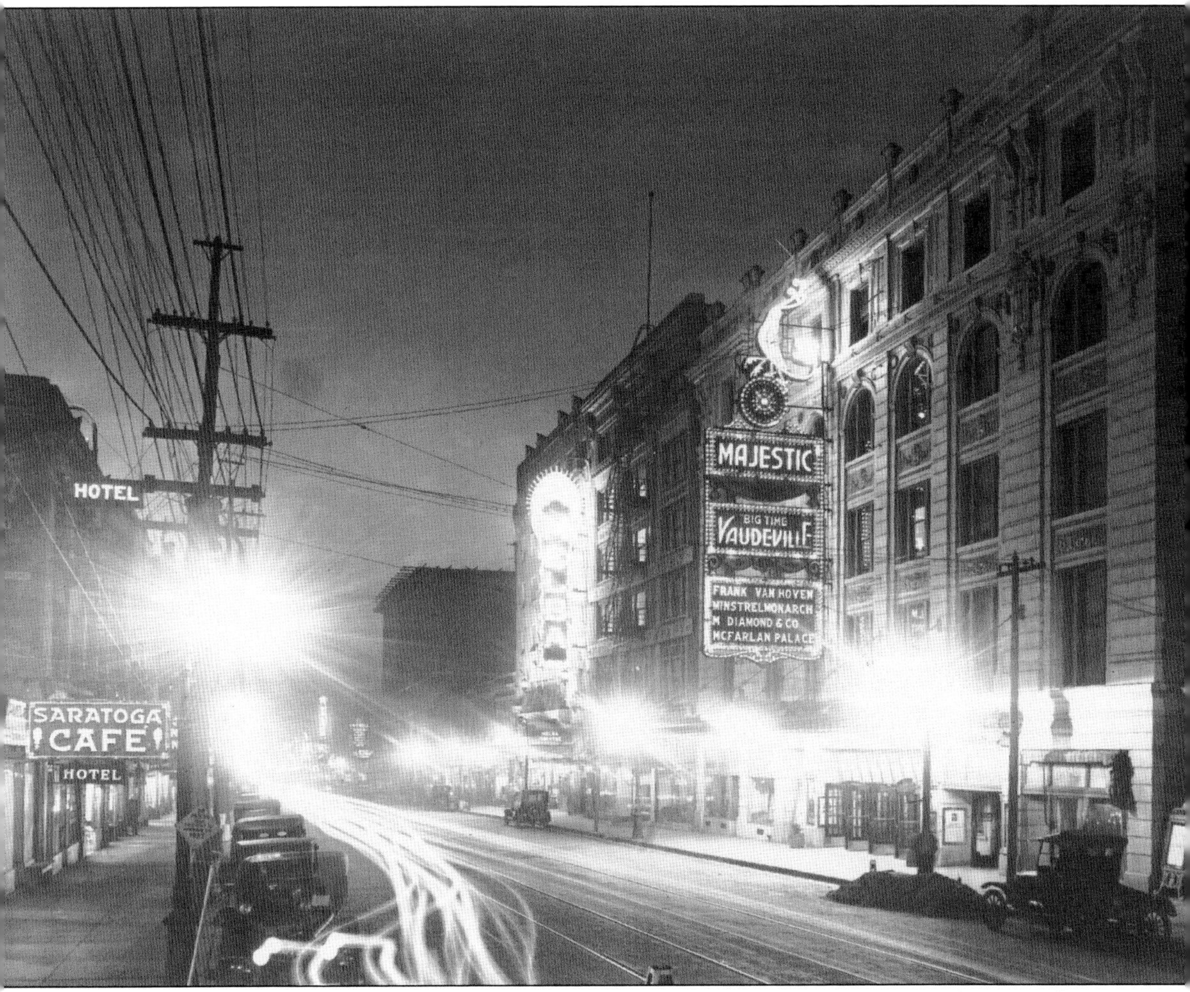


The Majestic Theatre was on Dallas's "Theater Row," on Elm Street west of Deep Ellum. In 1925, the Majestic presented vaudeville shows and films. During the years of racial segregation, African Americans sometimes mocked the strip as the "great white way." They were permitted to attend shows at the Majestic, but only by sitting in a high balcony known as the "buzzard roost." (Photograph by Frank Rogers; courtesy of the Texas/Dallas History and Archives Division, Dallas Public Library.)

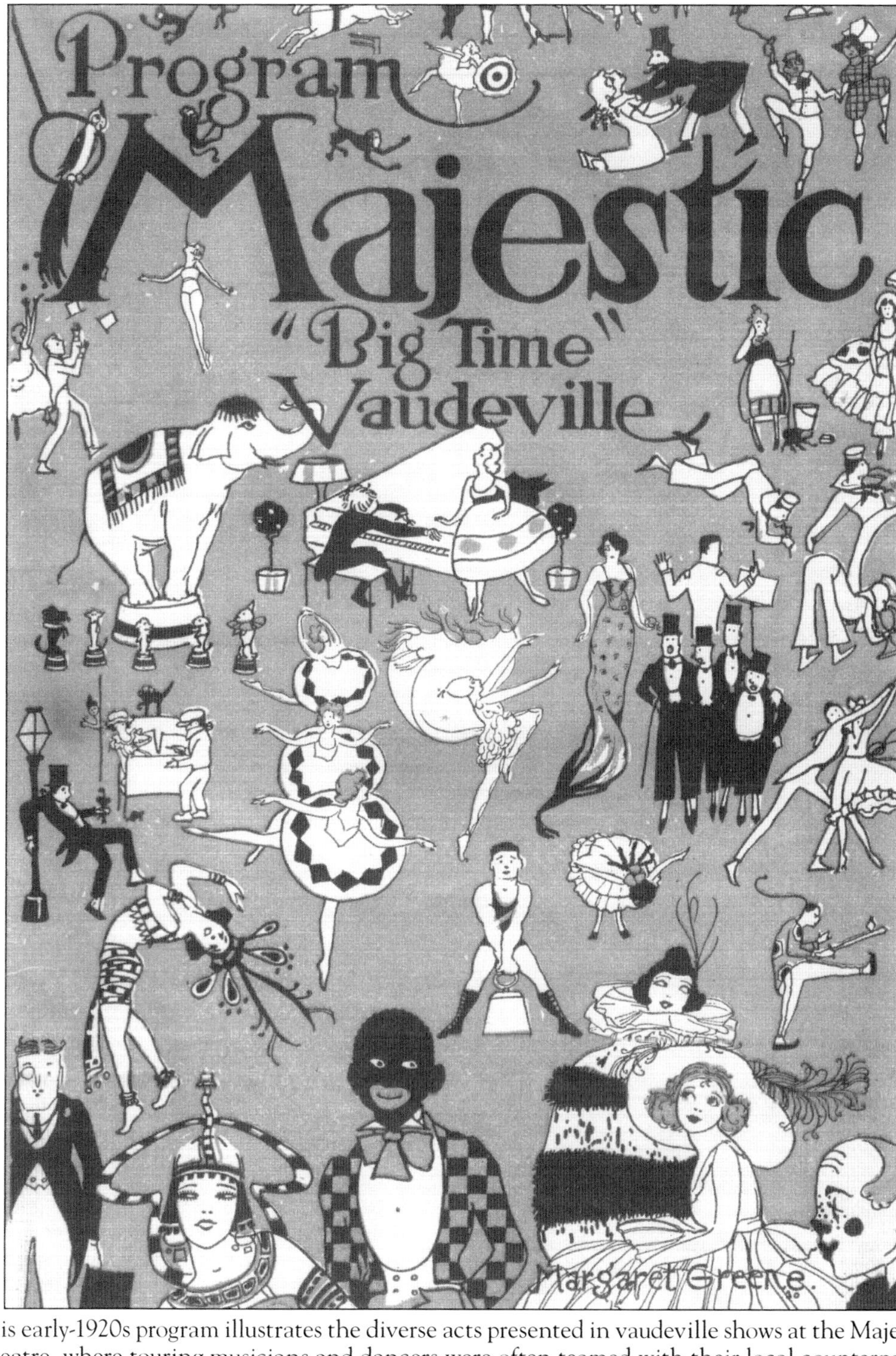


This early-1920s program illustrates the diverse acts presented in vaudeville shows at the Majestic Theatre, where touring musicians and dancers were often teamed with their local counterparts. Today, the Majestic, the sole remnant of Theater Row, presents a range of live theatrical and musical performances. The Dallas landmark is listed in the National Register of Historic Places. (Courtesy of the Texas African American Photography Archive.)

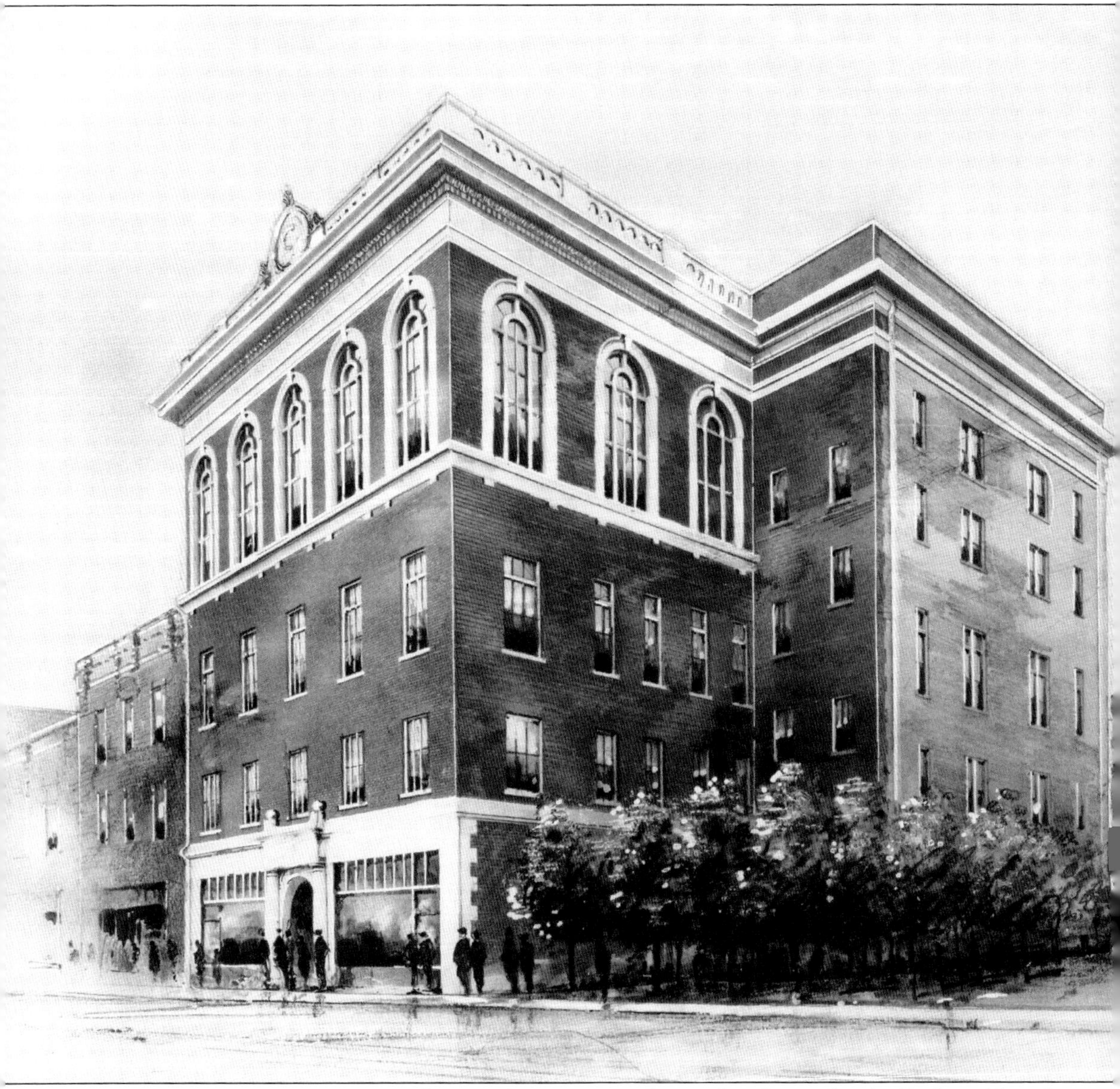

This rendering by architect William Sidney Pittman depicts his design for the Pythian Temple, the state headquarters of the Colored Knights of Pythias. It was completed in 1916 in the 2500 block of Elm and became a center of African American social and business life. Pittman, who was Booker T. Washington's son-in-law, was a brilliant, troubled man who lost his marriage and, in the 1940s, went to prison for fraud. The Pythians also fell on hard times and lost the temple. For a time, they maintained an office above Honest Joe's Pawn Shop, across the street. (Courtesy of Louis Bedford.)

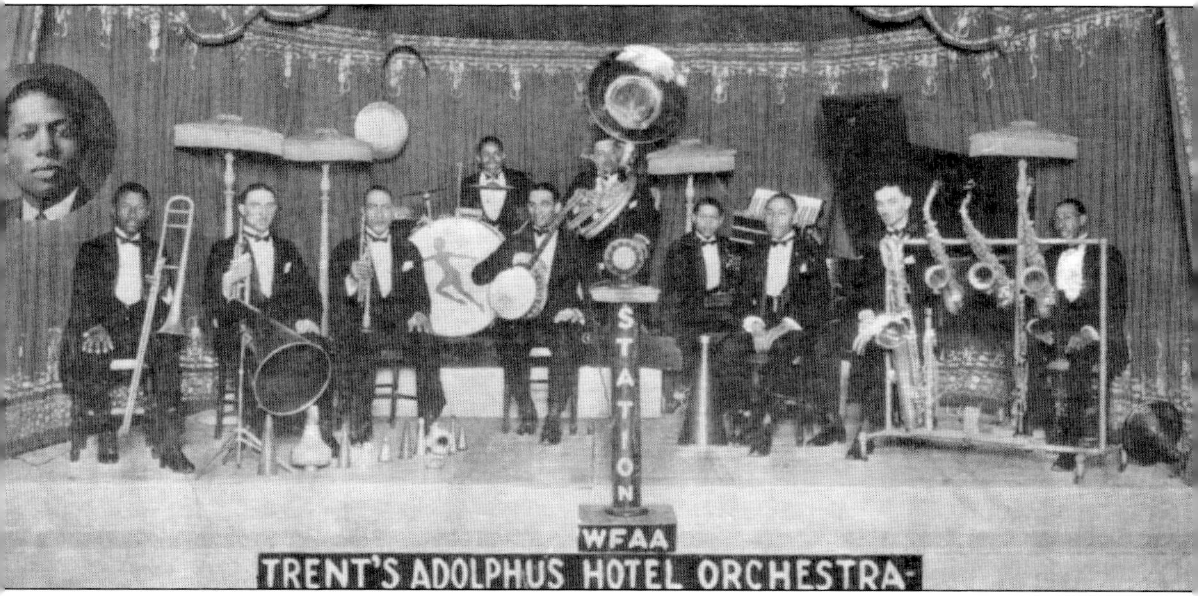


Alphonso Trent's Orchestra, one of the premier bands to tour the Southwest, was one of the most popular to perform at the Adolphus Hotel in downtown Dallas in the 1920s. However, blacks were not permitted to stay at the hotel. Trent's performances were often broadcast over radio station WFAA. (Courtesy of the Texas African American Photography Archive.)

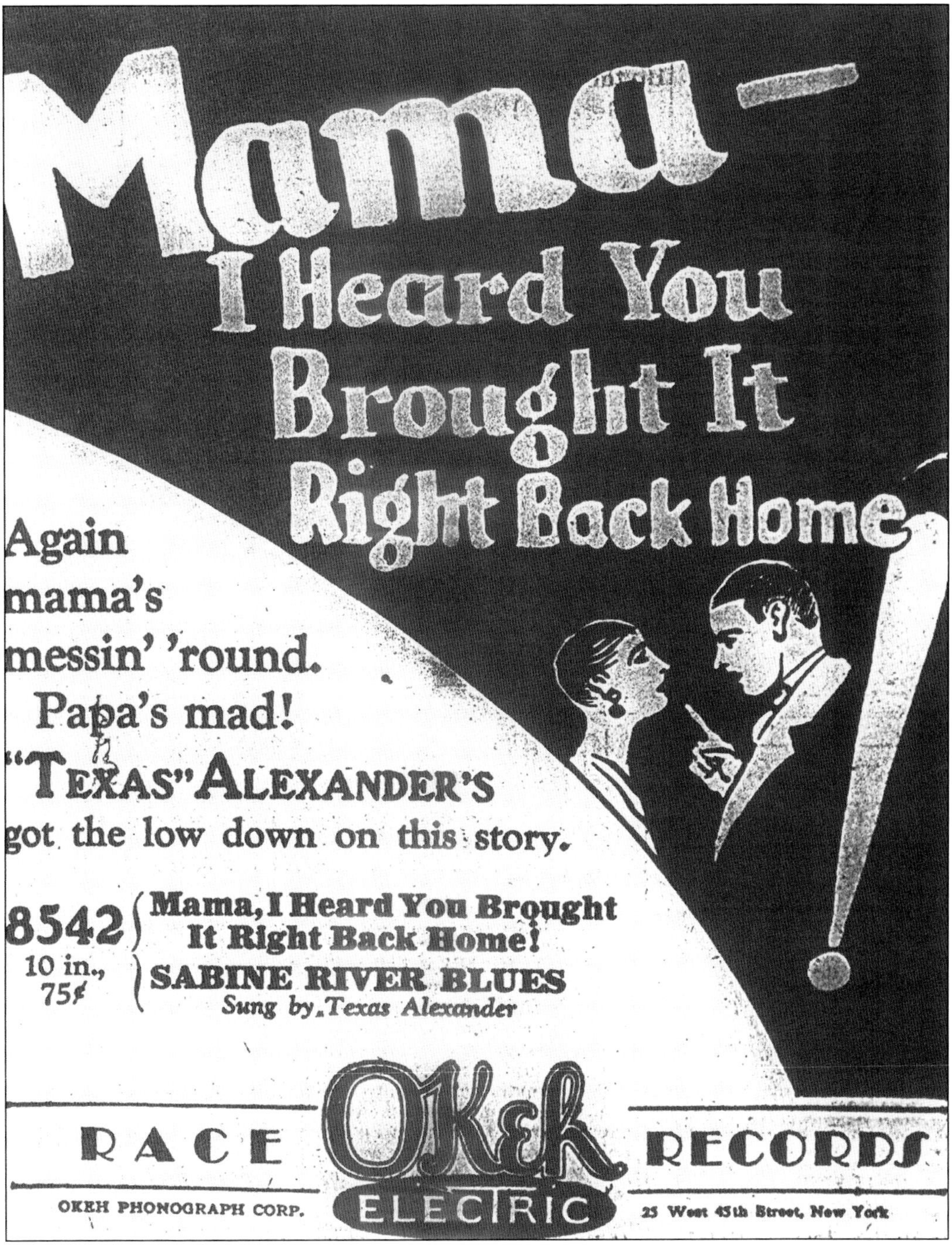


Alger "Texas" Alexander was a native of Leon County, also the birthplace of Sam "Lightnin' " Hopkins, who often identified Alexander as his cousin, though it is unclear whether they were related. Alexander did not play an instrument and was accompanied by a variety of musicians, from King Oliver's jazz combo to white guitarist Eddie Lang. (Courtesy of Kip Lornell.)

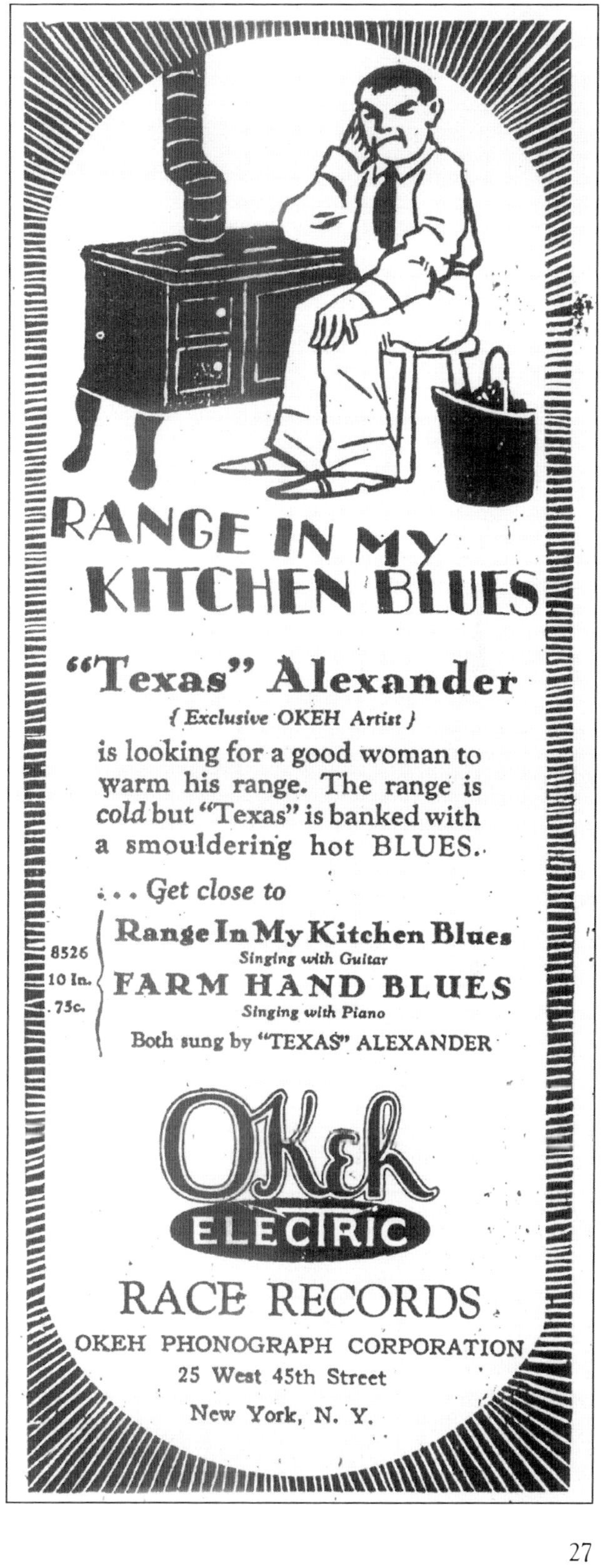


This advertisement's copy acknowledges, at least implicitly, the sexual metaphor of the lyrics ("I'm gonna get me a New York woman for to burn my Southern bread"). The illustration typifies artwork in race-record advertisements, in that the figure is racially ambiguous. The record was made in New York in August 1927, with Lonnie Johnson on guitar. Pianist Eddie Heywood accompanies the singer on the flip side, "Farm Hand Blues." (Courtesy of Kip Lornell.)

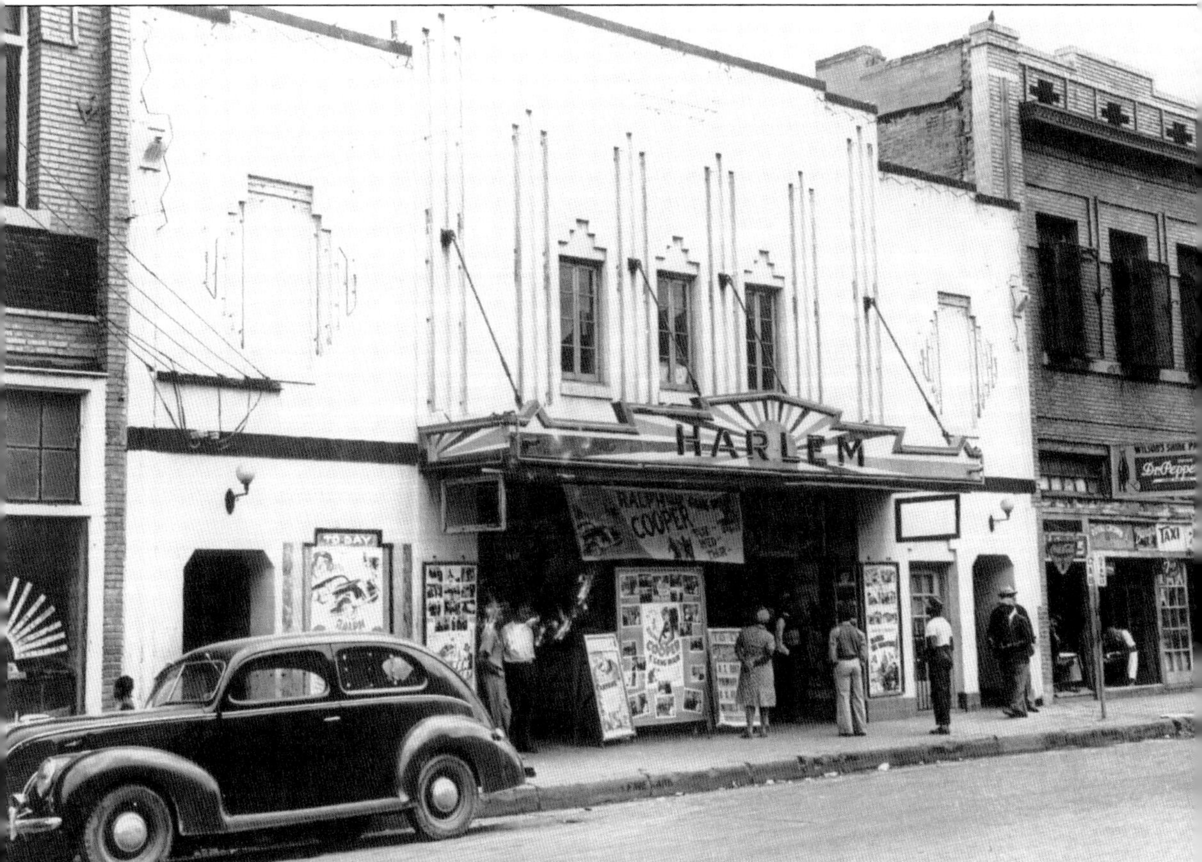


The Harlem Theater, at 2407 Elm Street, in the heart of Deep Ellum, screened films for African Americans, including movies with black casts, such as the feature in this photograph, *Gang War*. The 1940 crime saga was directed by Leo C. Popkin, a white native of Canada. African American moviegoers also enjoyed Westerns and other mainstream fare. The entire block was later razed to make way for Central Expressway. (Courtesy of the Texas/Dallas History and Archives Division, Dallas Public Library.)

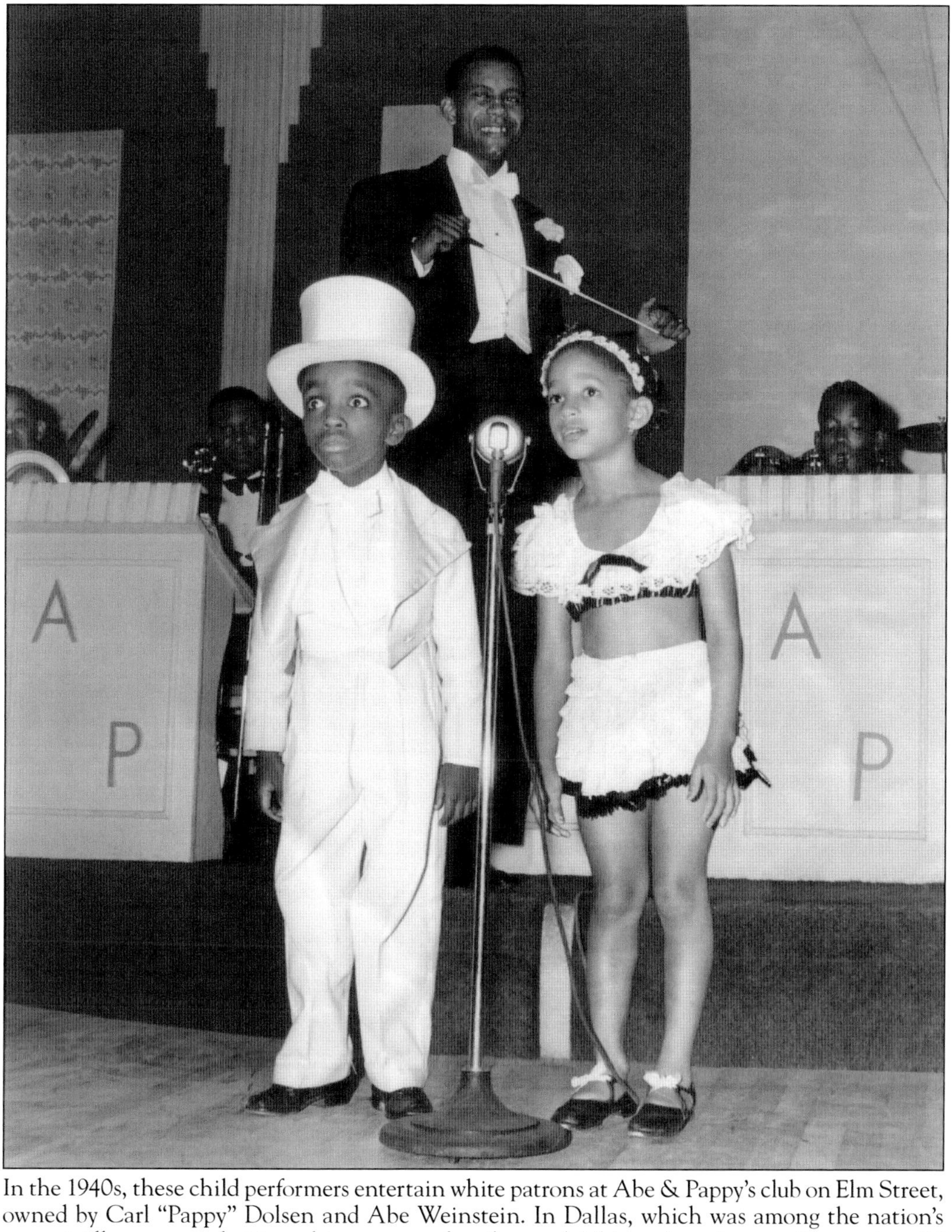


In the 1940s, these child performers entertain white patrons at Abe & Pappy's club on Elm Street, owned by Carl "Pappy" Dolsen and Abe Weinstein. In Dallas, which was among the nation's most rigidly segregated cities, white venues often featured African American performers but did not allow them to mix with customers. When not onstage, they were required to retreat to an offstage area such as the kitchen or to go outside. Black nightclub owner Big Bo Thomas recalled that in the 1960s, the Dallas police forced him to hire off-duty officers to provide security. "They had them out there so I wouldn't let the white folks in," he said. (Courtesy of the Texas African American Photography Archive.)

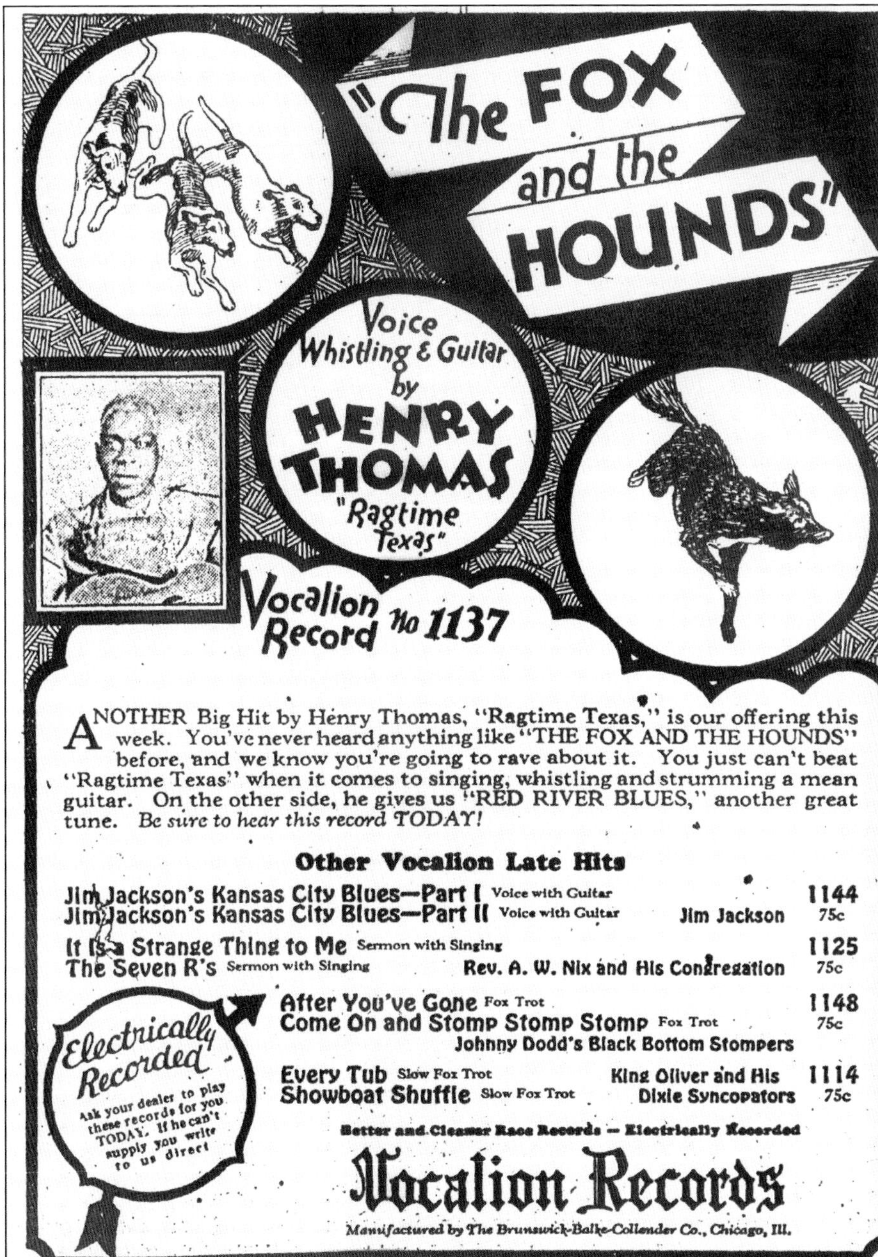


East Texan Henry "Ragtime Texas" Thomas was apparently in his 50s by the time he made his records in 1927–1929. Along with playing the blues, he was a songster and a musician whose repertoire included spirituals, ballads, and dance tunes. He accompanied himself by strumming a guitar and playing pan pipes, or quills, fashioned from cane and placed in a holder around his neck. In "The Fox and the Hounds," he vocally emulates the dogs of the title. This advertisement for his records on the Vocalion label fails to mention the quills, however, referring to "singing, whistling and strumming." Thomas apparently was a rambler; his songs often deal with train travel, and in "Railroadin' Some," he reels off the names of towns from Texas to Chicago, where he recorded. (Courtesy of Kip Lornell.)

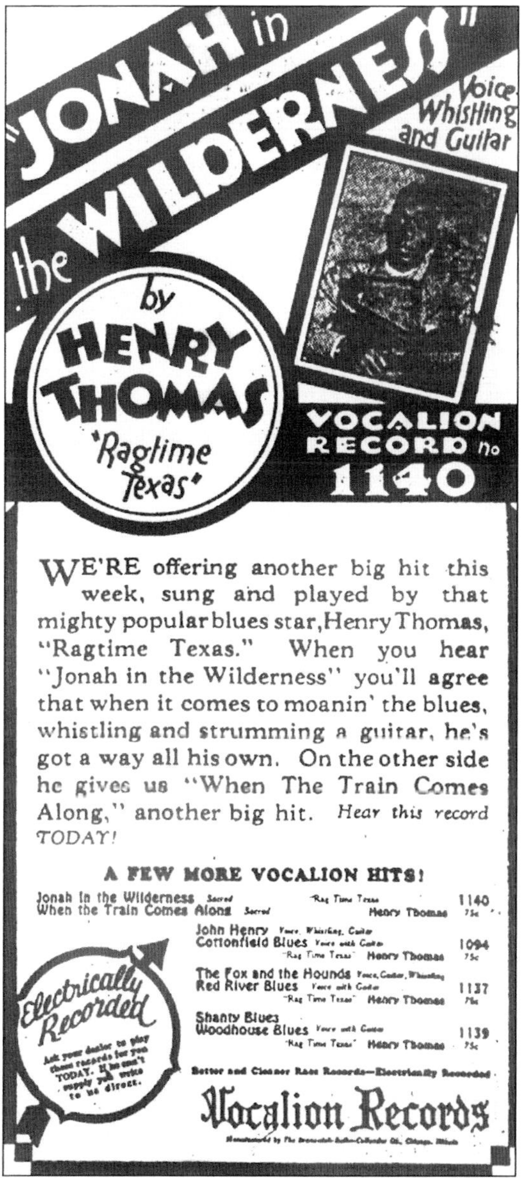


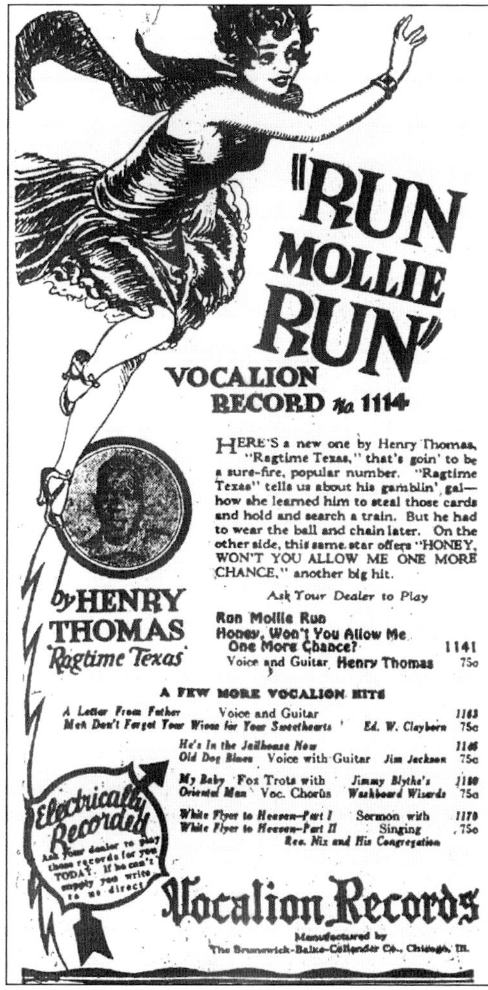


"Run Mollie Run," like some of Thomas's other songs, features guitar playing reminiscent of the banjo style he must have heard while growing up in East Texas. The song is indeed about gambling and going to prison: Thomas sings, "I went down to Huntsville; I did not go to stay," in a reference to the headquarters of the Texas prison system. But the copywriter appears to have misheard "trey" as "train." The flip side is one of Thomas's more enduring songs, "Honey Won't You Allow Me One More Chance," which was adapted by Bob Dylan on his second album. Contrary to the copy, Thomas does not moan the blues on "Jonah in the Wilderness," a fast-paced song with a biblical theme. (Courtesy of Kip Lornell.)

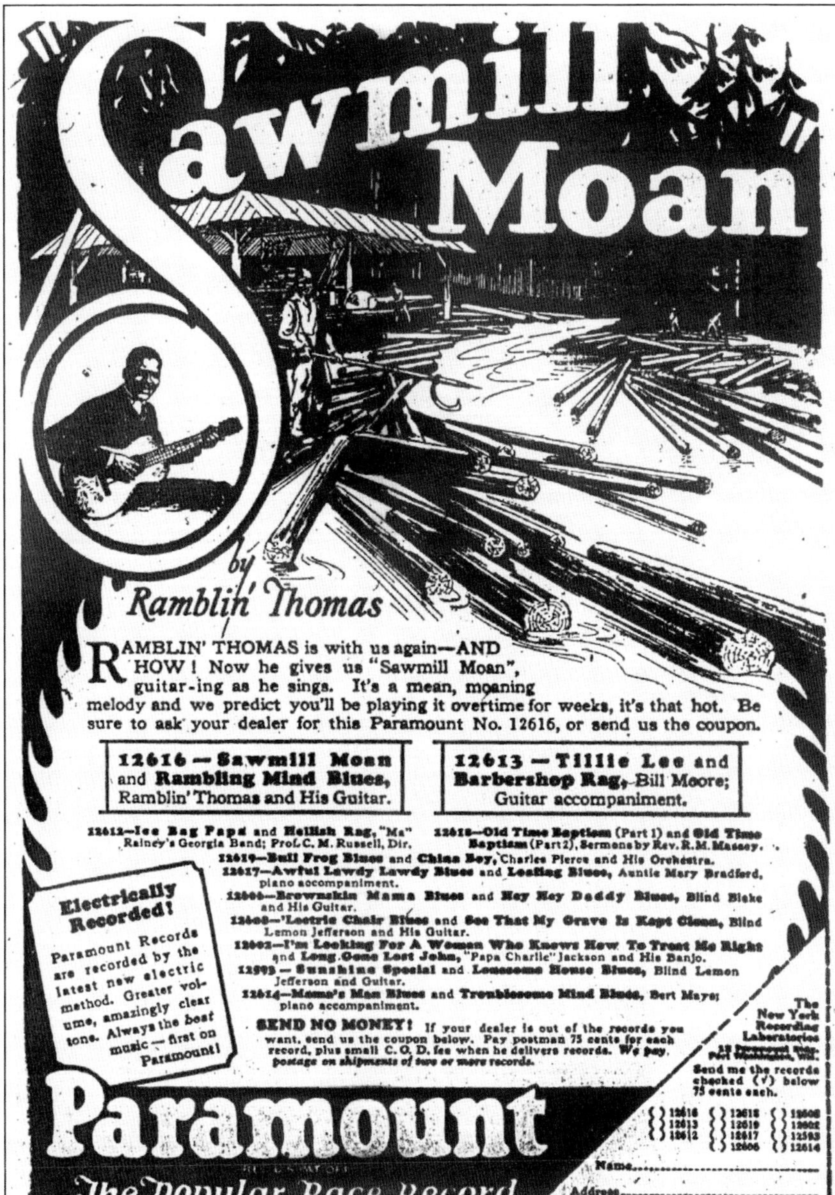


Willard "Ramblin' " Thomas, apparently no relation to Henry Thomas, was born in Logansport, Louisiana, in 1902. He was living in North Dallas in 1928 when his younger brother Jesse, also a blues musician, came to stay with him. Willard reportedly played with Blind Lemon Jefferson and, through him and merchant R.T. Ashford, got a contract with the Paramount record label. He recorded for Paramount in Chicago in 1928 and for Victor in Dallas in 1932 before rambling on, and Jesse Thomas heard little of his brother until Willard died in Memphis in 1945. The lyrics of "Sawmill Moan" make no reference to sawmills; perhaps the title was an effort to capitalize on the reputation of Southern sawmill camps as rough places where laborers were entertained by traveling bluesmen while drinking whiskey served on planks laid over barrels. (Courtesy of Kip Lornell.)

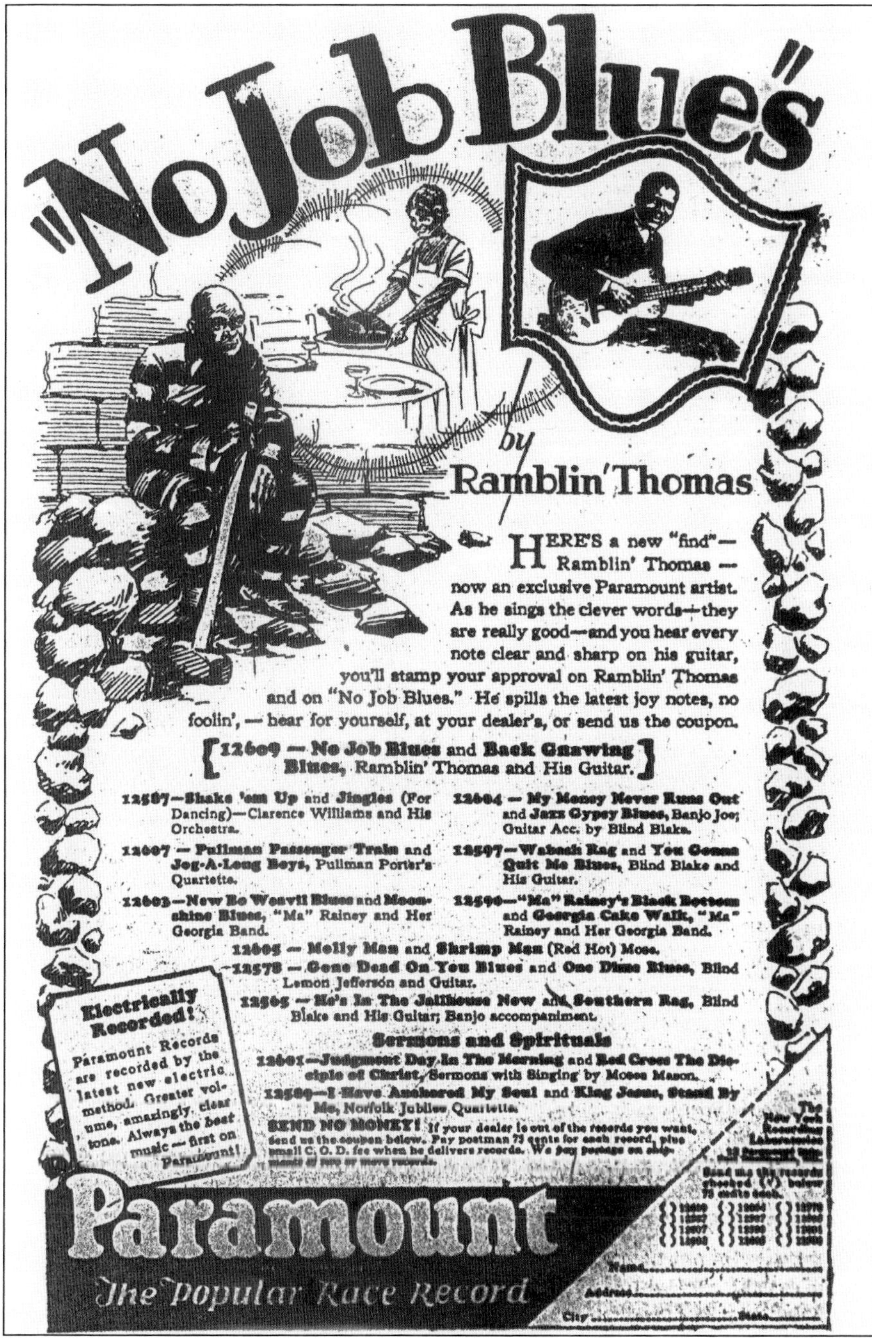


In "No Job Blues," Ramblin' Thomas laments the fact that his "meal-ticket woman" has quit him and he can find no work. A policeman arrests him for vag (vagrancy), and he ends up "working in the ice and snow"—hence the cartoon of a man in prison garb with a hammer for breaking rocks. It was common for black men to be arrested on trifling or fabricated charges and put to work, so a "meal-ticket woman" provided safety as well as food and shelter. This advertisement incongruously proclaims that Thomas "spills the latest joy notes, no foolin'." (Courtesy of Kip Lornell.)

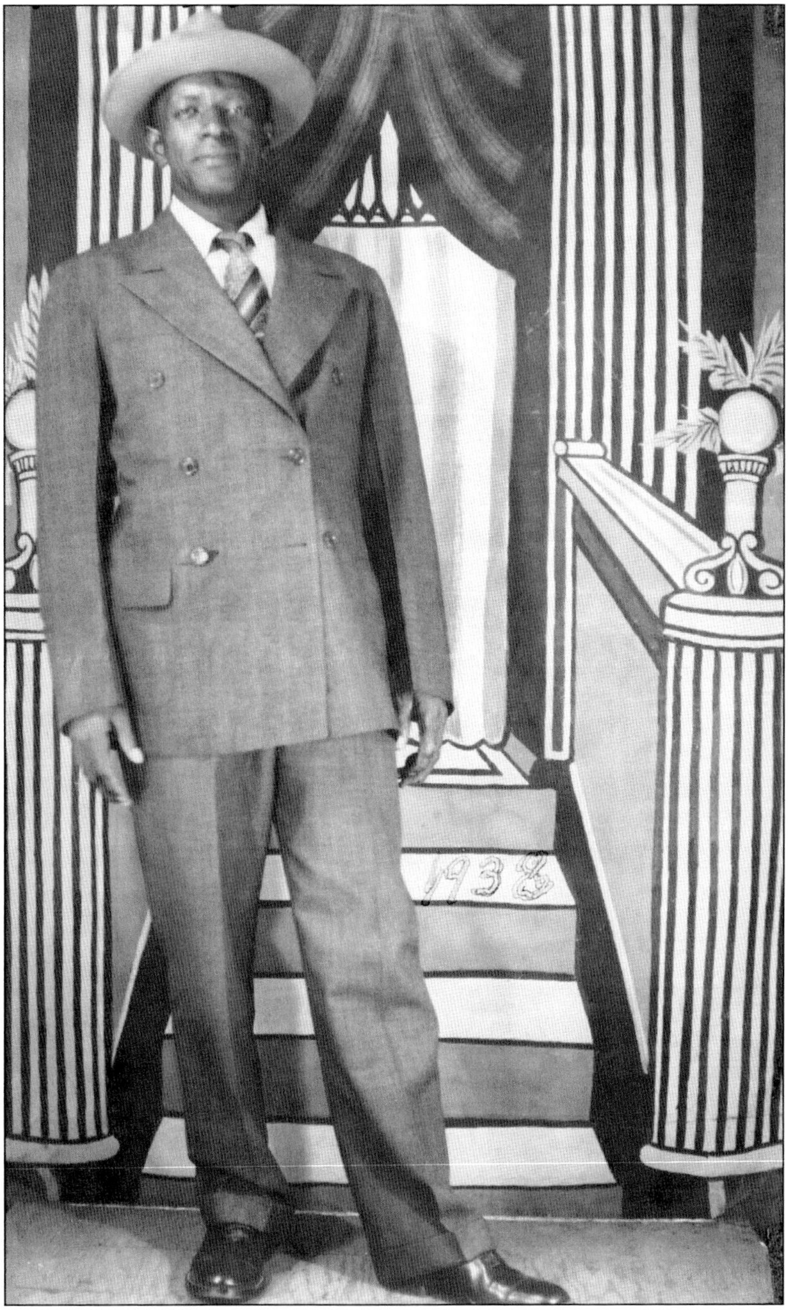


Blues pianist Alexander H. Moore posed for this portrait in 1938. Moore remained musically active all his life, but he always worked another job until his retirement in 1965. In the 1960s, he was discovered by white blues enthusiasts and made albums that mixed new material with re-creations of his records from the 1920s and 1930s. Known as "Whistlin' Alex Moore" for his habit of whistling as he played, he was revered late in life as the last living exponent of the rich musical life of Dallas in the 1920s, the heyday of Deep Ellum. In 1987, two years before he died at age 89, the National Endowment for the Arts awarded Moore a National Heritage Fellowship. (Courtesy of Documentary Arts.)

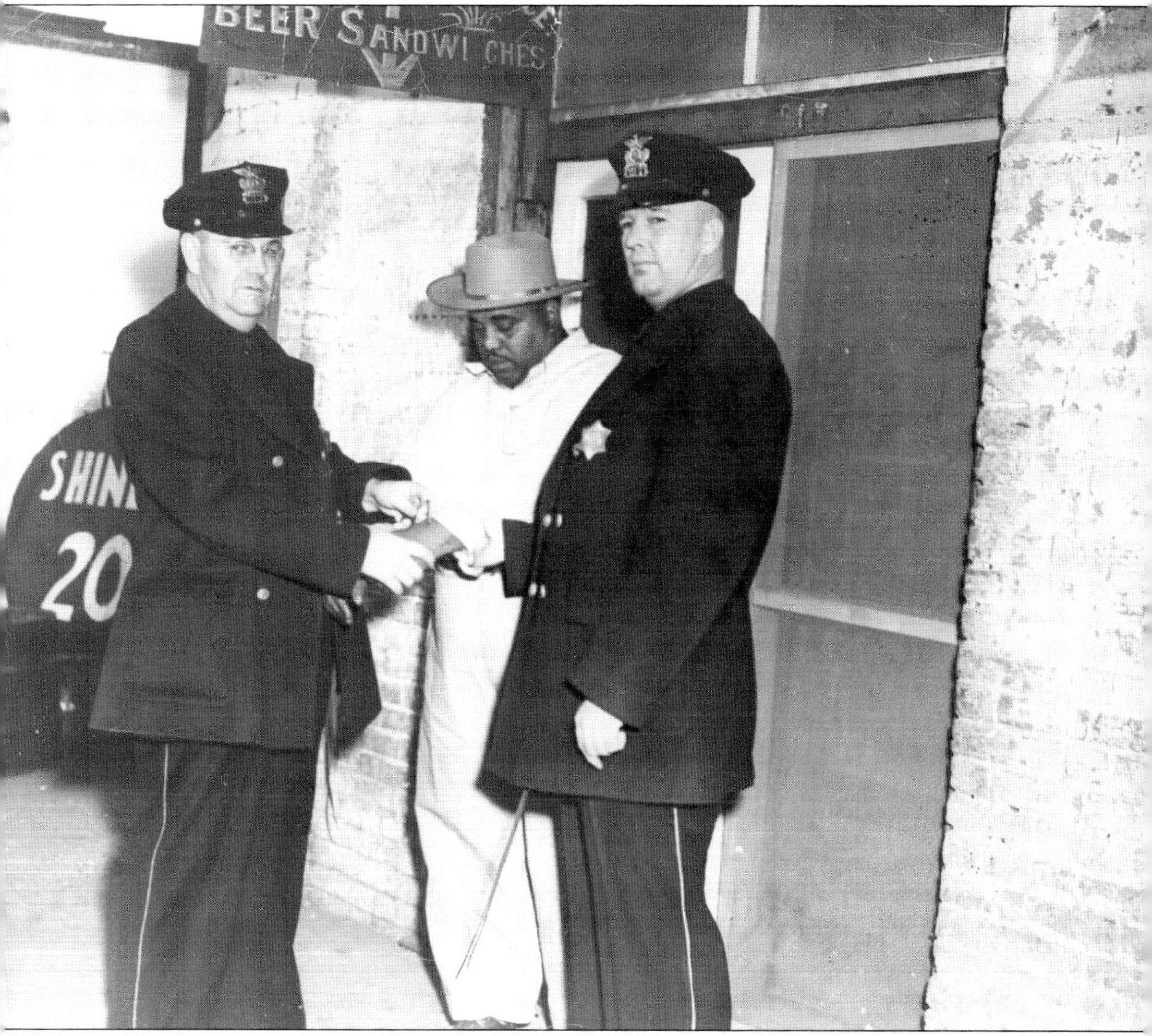


Dallas police officers Harry Stewart (left) and C.W. "Gus" Edwards playfully pretend to arrest George Edward Laffiton, better known as "Open the Door Richard," in the late 1940s. The foot patrolmen covered an area that stretched from Elm Street, up Central Track, to North Dallas, an area that had begun as a freed-slave community after the Civil War. Stewart and Edwards became friendly with business owners such as Laffiton, who operated a Central Track shine stand and other endeavors, legal and illegal. Laffiton opened his business in 1947 and took the name of a novelty song made popular that year by rhythm-and-blues artist Louis Jordan. Open the Door remained in business until 1963, when he accidentally shot himself while cleaning a pistol. He died two years later. A car dealership bought the property and tore down the shine stand, clearing the area behind it of a decades-long accumulation of broken wine bottles. (Courtesy of C.W. Edwards.)

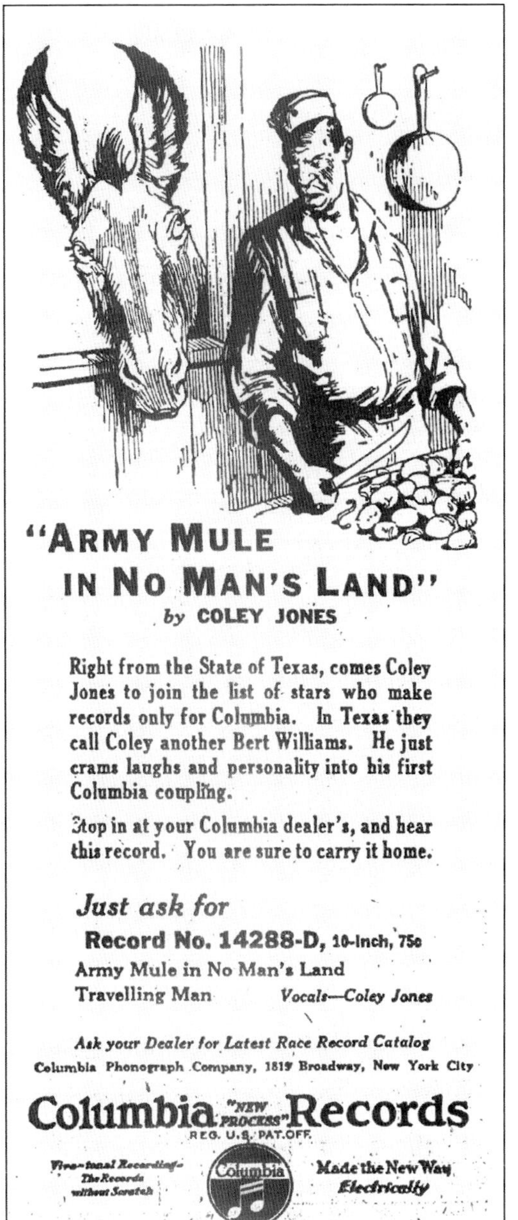


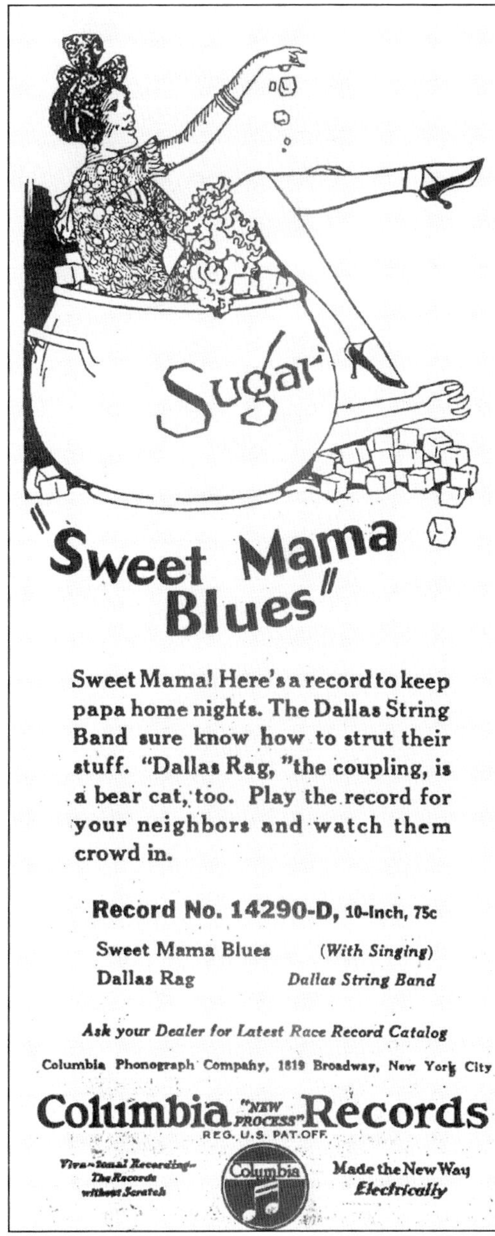


In "Army Mule in No Man's Land," Coley Jones protests being ordered to ride a mule pulling a cannon in World War I. The song is apparently a protest against racism, though it is adopted from one sung by Billy Beard of the white Al G. Fields Minstrels. Jones was a popular performer; the copy compares him to Bert Williams, the great black vaudevillian. On "Army Mule," Jones performs solo with his guitar, but "Sweet Mama Blues" features him in his role as bandleader. The Dallas String Band included bass player Marco Washington, stepfather of bluesman Aaron "T-Bone" Walker, an early exponent of the electric guitar. (Both, courtesy of Kip Lornell.)

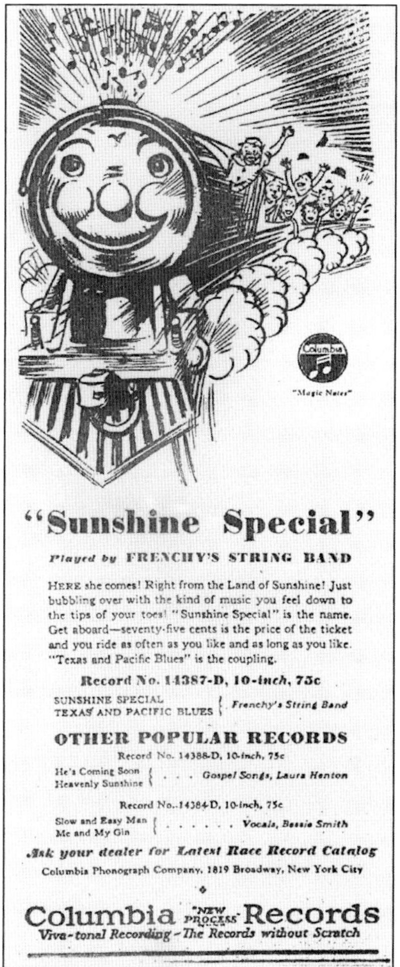


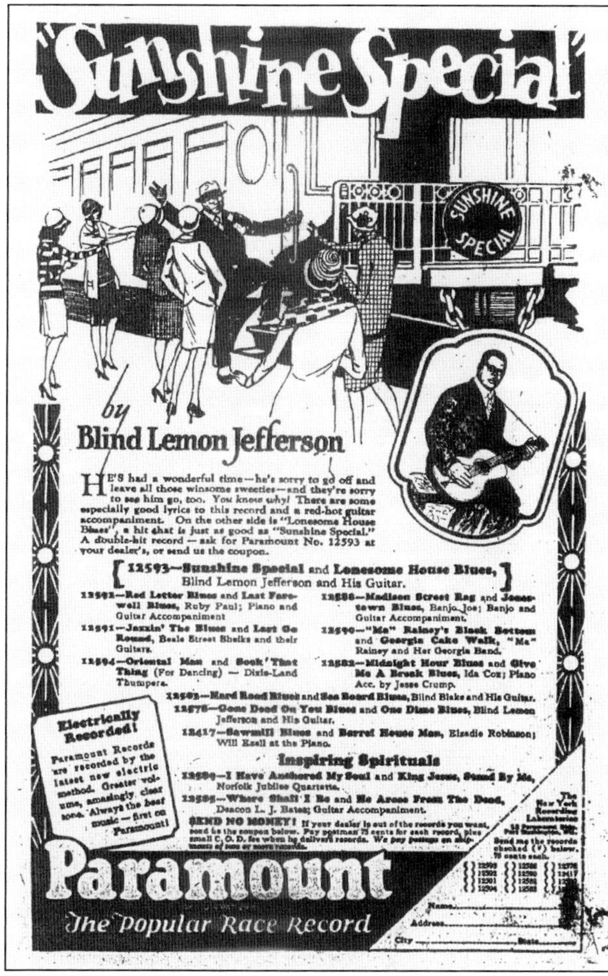


In the blues, trains can symbolize freedom or loss. These different songs about the fast daytime Sunshine Special have similar themes. In the advertisement above, Blind Lemon Jefferson sings, "Burn that railroad down so that Sunshine Special can't run. I got a gang of women, man, they ride from sun to sun." The vocalist in Frenchy's band, apparently clarinetist Jesse Hooker, proclaims, "That mean TP [Texas & Pacific] Railroad sure have done me wrong. It let that Sunshine Special carry my good girl from home." Contrary to the lyrics, the advertisement on the left exults, "Here she comes! Right from the Land of Sunshine! Just bubbling over with the kind of music you feel down to the tips of your toes!" Frenchy, whose real name was Polite Christian, was a trumpet player from New Orleans who lived and recorded in Dallas in the late 1920s. (Both, courtesy of Kip Lornell.)

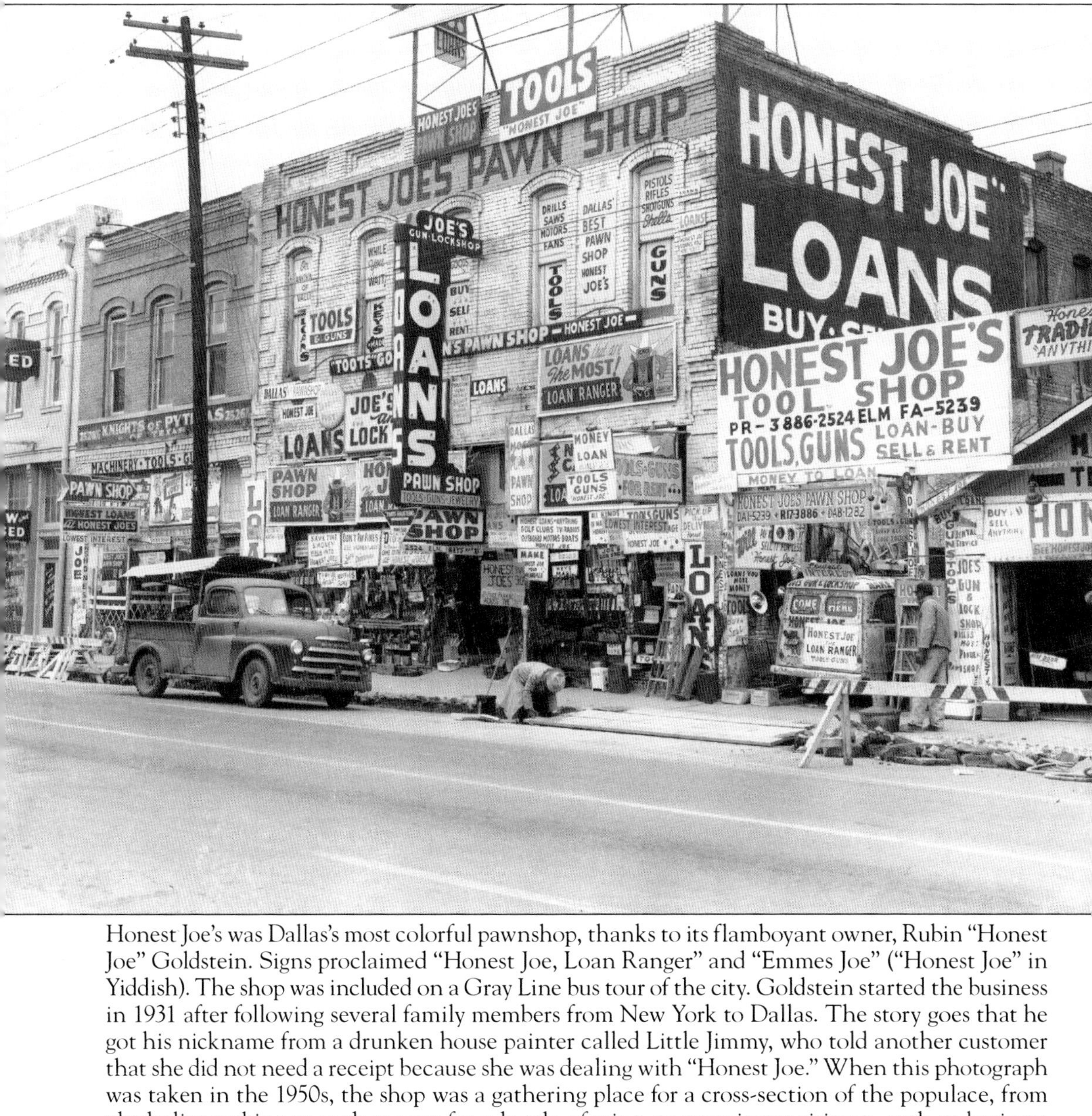


Honest Joe's was Dallas's most colorful pawnshop, thanks to its flamboyant owner, Rubin "Honest Joe" Goldstein. Signs proclaimed "Honest Joe, Loan Ranger" and "Emmes Joe" ("Honest Joe" in Yiddish). The shop was included on a Gray Line bus tour of the city. Goldstein started the business in 1931 after following several family members from New York to Dallas. The story goes that he got his nickname from a drunken house painter called Little Jimmy, who told another customer that she did not need a receipt because she was dealing with "Honest Joe." When this photograph was taken in the 1950s, the shop was a gathering place for a cross-section of the populace, from alcoholics seeking enough money for a bottle of wine, to prominent citizens, such as business executive John W. Carpenter and Mayor Robert Thornton. Goldstein's brothers, "Good Old" Dave and Isaac "Rocky" Goldstein, also owned pawnshops on Elm Street. (Courtesy of the Texas/Dallas History and Archives Division, Dallas Public Library.)

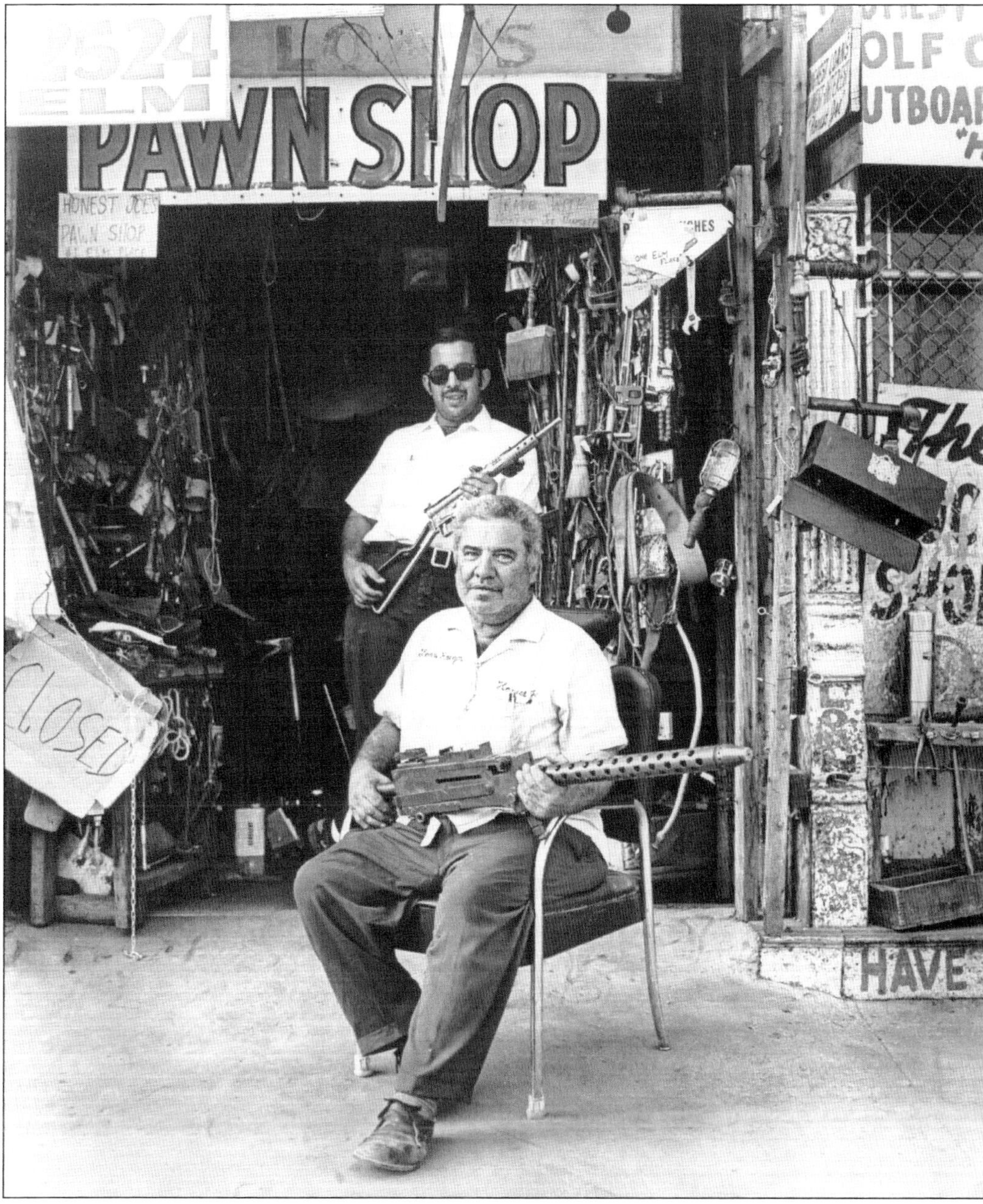


Rubin Goldstein (seated) and his son Eddie pose with weapons outside the Elm Street pawnshop in the 1960s. Honest Joe sometimes drew attention by driving downtown in a vehicle sporting a disabled machine gun, parking illegally, and staging shouting matches with the officers who wrote him tickets. One of his signs read "YCMMSOYA," an acronym for "You can't make money sitting on your Afghanistan." The store's fortunes declined with Deep Ellum, but Honest Joe sold other properties to keep it going and ran it until he died in 1972. For years after his father's death, Eddie Goldstein owned and operated an East Dallas business called King Edward Swap Shop, whose signage proclaimed it "Little Honest Joe's, 'Deeep' East Grand." The cluttered interior was modeled on the original Honest Joe's, and Eddie Goldstein loved to haggle with customers and hold court about the old days in Deep Ellum. After years of ill health, he died in 2013. (Courtesy of Eddie Goldstein.)

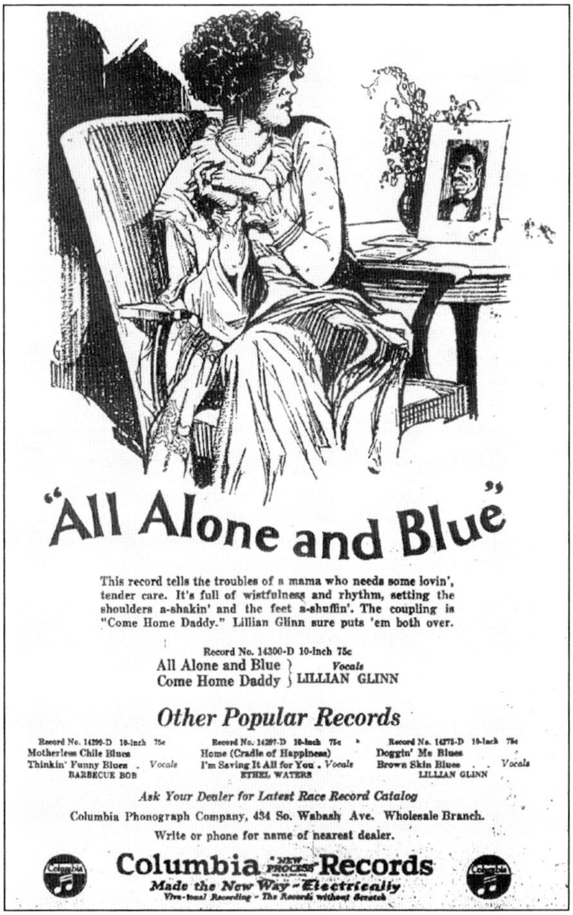


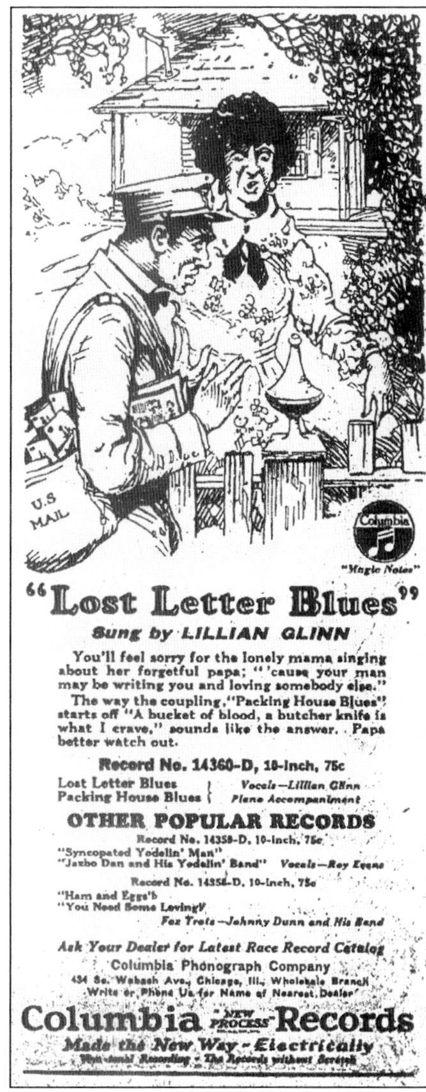


Lillian Glinn, born about 1902 in a small town near Dallas, moved to the city in her early 20s and performed at Ella B. Moore's Park Theatre. African American businessman R.T. Ashford became her manager and helped her get a record contract. Her first session, in Dallas in December 1927, yielded "All Alone and Blue" and her first hit, "Doggin' Me Blues." Glinn was often accompanied by piano, a dominant instrument in Dallas blues, but also by instruments more commonly associated with New Orleans, including cornet, banjo, and brass bass. On "Lost Letter Blues," recorded at her second session, in New Orleans in April 1928, she was backed only by pianist Willie Tyson. (Both, courtesy of Kip Lornell.)

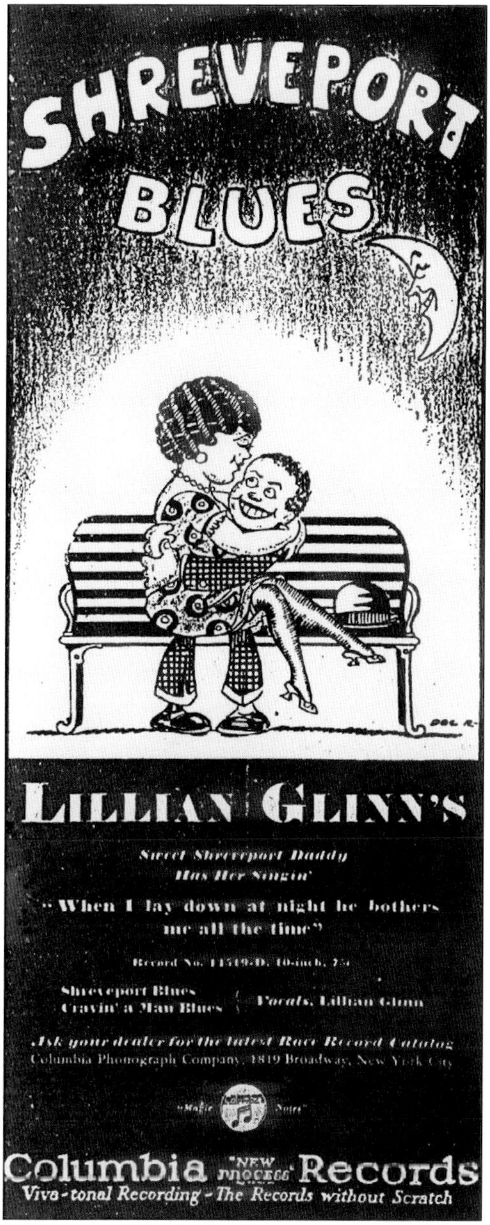


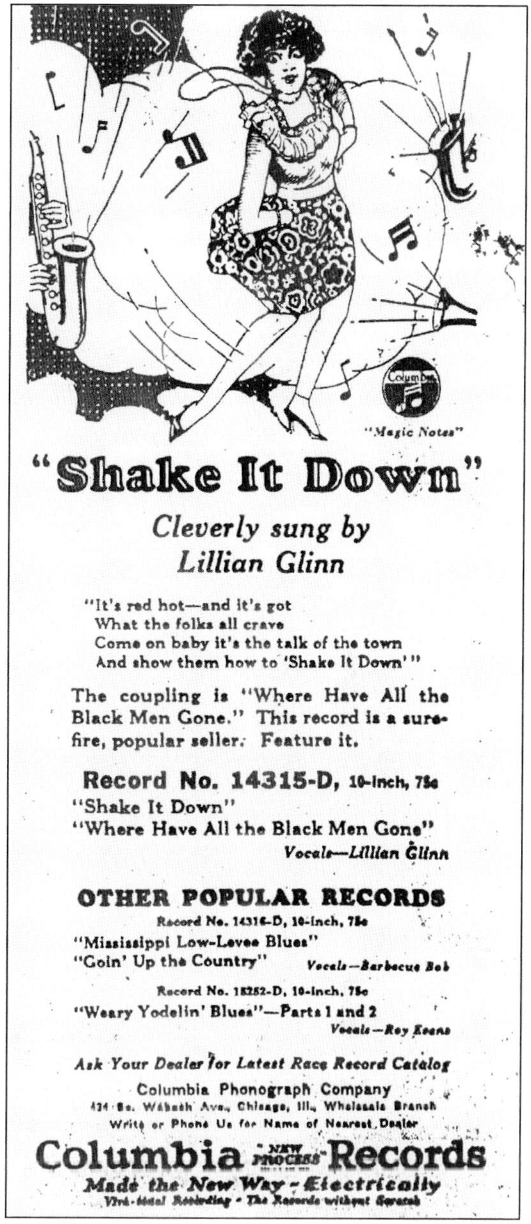


The raucous "Shake It Down" was also recorded at the April 1928 New Orleans session. The advertisement proclaims that the flip side, "Where Have All the Black Men Gone," "is a sure-fire, popular seller," while steering clear of its theme of intraracial prejudice ("yellows, they give out; brownskins fade so quick"). Glinn recorded once more, in Dallas in December 1929. On "Shreveport Blues," made at that session, she sang of a "long tall papa, lives mostly on Texas Avenue," then at the heart of the north Louisiana city's black business and social life. Glinn subsequently renounced the blues, moved to California, and married a minister. In the early 1970s, British blues historian Paul Oliver saw her name on a church marquee and interviewed her, though she was initially reluctant to talk about her days as a blues singer. (Both, courtesy of Kip Lornell.)

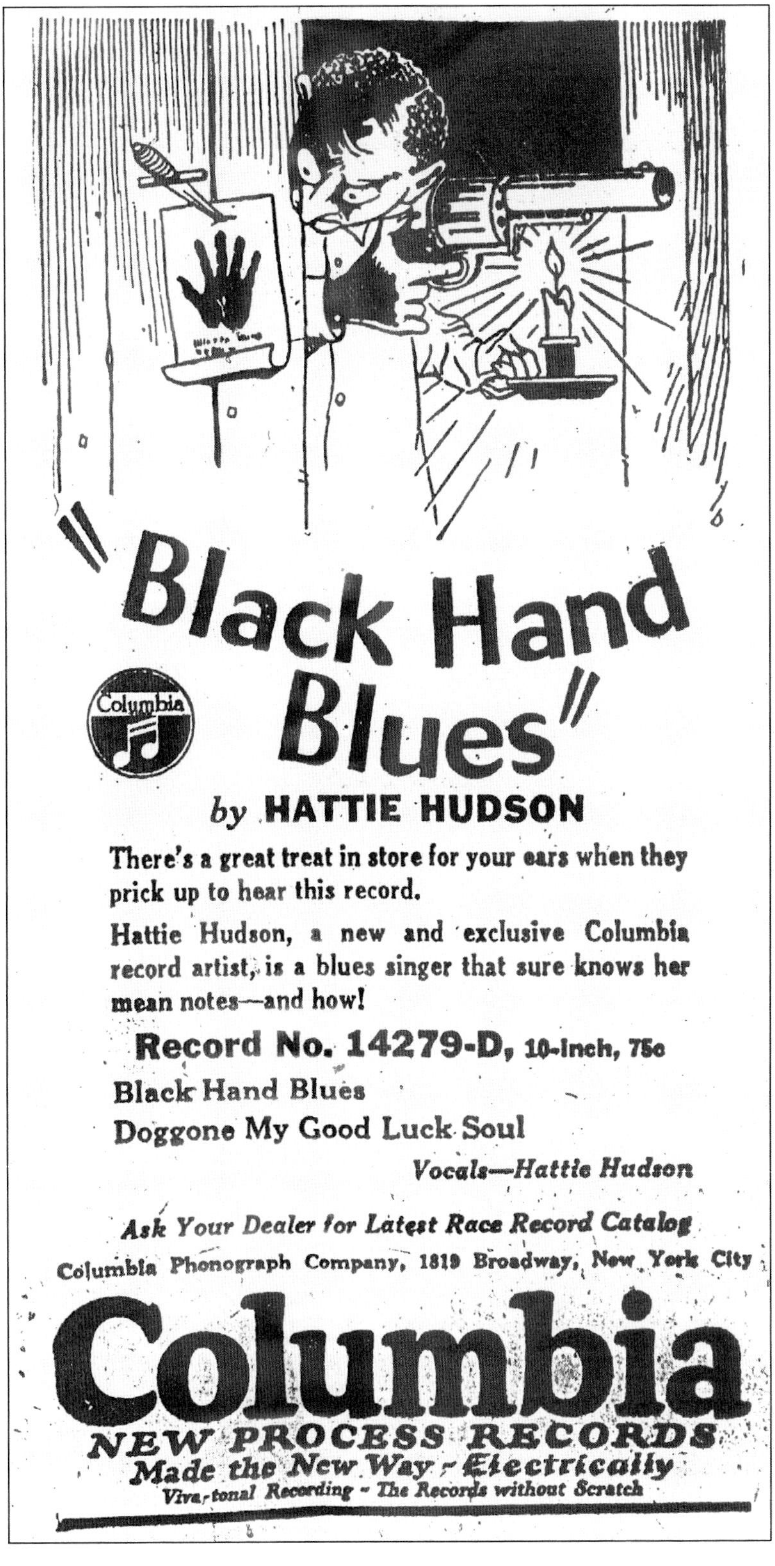


In "Black Hand Blues," the command "take your black hand down" apparently refers to the black hand of luck, a gambling charm, but the advertisement depicts an organized-crime death threat. Pianist Willie Tyson is the accompanist on these two songs, the only ones recorded under the name Hattie Hudson. The name may have been a pseudonym for Hattie Burleson, who recorded for Brunswick and Paramount. (Courtesy of Kip Lornell.)

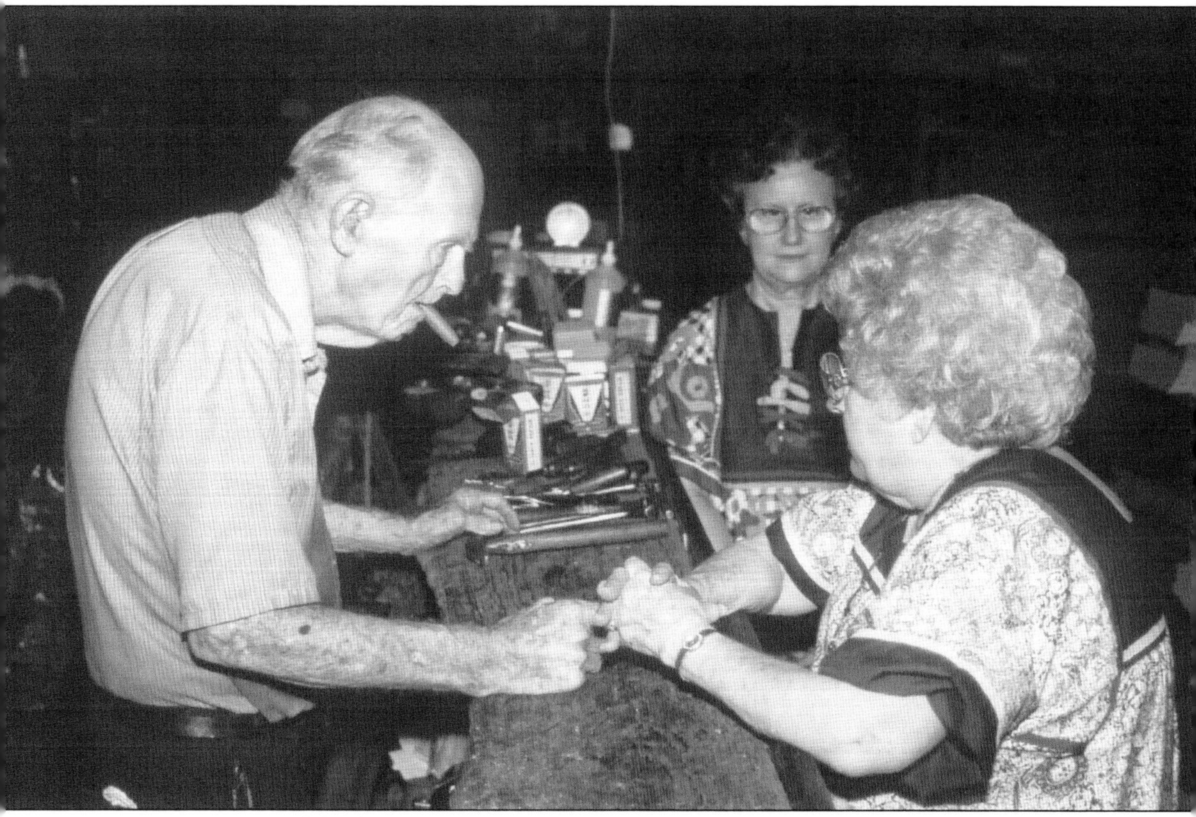

C.A. Spain was one of the longest-surviving Deep Ellum business owners. In 1990, he was still repairing shoes in the building at 2642 Elm Street that his father had built in 1919. The place still bore the original name, Spain & Son Shoe Store, though it had not sold shoes in years. Business was slow, though some old customers still came to Deep Ellum to have Spain repair their shoes, and vandalism had become a problem. Spain married once, briefly, and spent his entire life in Dallas except for service in the Army, which put him to work as a cobbler. He finally retired in 1992, telling a newspaper reporter, "I hate to leave Deep Ellum because it's a home to me. I've been here for a long time." The leaky old building was cleaned up and converted into an art gallery. Spain died in 1995, at age 91. (Photograph by Alan Govenar.)

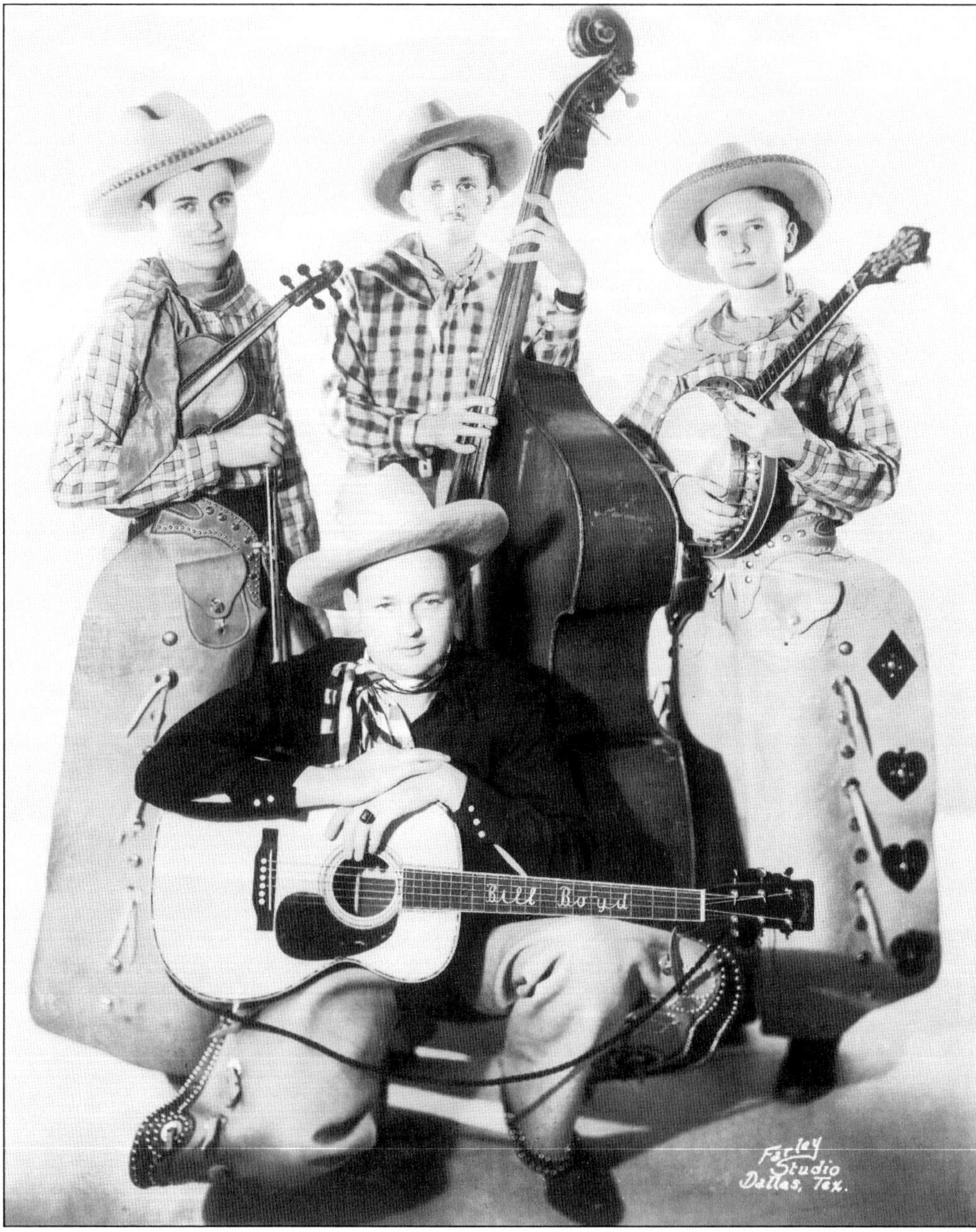


Bill Boyd (kneeling) led a Dallas string band, the Cowboy Ramblers. The group moved toward Western swing in the late 1930s by recording with hot players such as pianist John "Knocky" Parker and guitarist Muryel "Zeke" Campbell. Shown here with Boyd are, from left to right, fiddler Audrey "Art" Davis, bass player and singer Jim Boyd, and tenor banjo player Walker Kirkes. Brothers Bill and Jim Boyd moved from Fannin County, in northeast Texas, to Dallas in 1929 and soon became part of the city's lively musical scene. Bill Boyd formed his band in 1932, the same year he backed country star Jimmie Rodgers on recordings in Dallas. Members of the Ramblers worked as studio musicians at radio station WRR and made their first recordings, on the Victor label, in 1934. The Boyds toured occasionally, but for the most part they lived and worked in Dallas. (Courtesy of Walker Kirkes.)

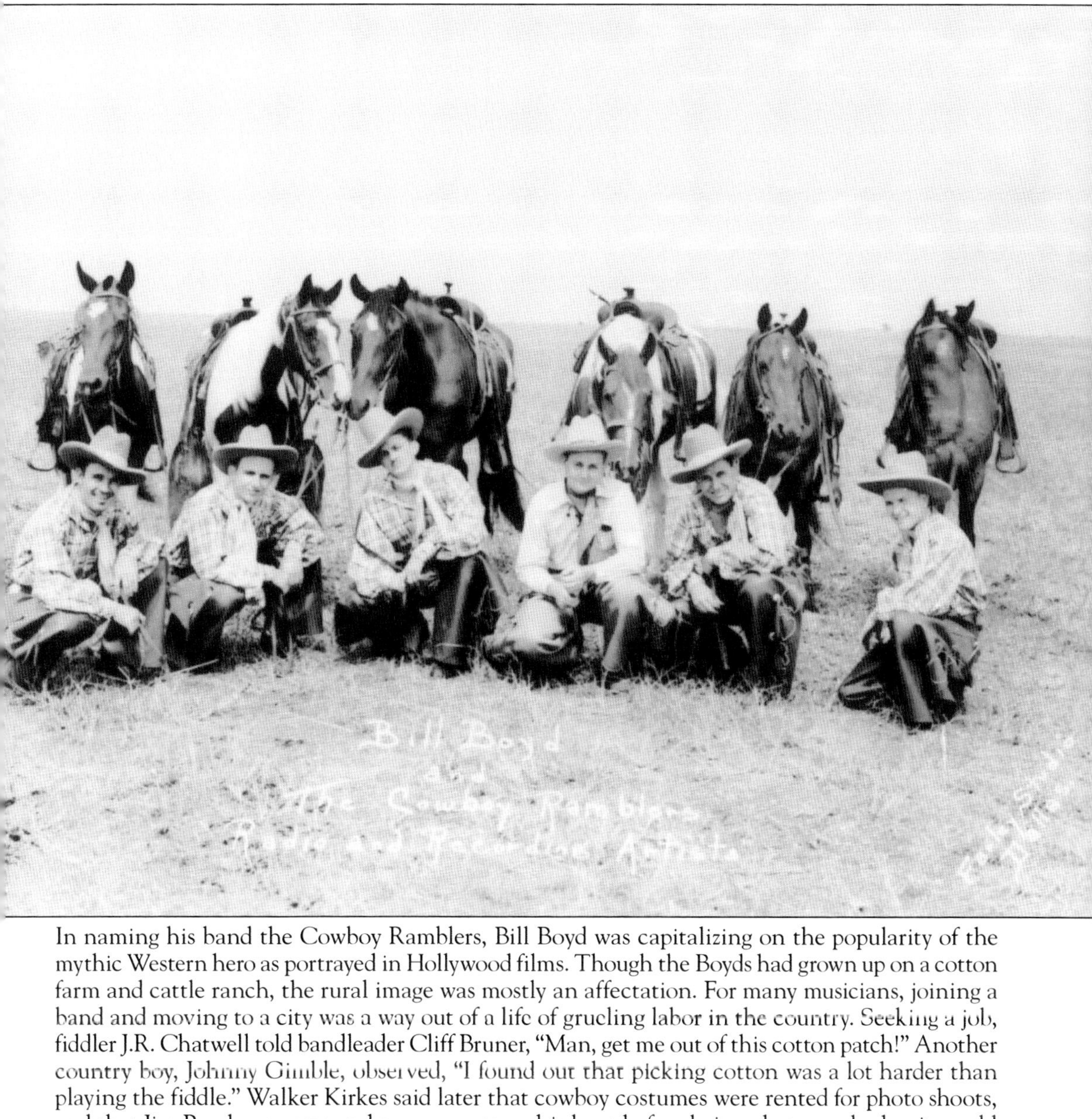


In naming his band the Cowboy Ramblers, Bill Boyd was capitalizing on the popularity of the mythic Western hero as portrayed in Hollywood films. Though the Boyds had grown up on a cotton farm and cattle ranch, the rural image was mostly an affectation. For many musicians, joining a band and moving to a city was a way out of a life of grueling labor in the country. Seeking a job, fiddler J.R. Chatwell told bandleader Cliff Bruner, "Man, get me out of this cotton patch!" Another country boy, Johnny Gimble, observed, "I found out that picking cotton was a lot harder than playing the fiddle." Walker Kirkes said later that cowboy costumes were rented for photo shoots, and that Jim Boyd once smeared cow manure on his boot before being photographed so it would appear that he had just come in from the pasture. (Courtesy of Walker Kirkes.)

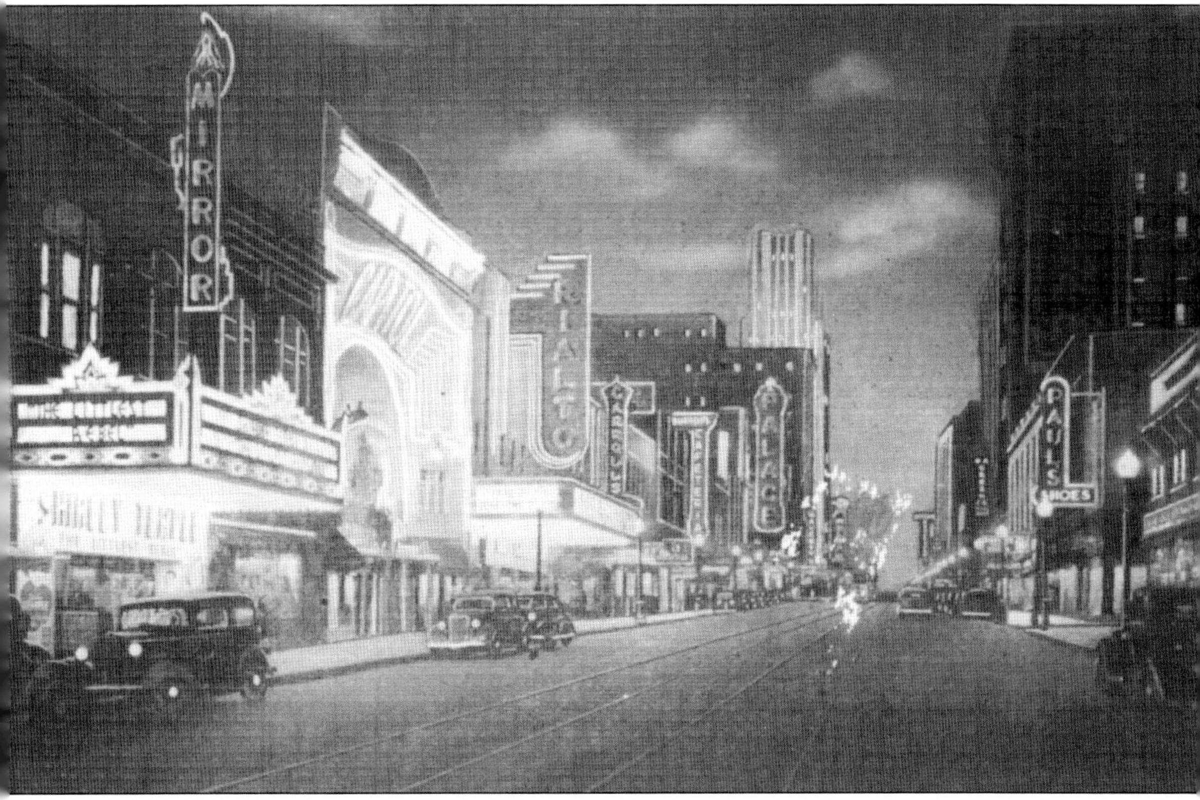


Dallas's "Theater Row" came alive with neon at night, as shown in this 1930s postcard. The view looks east from the 1500 block of Elm Street. The Palace, with a seating capacity of almost 3,000, a domed ceiling, and an elevator orchestra pit, rivaled the Majestic in grandeur when both opened in 1921. The movie houses thrived when downtown Dallas was a lively place where people worked, shopped, and came to eat and be entertained. Growth and changing times, though, spelled the theaters' demise, and the Palace was closed and demolished in the early 1970s. For years, downtown was virtually deserted after dark; the growth of urban lofts and condominiums has revived historic structures, such as the 1904 J.B. Wilson Building at 1800 Main Street. Such renovation has brought people back to the city's core, but nothing so grand as Theater Row has resulted.

# *Two*

# 508 Park

In 1929, when Warner Bros. started construction of a film exchange building at 508 Park Avenue in Dallas, the company never envisioned that some of the most important recordings of Western swing and blues would be produced there. In 1930, when the film exchange opened, the first floor was fitted with film vaults, the second was devoted to offices, and the third was left for expansion. On the roof was a small screening room where theater operators could preview films for rental. There was also a Warner Club in the building, a lounge for executives and traveling movie stars.

With the advent of the "talkies," Warner Bros. realized the potential of the burgeoning record industry and bought the Brunswick phonograph division from the Brunswick-Balke-Collender Company, a manufacturer of pool tables and phonographs. Warner Bros. planned to record its movie stars, but by late 1931, it had abandoned its efforts as record sales dropped sharply during the Depression. Warner Bros. sold (while retaining certain rights) its record business to Consolidated Film Industries (CFI), parent of American Record Corporation (ARC). CFI changed the name to Brunswick Record Corporation and operated Brunswick as part of ARC.

ARC's regional field-recording activities included sessions in San Antonio, Dallas, Fort Worth, Saginaw, and El Paso, Texas, and Hot Springs, Arkansas. It is believed that the introduction of the DAL matrix series (recording IDs) coincided with the first sessions conducted at 508 Park in 1935. The first side recorded, DAL 100, was Cargill and Keenan's "I'm Goin' to Where the Blues Ain't Never Known." It was followed by numerous recordings by hillbilly and Western swing bands, most notably the Light Crust Doughboys and Bob Wills and his Texas Playboys; those two bands made more recordings in the building than anyone else. Other groups included the Dallas Jamboree Jug Band, Roy Newman and his Boys, Zeke Williams and his Rambling Cowboys, the Crystal Springs Ramblers, W. Lee O'Daniel and his Hillbilly Boys, and Mexican musicians such as Lolo Cavazos and José Almeida, Los Tres Manueles con Orquesta, and Orquesta Vocalion Internacional.

Among the blues musicians who found their way to 508 Park were Willie Reed, Black Boy Shine, and the legendary Robert Johnson, whose recordings on June 19 and 20, 1937, are considered among the finest ever made.

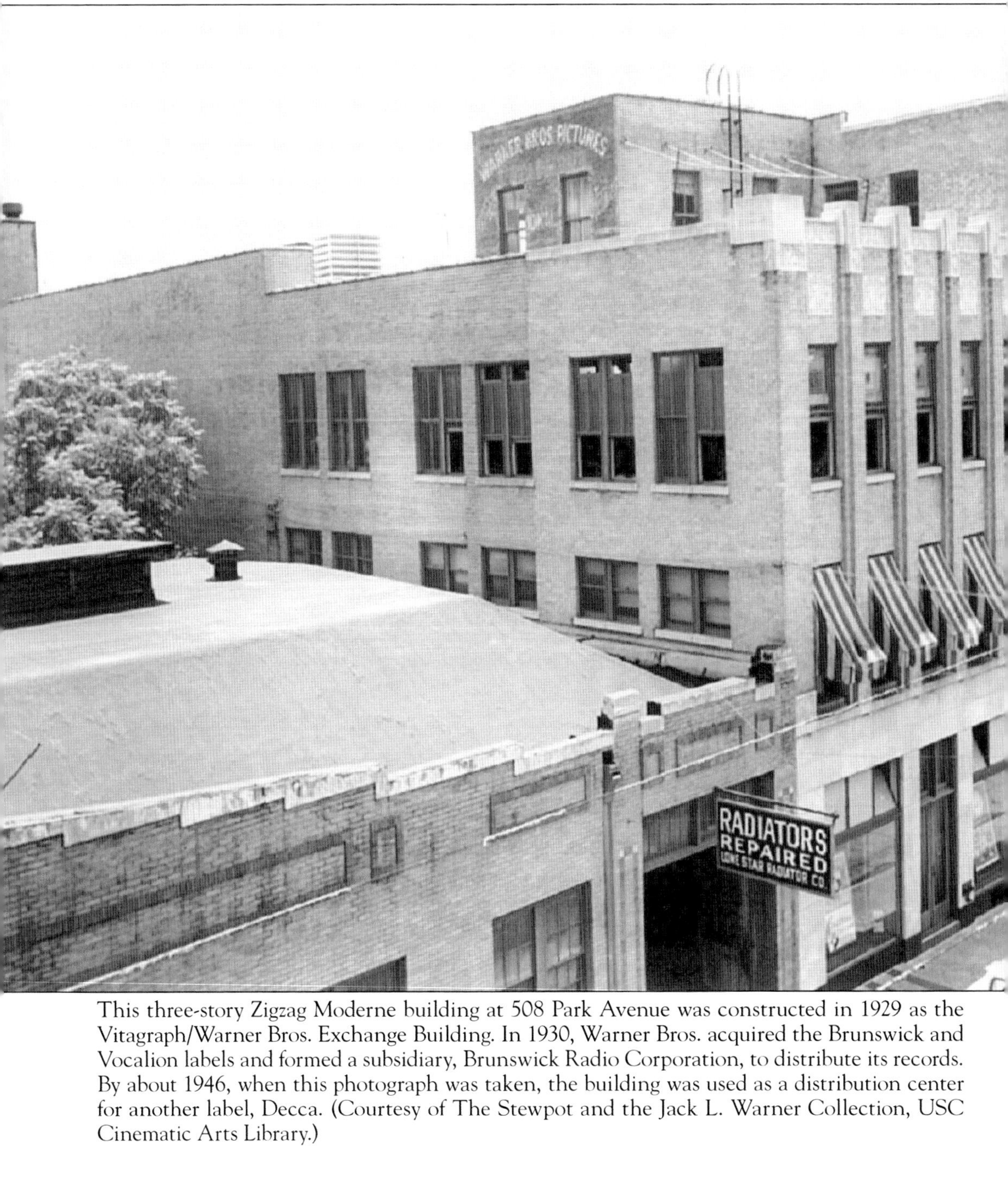


This three-story Zigzag Moderne building at 508 Park Avenue was constructed in 1929 as the Vitagraph/Warner Bros. Exchange Building. In 1930, Warner Bros. acquired the Brunswick and Vocalion labels and formed a subsidiary, Brunswick Radio Corporation, to distribute its records. By about 1946, when this photograph was taken, the building was used as a distribution center for another label, Decca. (Courtesy of The Stewpot and the Jack L. Warner Collection, USC Cinematic Arts Library.)

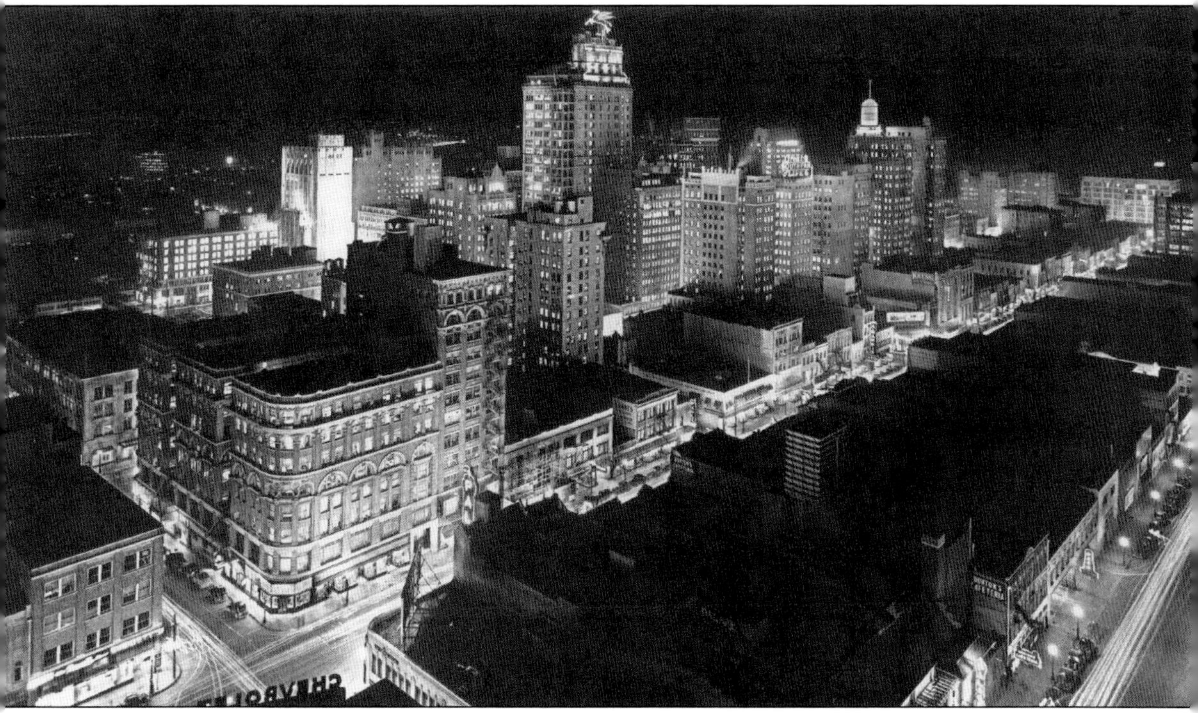

A postcard proclaiming Dallas as "brilliant in achievement" illustrates the North Texas city's efforts to promote itself as an exceptional place created out of nothing by visionary business leaders. Towering over the skyline is the red neon Pegasus, inspired by the winged horse from Greek mythology. The sign was installed on the roof of the Magnolia Building, the city's first skyscraper, in 1934. Derived from the Magnolia Oil Company logo, it greeted those attending the first meeting of the American Petroleum Institute. After the discovery of the huge East Texas Oil Field in 1930, Dallas had become a center of petroleum business and home to figures such as the legendary wildcatter H.L. Hunt. Pegasus came to symbolize Dallas's "can-do" spirit and once was visible for miles across the surrounding prairie. Though it no longer dominates the skyline as it once did, the sign, now owned by the city, has been renovated and still flies at Pegasus Plaza at City Center. (Courtesy of the Texas/Dallas History and Archives Division, Dallas Public Library.)

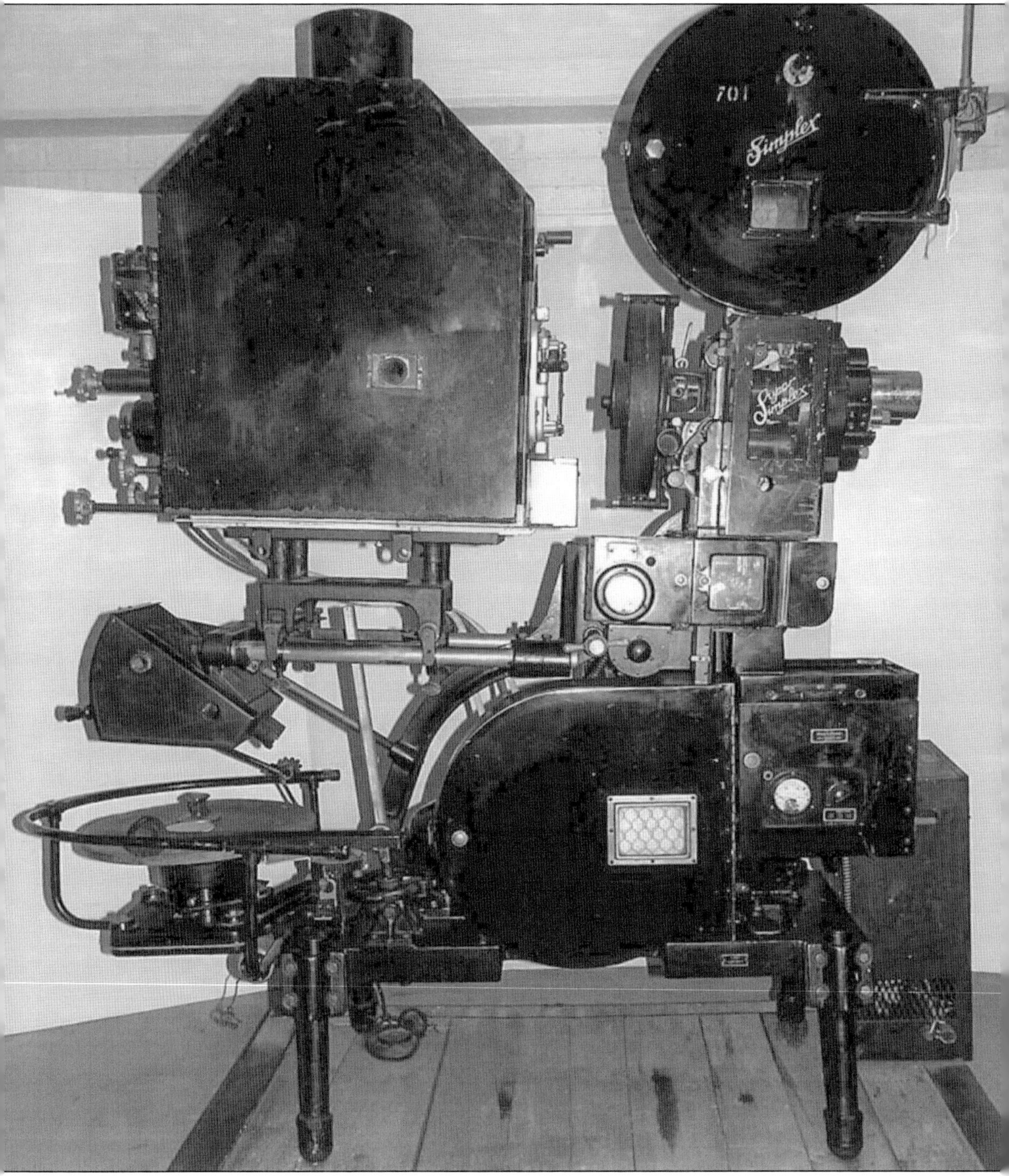


The Universal Base projector gave theaters the flexibility to run full-aperture silent, sound-on-disc, or sound-on-film movies in a time when the studios were uncertain about the future of synchronized films. Western Electric developed the sound-on-disc process and presented it to Warner Bros. After the movie studio acquired the Brunswick and Vocalion record labels, it used 508 Park as a distribution center. (Courtesy of Tom Wilson.)

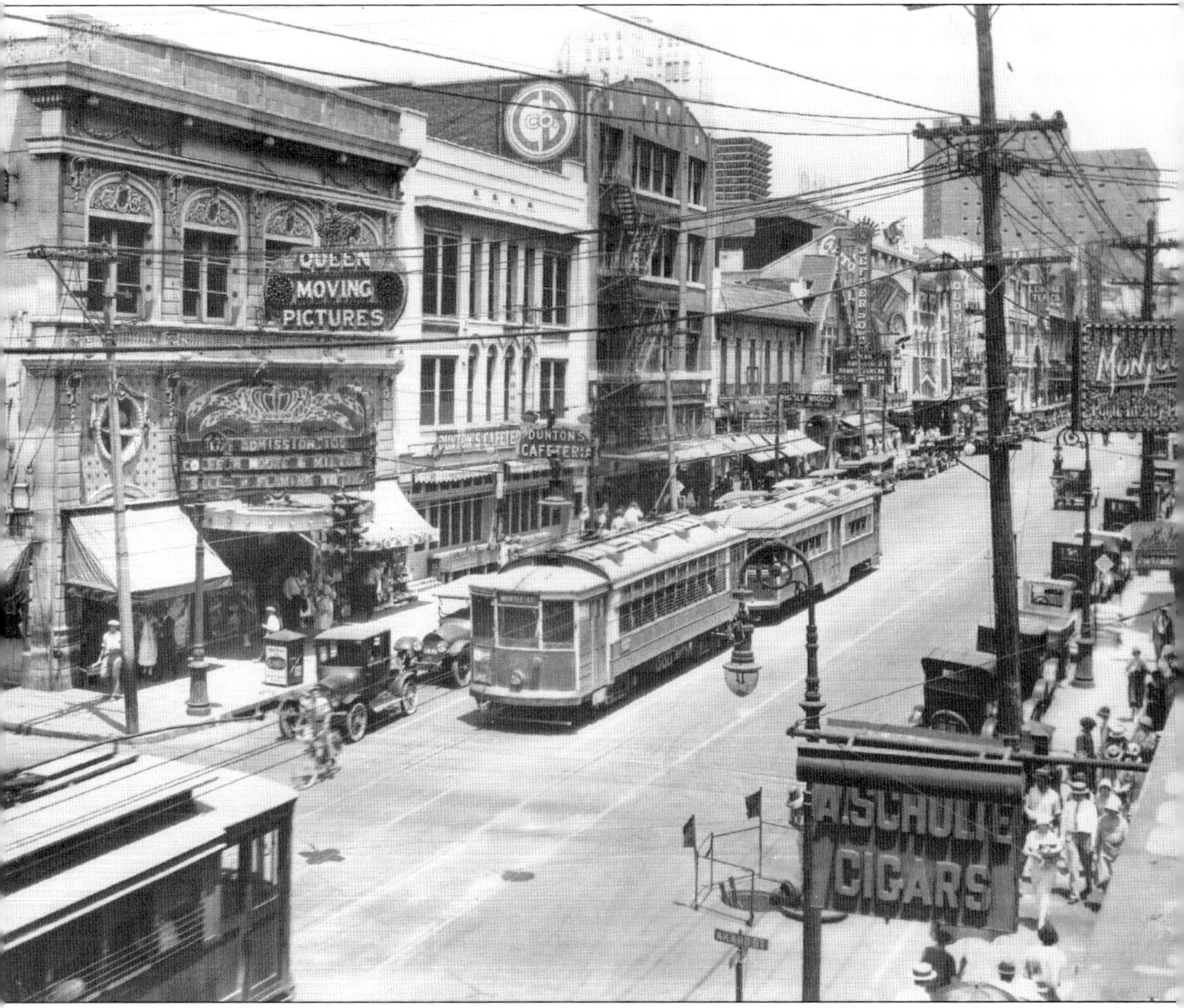


The Queen Theater opened at 1501 Elm Street, at the intersection with Akard Street, in 1913 as a showplace. It featured life-sized statues of historical figures such as Cleopatra, a $20,000 pipe organ with special effects, a grand piano, and an orchestra. Patrons sitting in boxes had access to a cigar parlor. Management promised to ensure the moral protection of child patrons. The Queen promoted itself as "crowned with public favor," but it was eclipsed by newer, more modern movie houses and became a second-run venue in 1926. Four years later, the Queen showed its first talking picture, *The Cock-Eyed World*, using the Western Electric sound-on-film technology. The theater was renovated and renamed the Leo in 1948. It struggled to survive, offering "adult" films and vaudeville and burlesque shows. But time had passed the theater by, and it closed in 1953 and was demolished in 1955. (Courtesy of the Texas/Dallas History and Archives Division, Dallas Public Library.)

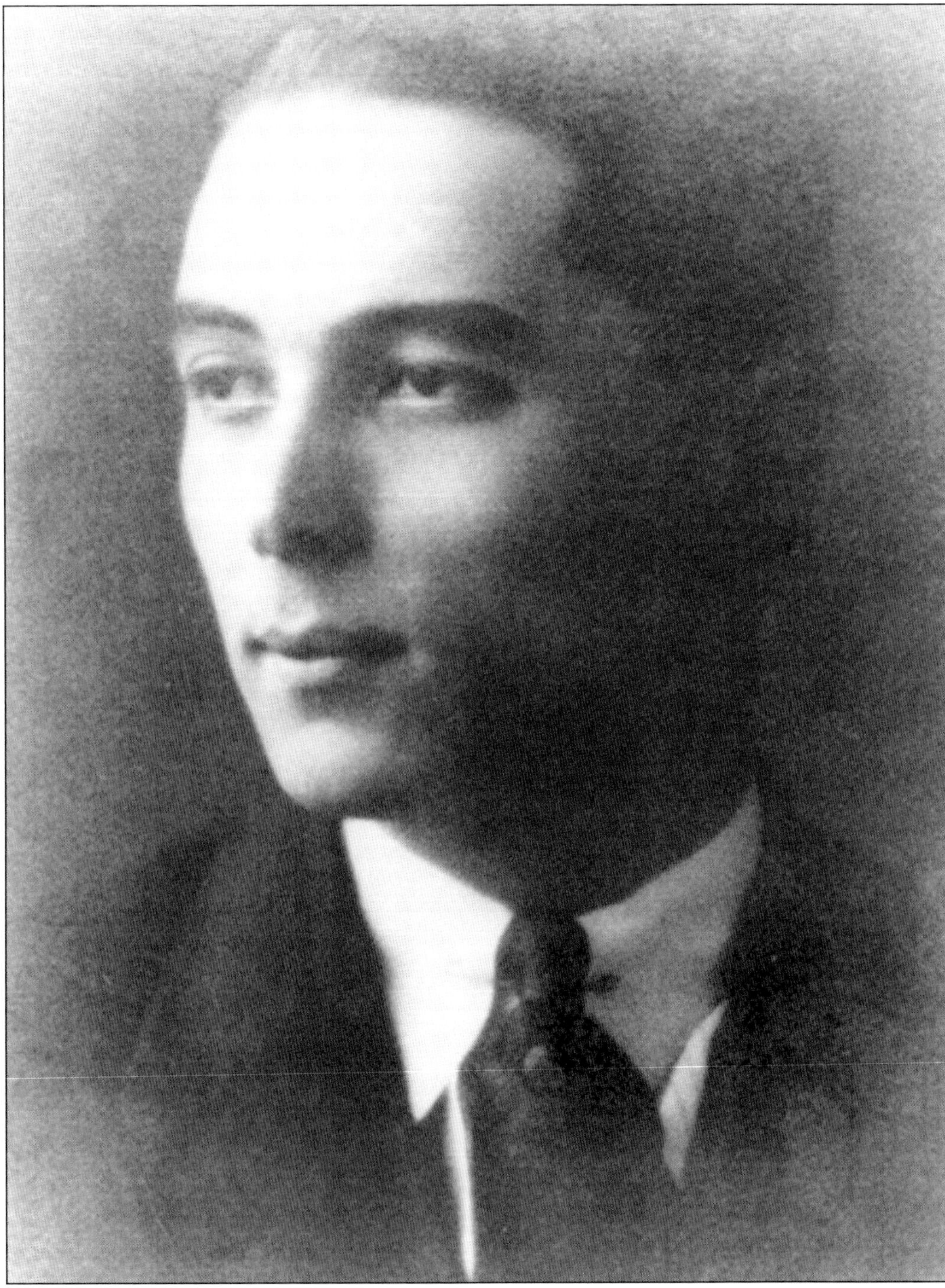

Don Law, born in England in 1902, immigrated to the United States in 1924. By 1930, he was working as an accounting clerk for Brunswick Radio Corporation at 508 Park Avenue in Dallas. When the American Record Corporation took over Brunswick in 1931, Law found a mentor in a fellow Englishman, "Uncle" Art Satherley, and became involved in producing records, including those of Robert Johnson. (Courtesy of Don Law Jr.)

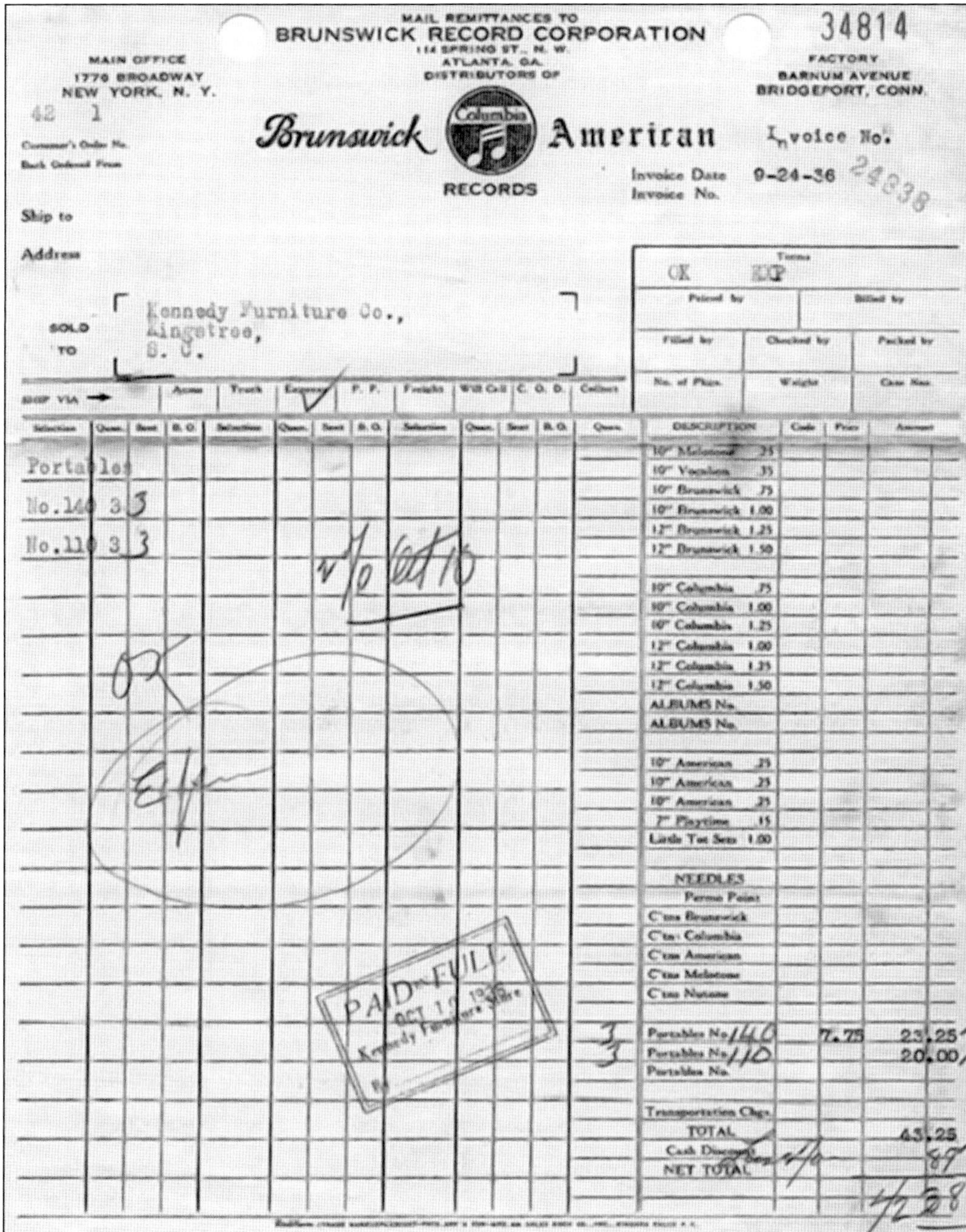

MAIL REMITTANCES TO
BRUNSWICK RECORD CORPORATION
114 SPRING ST., N. W.
ATLANTA, GA.
DISTRIBUTORS OF

34814

MAIN OFFICE
1776 BROADWAY
NEW YORK, N. Y.

FACTORY
BARNUM AVENUE
BRIDGEPORT, CONN.

42 1

Customer's Order No.
Back Ordered From

Brunswick Columbia American
RECORDS

Invoice No.
Invoice Date 9-24-36
Invoice No. 24838

Ship to
Address

SOLD TO Kennedy Furniture Co.,
Kingstree,
S. C.

SHIP VIA → Express

Terms: OK EXP

Portables
No.140 3 3
No.110 3 3

| DESCRIPTION | Code | Price | Amount |
|---|---|---|---|
| 10" Melotone .35 | | | |
| 10" Vocalion .35 | | | |
| 10" Brunswick .75 | | | |
| 10" Brunswick 1.00 | | | |
| 12" Brunswick 1.25 | | | |
| 12" Brunswick 1.50 | | | |
| 10" Columbia .75 | | | |
| 10" Columbia 1.00 | | | |
| 10" Columbia 1.25 | | | |
| 12" Columbia 1.00 | | | |
| 12" Columbia 1.25 | | | |
| 12" Columbia 1.50 | | | |
| ALBUMS No. | | | |
| ALBUMS No. | | | |
| 10" American .25 | | | |
| 10" American .25 | | | |
| 10" American .25 | | | |
| 7" Playtime .15 | | | |
| Little Tot Sets 1.00 | | | |
| NEEDLES | | | |
| Permo Point | | | |
| C'ns Brunswick | | | |
| C'ns Columbia | | | |
| C'ns American | | | |
| C'ns Melotone | | | |
| C'ns Nutone | | | |
| Portables No. 140 | | 7.75 | 23.25 |
| Portables No. 110 | | | 20.00 |
| Portables No. | | | |
| Transportation Chgs. | | | |
| TOTAL | | | 43.25 |
| Cash Discount | | | .87 |
| NET TOTAL | | | 42.38 |

PAID IN FULL
OCT 1 1936
Kennedy Furniture Store

This 1936 Brunswick Record Corporation invoice to a South Carolina furniture company also bears the "Magic Notes" logo of the Columbia Phonograph Company, which had been acquired out of bankruptcy from Grigsby-Grunow by Brunswick's parent company, Consolidated Film Industries (CFI), two years before. It is believed that CFI operated Brunswick, Columbia, and American Records as one business (historically referred to as the American Record Corporation) from 1934 to 1938, when Columbia Broadcasting System acquired the business and renamed it Columbia Recording Corporation. (Courtesy of the 508 Park Collection.)

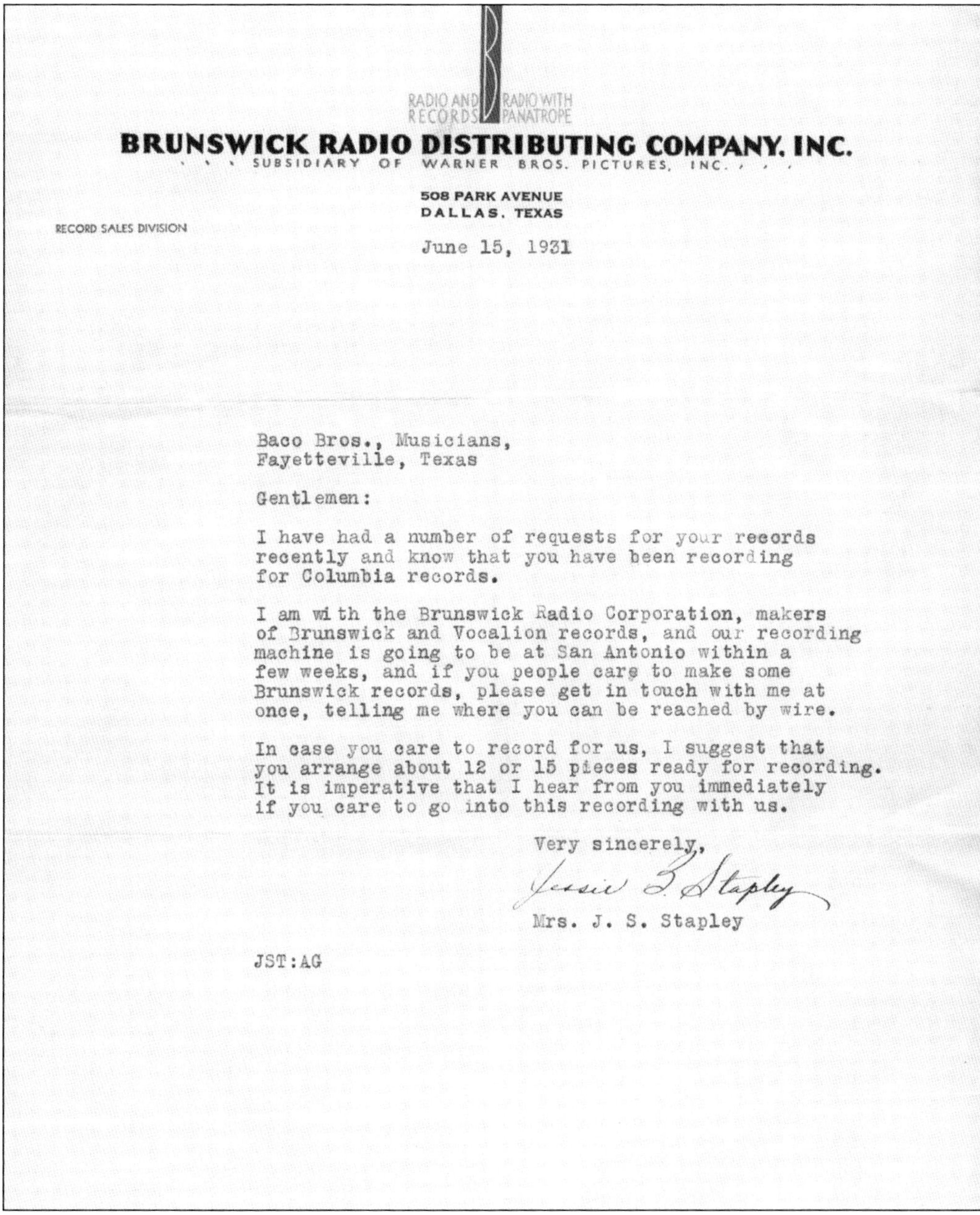

RADIO AND RECORDS | RADIO WITH PANATROPE

**BRUNSWICK RADIO DISTRIBUTING COMPANY, INC.**

SUBSIDIARY OF WARNER BROS. PICTURES, INC.

508 PARK AVENUE
DALLAS, TEXAS

RECORD SALES DIVISION

June 15, 1931

Baco Bros., Musicians,
Fayetteville, Texas

Gentlemen:

I have had a number of requests for your records recently and know that you have been recording for Columbia records.

I am with the Brunswick Radio Corporation, makers of Brunswick and Vocalion records, and our recording machine is going to be at San Antonio within a few weeks, and if you people care to make some Brunswick records, please get in touch with me at once, telling me where you can be reached by wire.

In case you care to record for us, I suggest that you arrange about 12 or 15 pieces ready for recording. It is imperative that I hear from you immediately if you care to go into this recording with us.

Very sincerely,

Jessie S. Stapley

Mrs. J. S. Stapley

JST:AG

A June 1931 letter from Brunswick seeks to interest the Baca Brothers Band, a Czech American group from Fayetteville, Texas, in recording in San Antonio. The Bacas did record for Brunswick, but not until 1935. (Courtesy of Andrew Brown and The Clarence Baca Collection.)

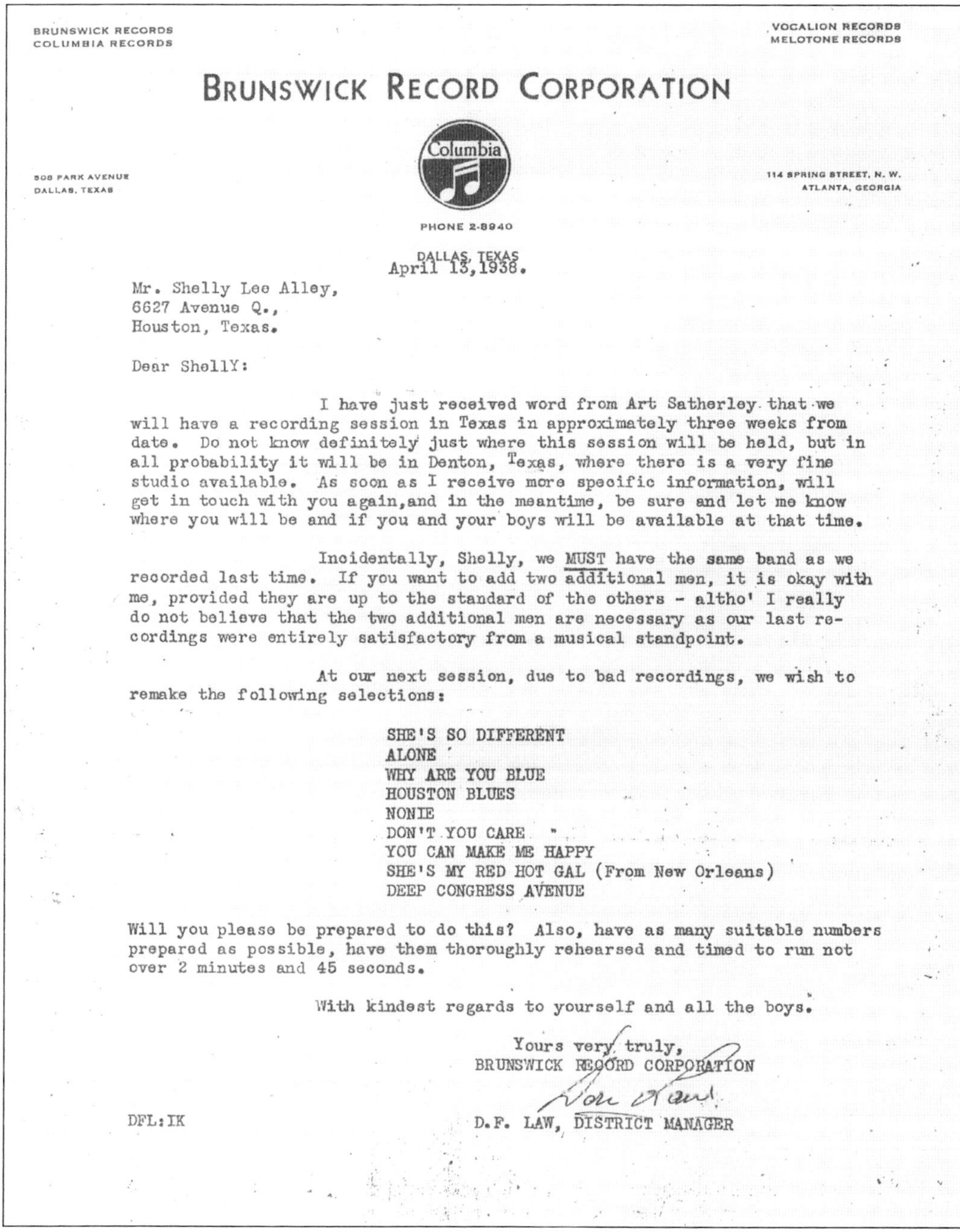

BRUNSWICK RECORDS
COLUMBIA RECORDS

VOCALION RECORDS
MELOTONE RECORDS

# BRUNSWICK RECORD CORPORATION

Columbia

508 PARK AVENUE
DALLAS, TEXAS

114 SPRING STREET, N. W.
ATLANTA, GEORGIA

PHONE 2-8940

DALLAS, TEXAS
April 13,1938.

Mr. Shelly Lee Alley,
6627 Avenue Q.,
Houston, Texas.

Dear ShellY:

I have just received word from Art Satherley that we will have a recording session in Texas in approximately three weeks from date. Do not know definitely just where this session will be held, but in all probability it will be in Denton, Texas, where there is a very fine studio available. As soon as I receive more specific information, will get in touch with you again,and in the meantime, be sure and let me know where you will be and if you and your boys will be available at that time.

Incidentally, Shelly, we MUST have the same band as we recorded last time. If you want to add two additional men, it is okay with me, provided they are up to the standard of the others - altho' I really do not believe that the two additional men are necessary as our last recordings were entirely satisfactory from a musical standpoint.

At our next session, due to bad recordings, we wish to remake the following selections:

SHE'S SO DIFFERENT
ALONE
WHY ARE YOU BLUE
HOUSTON BLUES
NONIE
DON'T YOU CARE
YOU CAN MAKE ME HAPPY
SHE'S MY RED HOT GAL (From New Orleans)
DEEP CONGRESS AVENUE

Will you please be prepared to do this? Also, have as many suitable numbers prepared as possible, have them thoroughly rehearsed and timed to run not over 2 minutes and 45 seconds.

With kindest regards to yourself and all the boys.

Yours very truly,
BRUNSWICK RECORD CORPORATION

Don Law

DFL:IK

D.F. LAW, DISTRICT MANAGER

In an April 1938 letter, Don Law asks Houston bandleader Shelly Lee Alley to take part in a recording session in about three weeks, probably at a studio in Denton, north of Dallas. Law lists songs to be recorded, including "Deep Congress Avenue," about a notorious part of Houston, and "She's My Red Hot Gal." These were among songs the band recorded on May 10, 1938, and issued on Vocalion. The session was held not in Denton but in Dallas, at 508 Park Avenue. The bass player on "Red Hot Gal," "Deep Congress," and several other tunes was Pinkie Dawson, father of rockabilly performer Ronnie Dawson, who later became a regular on the *Big "D" Jamboree*. Alley continued to record for ARC labels in Dallas for several years. (Courtesy of Shelly Lee Alley Jr.)

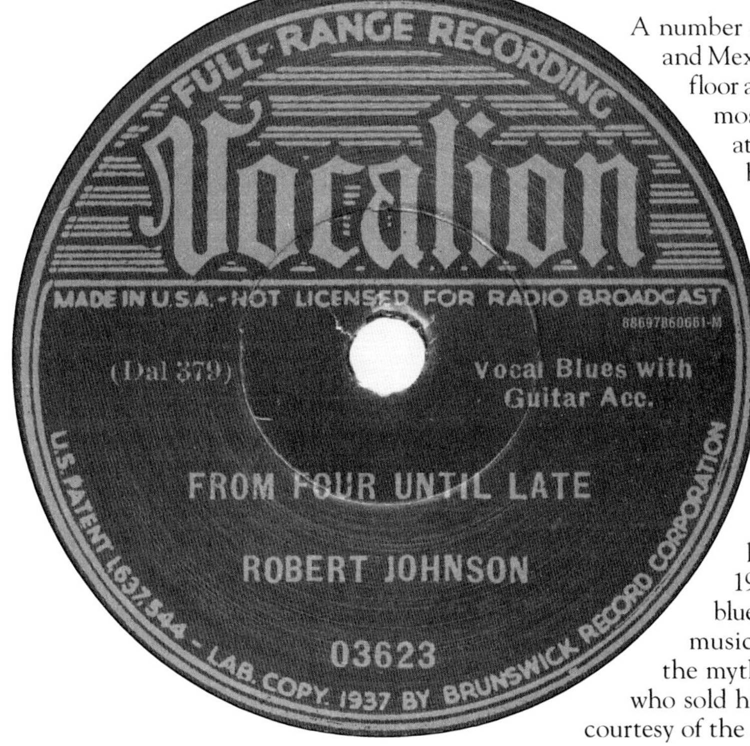


A number of musicians, white, black, and Mexican, recorded on the third floor at 508 Park, but no doubt the most famous—posthumously, at least—was the Mississippi blues singer Robert Johnson. He made his first recordings in San Antonio in 1936 and his final ones, including "From Four Until Late" and "Hell Hound on My Trail," at 508 Park on June 19 and 20, 1937. Johnson died the next year at 27, apparently poisoned by a jealous husband at a Delta juke joint. He was largely forgotten until the 1960s, when young folk and blues fans seized on his powerful music and haunting lyrics and the myth of the doomed bluesman who sold his soul to the devil. (Both, courtesy of the 508 Park Collection.)

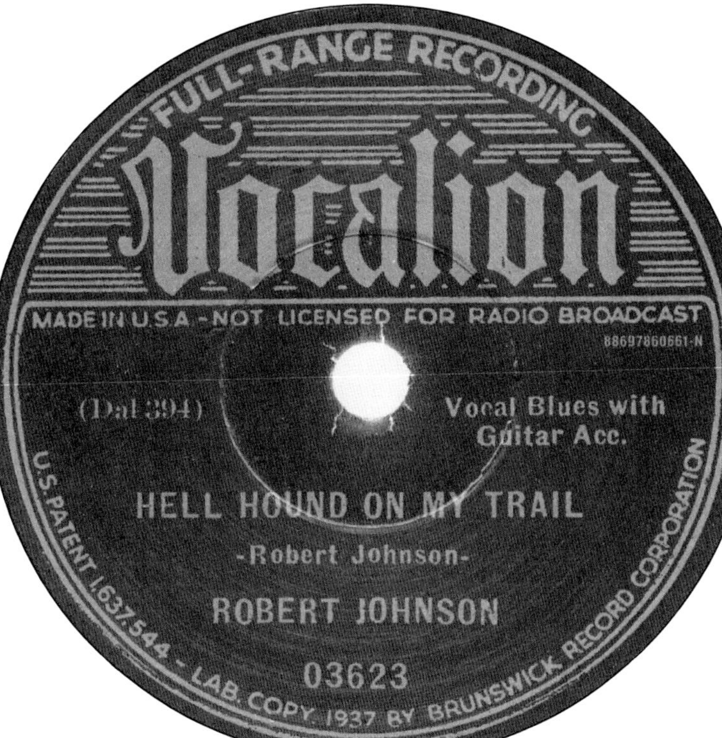

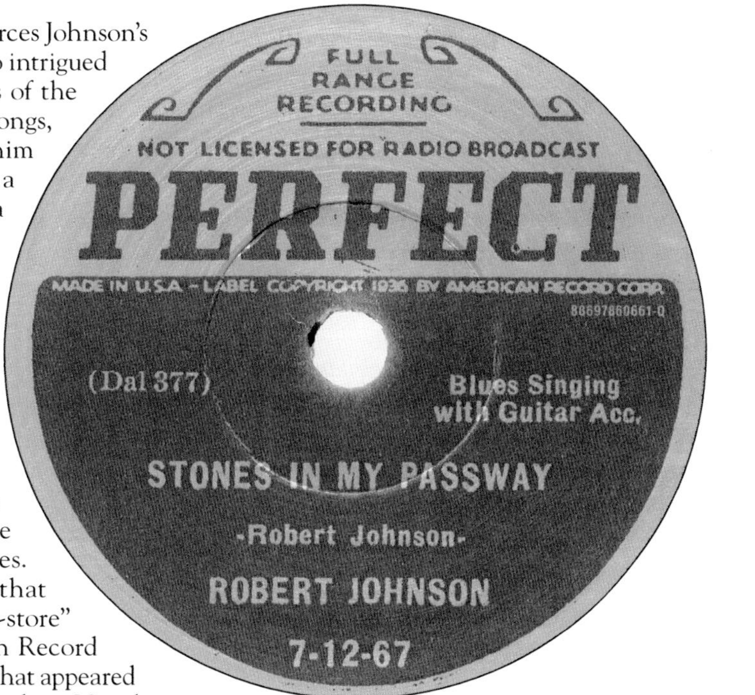


“Stones in My Passway” reinforces Johnson’s mysterious image, which has so intrigued modern fans. The liner notes of the first Columbia album of his songs, released in 1961, referred to him as “little, very little more than a name on aging index cards and a few dusty master records in the files of a phonograph company that no longer exists.” In “I’m a Steady Rollin’ Man,” he boasts of being a hard worker, which seems ironic, considering his reputation for avoiding physical labor. But “rolling” and “working” had sexual overtones as well, so he may have been engaging in the bragging common in the blues. These are among the songs that appeared on Perfect, a “dime-store” label owned by the American Record Corporation. Generally, songs that appeared on such labels also were issued on Vocalion. (Both, courtesy of the 508 Park Collection.)

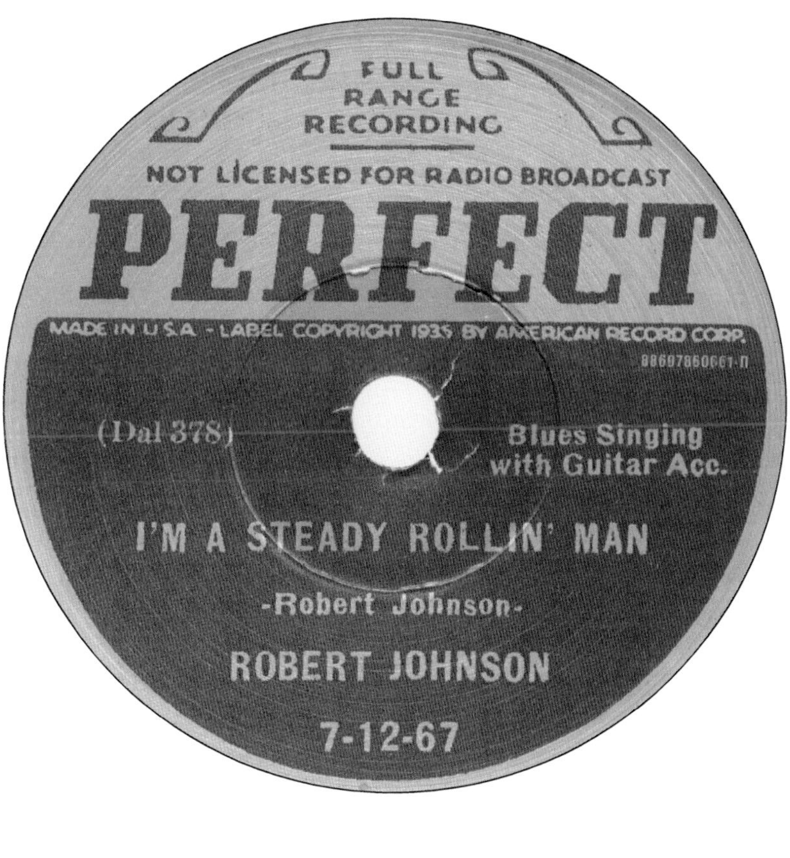

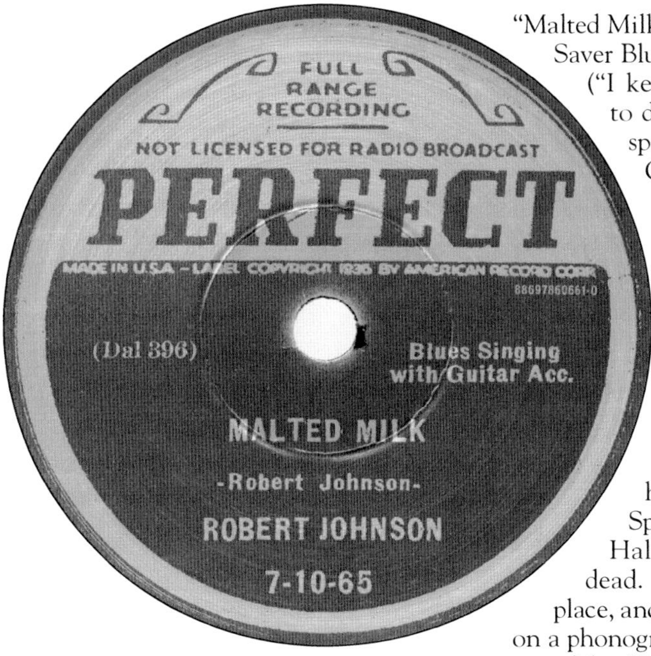


"Malted Milk," based on Lonnie Johnson's "Life Saver Blues," refers to an alcoholic beverage ("I keep drinking malted milk, trying to drive my blues away"), though the specific reference is unclear. "Milkcow's Calf Blues" is a follow-up to "Milk Cow Blues" by Kokomo Arnold, a model for several of Johnson's guitar accompaniments. Johnson waxed only three songs in his first Dallas session, but he recorded 10 on the second day. "Milkcow's Calf" was the last song he recorded. Johnson may have just missed national fame. In 1938, Columbia producer and talent scout John Hammond sought him for an appearance in the first Spirituals to Swing concert at Carnegie Hall, only to learn that Johnson was dead. Big Bill Broonzy performed in his place, and two of Johnson's songs were played on a phonograph onstage at the concert. (Both, courtesy of the 508 Park Collection.)

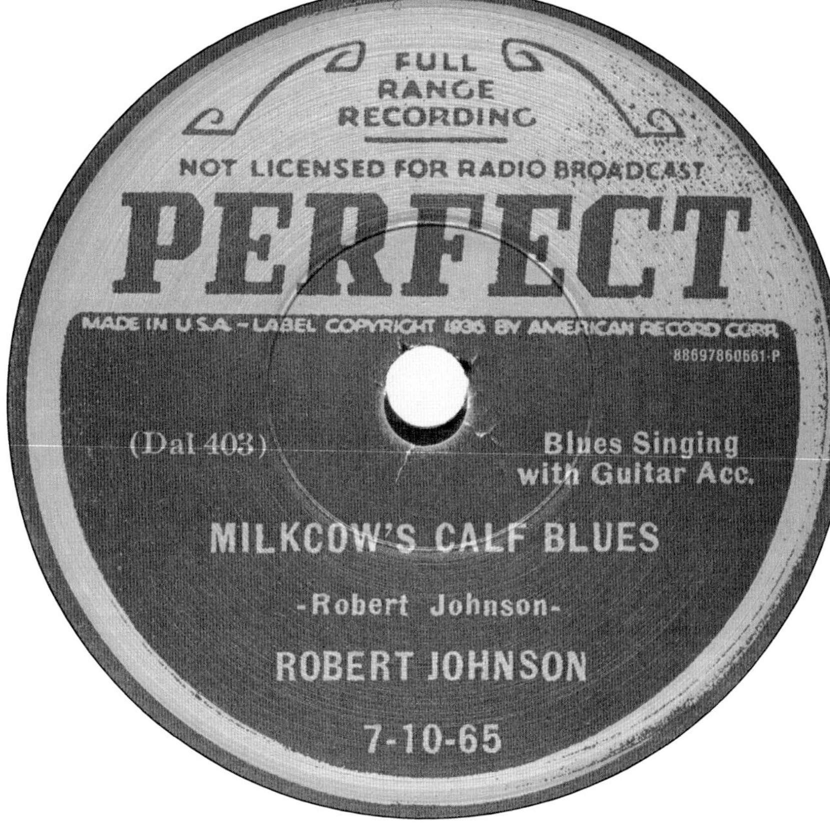

“Love in Vain Blues” is among Johnson’s most moving songs, with its image of a man following his woman to the railroad station to bid her farewell. The melody is based on a song by the very popular singer Leroy Carr, “When the Sun Goes Down”; one of its most powerful lines, “The blue light was my blues / The red light was my mind,” is derived from “Dry Southern Blues,” recorded in 1926 by Texas singer Blind Lemon Jefferson. Johnson often engaged in such borrowing, which was common in the blues, but he made the resulting songs his own. He transformed Son House’s “Preaching the Blues” into his own “Preachin’ Blues,” which was recorded in San Antonio but released as the flip side of “Love in Vain.” The Rolling Stones, among the rock groups smitten by Johnson, recorded “Love in Vain” for their 1969 album *Let It Bleed.* (Both, courtesy of the 508 Park Collection.)

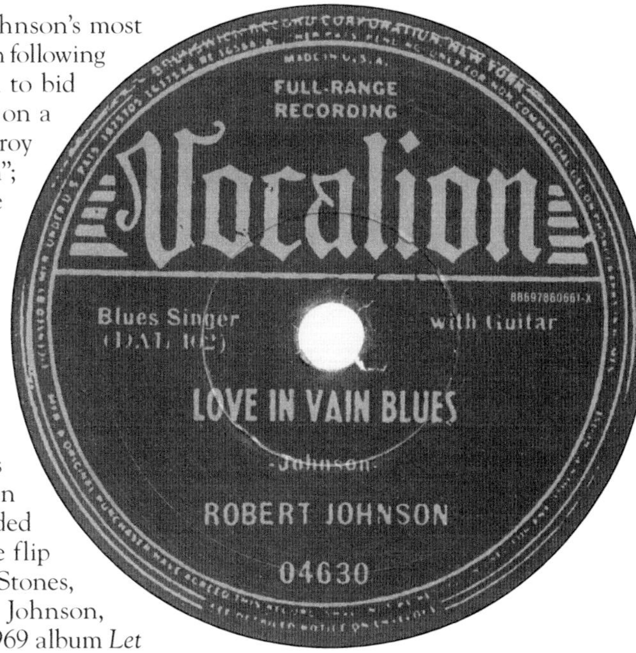


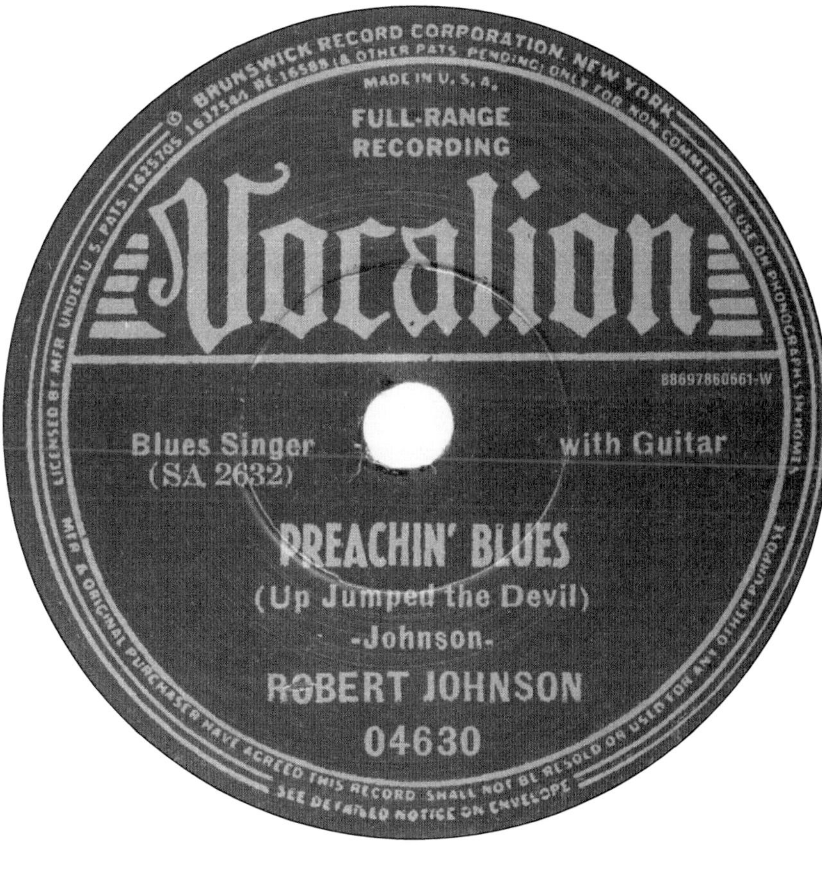

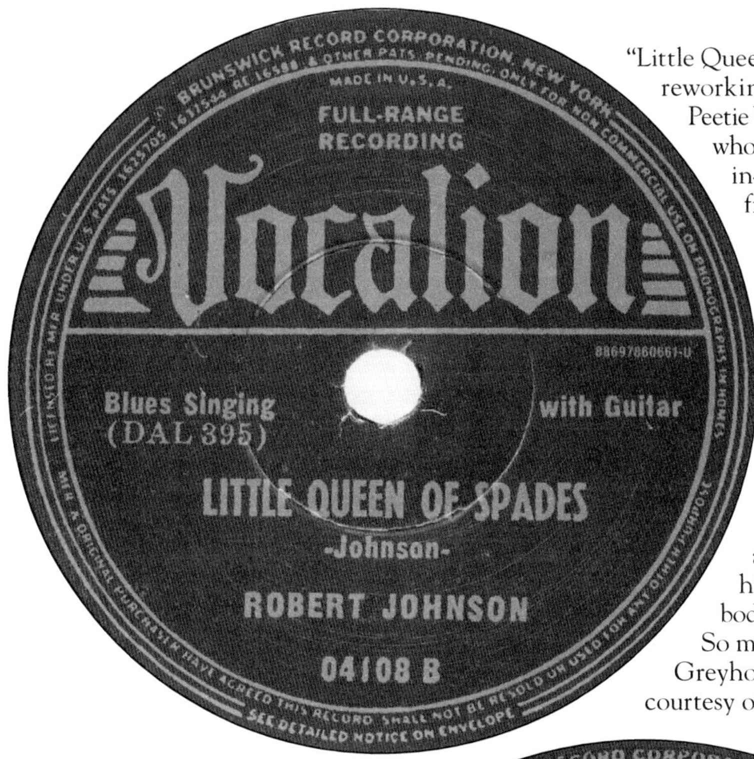


"Little Queen of Spades" was Johnson's reworking of "King of Spades" by Peetie Wheatstraw, a popular singer who was called "the Devil's Son-in-Law" and "the High Sheriff from Hell." Johnson shifted the song to a woman's perspective but employed some of Wheatstraw's vocal interjections. "Me and the Devil Blues," also inspired by Wheatstraw, opens with a casual greeting, "Hello, Satan, I believe it's time to go," and includes one of Johnson's signature lines that took on added resonance in view of his death: "You may bury my body down by the highway side / So my old evil spirit can catch a Greyhound bus and ride." (Both, courtesy of the 508 Park Collection.)

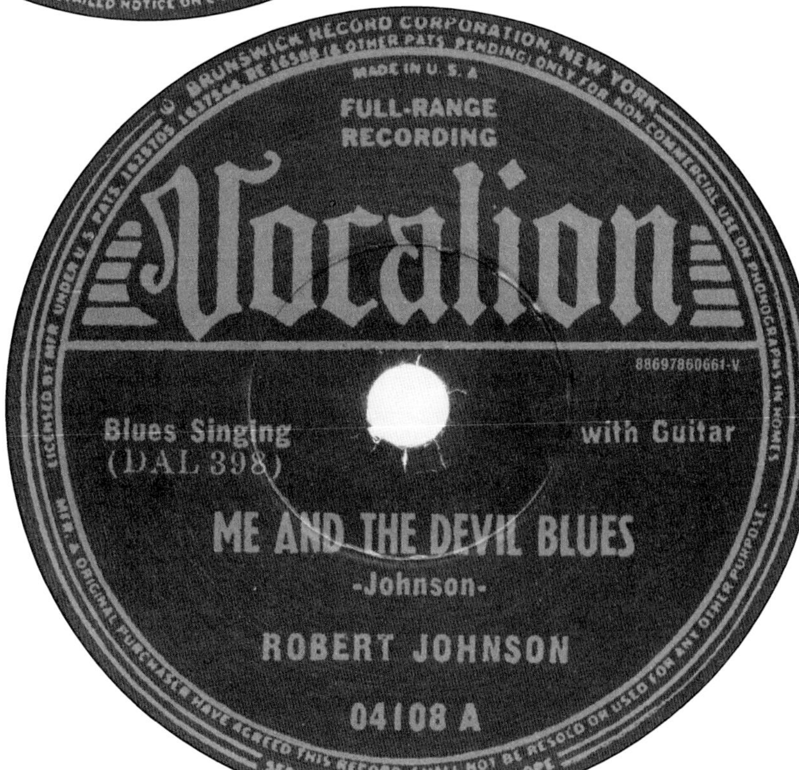

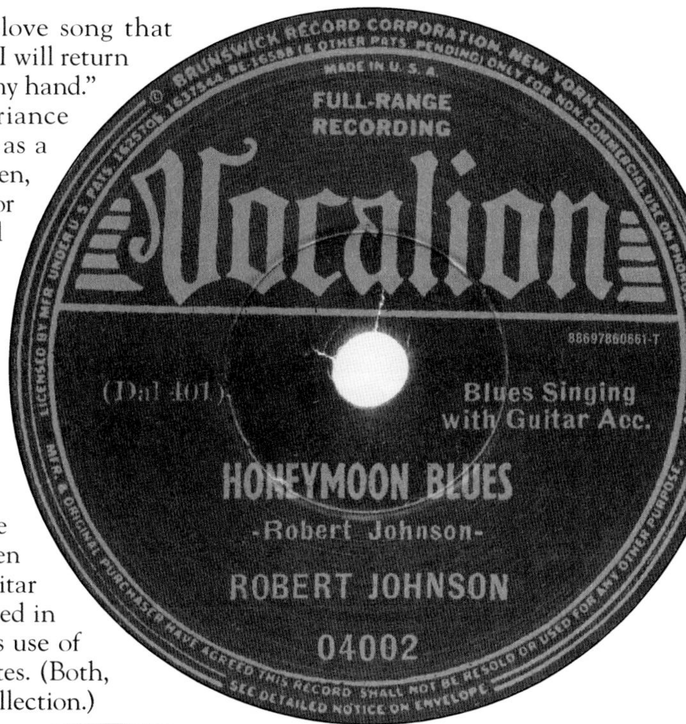


"Honeymoon Blues" is a love song that includes the line "Someday I will return with a marriage license in my hand." It seems somewhat at variance with Johnson's reputation as a rambling womanizer. "Women, to Robert, were like motel or hotel rooms," his musical traveling companion Johnny Shines recalled years later. "Even if he used them repeatedly, he left them where he found them." Yet Johnson was known to have been married at least once and lost a wife and child in childbirth. "Stop Breakin' Down Blues," whose title means roughly "straighten up," features an unusual guitar accompaniment that is played in an open tuning and makes use of slide only in its last four notes. (Both, courtesy of the 508 Park Collection.)

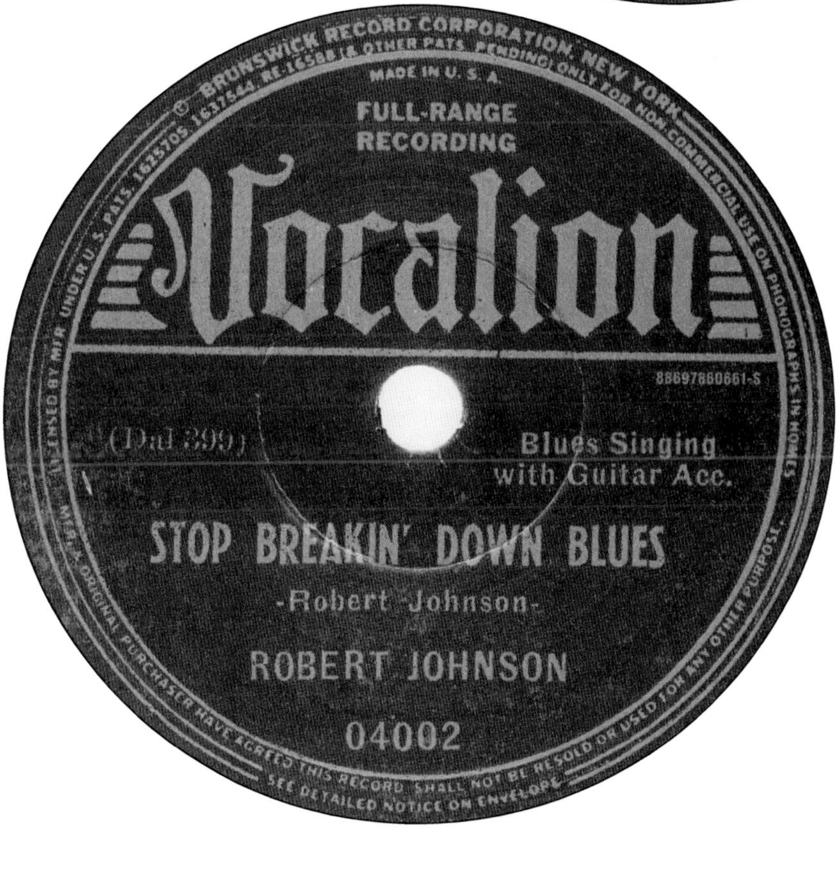

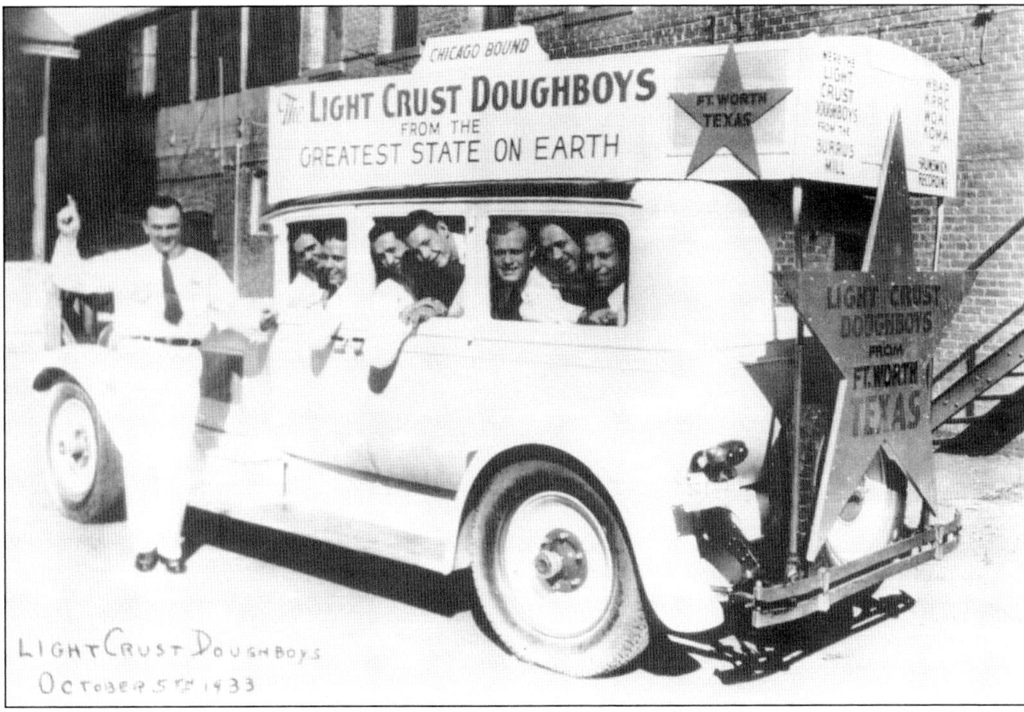


The Light Crust Doughboys originated as an advertising vehicle for Burrus Mill & Elevator Company, a Fort Worth flour company. The band originally included Western swing pioneers Bob Wills and Milton Brown, but both had left by the time the Doughboys were photographed in a company station wagon on October 5, 1933 (above). In 1936, the band visited Dallas's Fair Park to promote the Texas Centennial (below). Iowa native Marvin "Smokey" Montgomery, the longtime banjo player and leader who joined in 1935, learned about the blues when fellow band member Dick Reinhart took him to Deep Ellum. Reinhart sat in with black musicians and learned songs that were soon added to the group's repertoire. (Courtesy of Marvin Montgomery.)

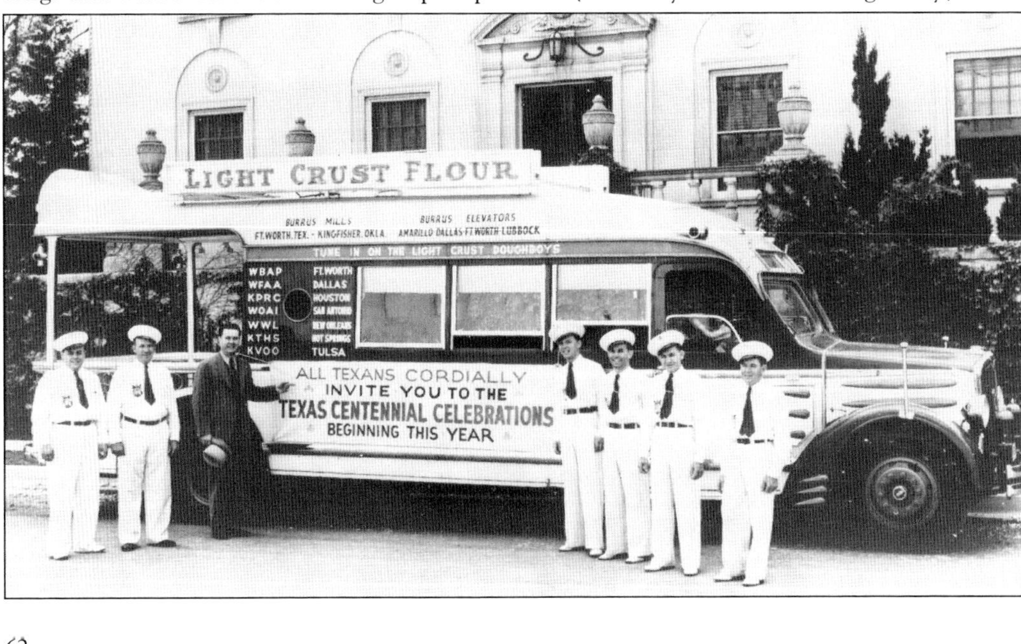

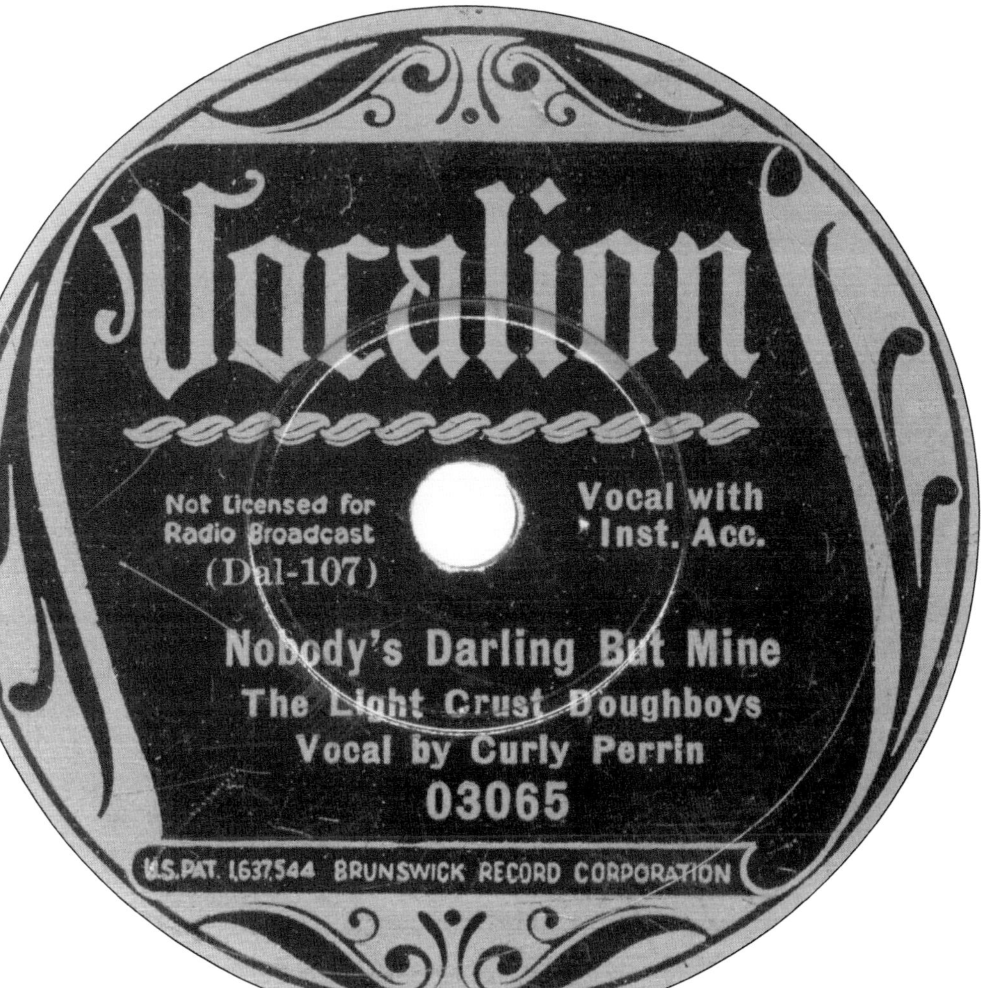


"Nobody's Darling But Mine," recorded at 508 Park Avenue on September 20, 1935, featured a vocal by William "Curly" Perrin. The guitarist and singer belonged to a pool of musicians who often moved from band to band. Perrin also recorded with Bill Boyd and his Cowboys Ramblers, W. Lee O'Daniel's Hillbilly Boys, and Ross Rhythm Rascals. The songs recorded at the session that produced "Nobody's Darling" illustrate the Doughboys' wide-ranging repertoire; they included "My Blue Heaven," "My Carolina Mountain Rose," "My Buddy," "My Melancholy Baby," "Rural Rhythm," "The Waltz You Saved for Me," and "In a Little Gypsy Tea Room," a pop tune that had been a hit for bandleader Bob Crosby months earlier. There were a number of Gypsy Tea Room establishments around the country, including one on Central Track, then the main stem of Dallas's black business district. (Courtesy of the 508 Park Collection.)

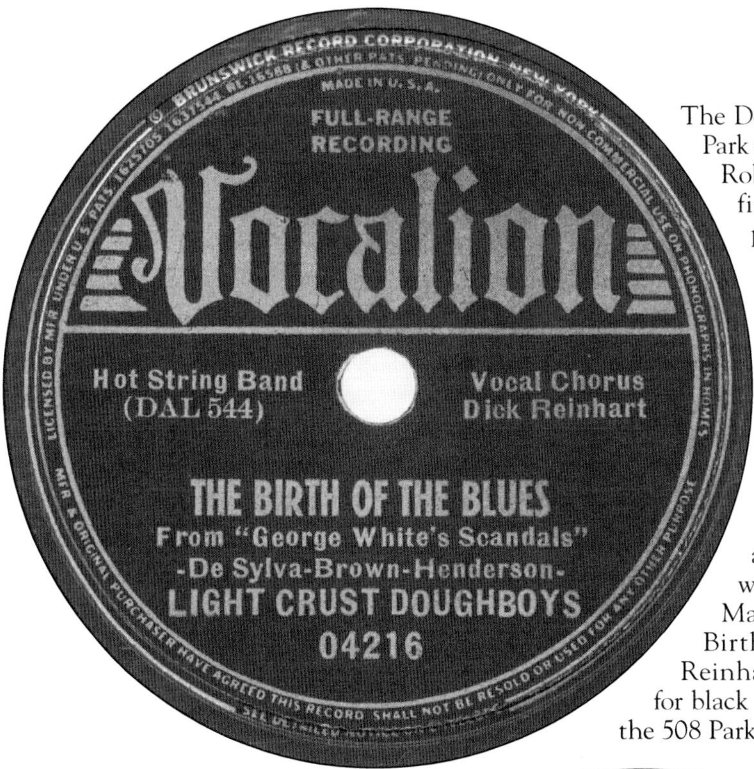


The Doughboys recorded at 508 Park on June 20, 1937, the day of Robert Johnson's second and final Dallas session. Banjo player Marvin "Smokey" Montgomery, who played with the group off and on from 1935 until his death in 2001, said he remembered seeing a blues musician at the building, but paid little attention because he had no idea that the young man would later become an icon. These records were made the following May. The vocalist on "The Birth of the Blues" is Dick Reinhart, who had an affinity for black music. (Both, courtesy of the 508 Park Collection.)

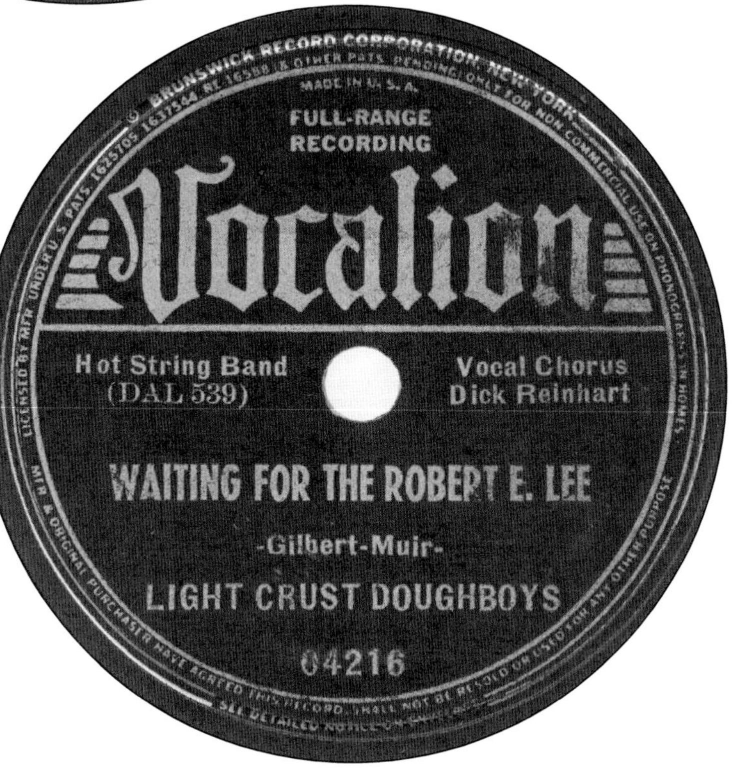

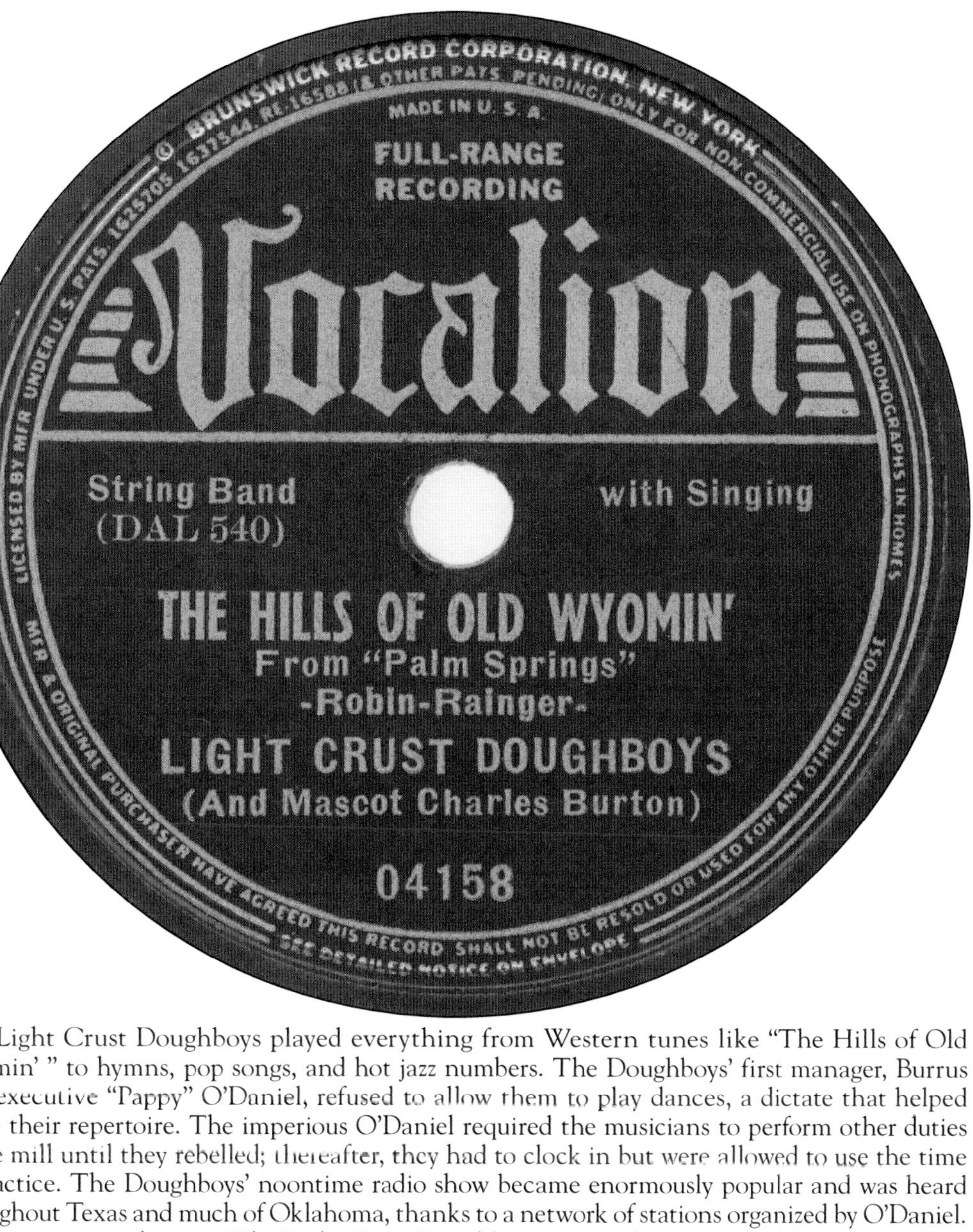


The Light Crust Doughboys played everything from Western tunes like "The Hills of Old Wyomin' " to hymns, pop songs, and hot jazz numbers. The Doughboys' first manager, Burrus Mill executive "Pappy" O'Daniel, refused to allow them to play dances, a dictate that helped shape their repertoire. The imperious O'Daniel required the musicians to perform other duties at the mill until they rebelled; thereafter, they had to clock in but were allowed to use the time to practice. The Doughboys' noontime radio show became enormously popular and was heard throughout Texas and much of Oklahoma, thanks to a network of stations organized by O'Daniel. The ringing introduction "The Light Crust Doughboys are on the air!" called listeners to their radios, and it was said that one could walk through a neighborhood when the show was on and never miss a note—everyone had the Doughboys tuned in and the windows open. (Courtesy of the 508 Park Collection.)

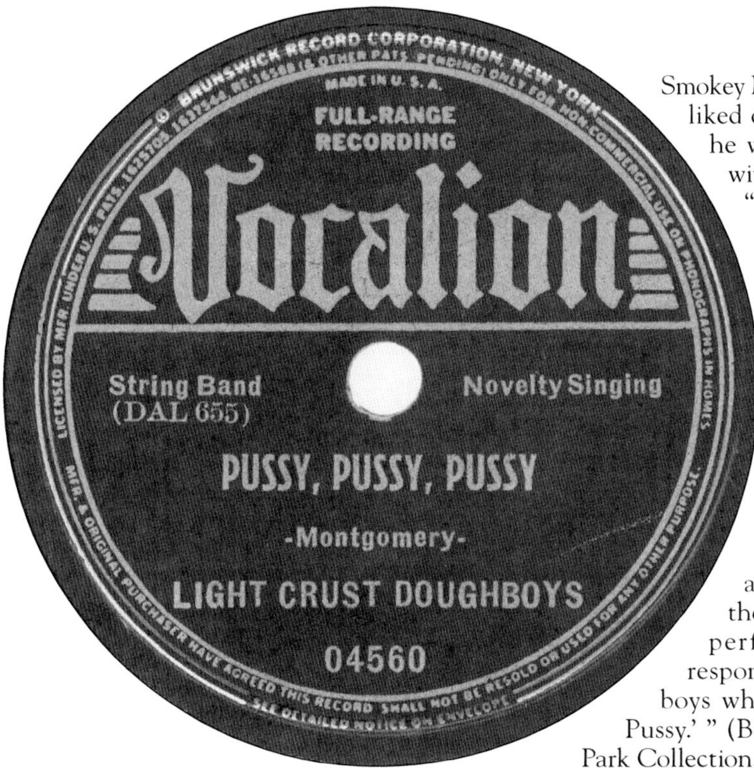


Smokey Montgomery said he never liked cats but his wife did, and he wrote a number of songs with feline themes, including "Three Naughty Kittens" and "Pussy, Pussy, Pussy," a double-entendre tune that has been covered by a number of other groups over the years and even turned up in a movie soundtrack. The 1938 record became so popular that when pianist John "Knocky" Parker met Fats Waller and introduced himself as a member of the Doughboys, the great African American performer and composer responded, "Oh, you were the boys who put out 'Pussy, Pussy, Pussy.' " (Both, courtesy of the 508 Park Collection.)

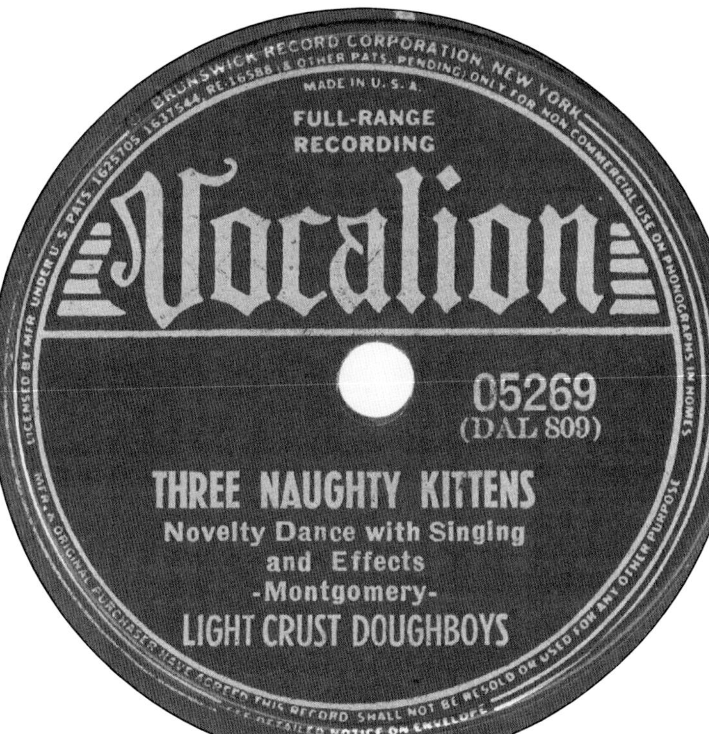

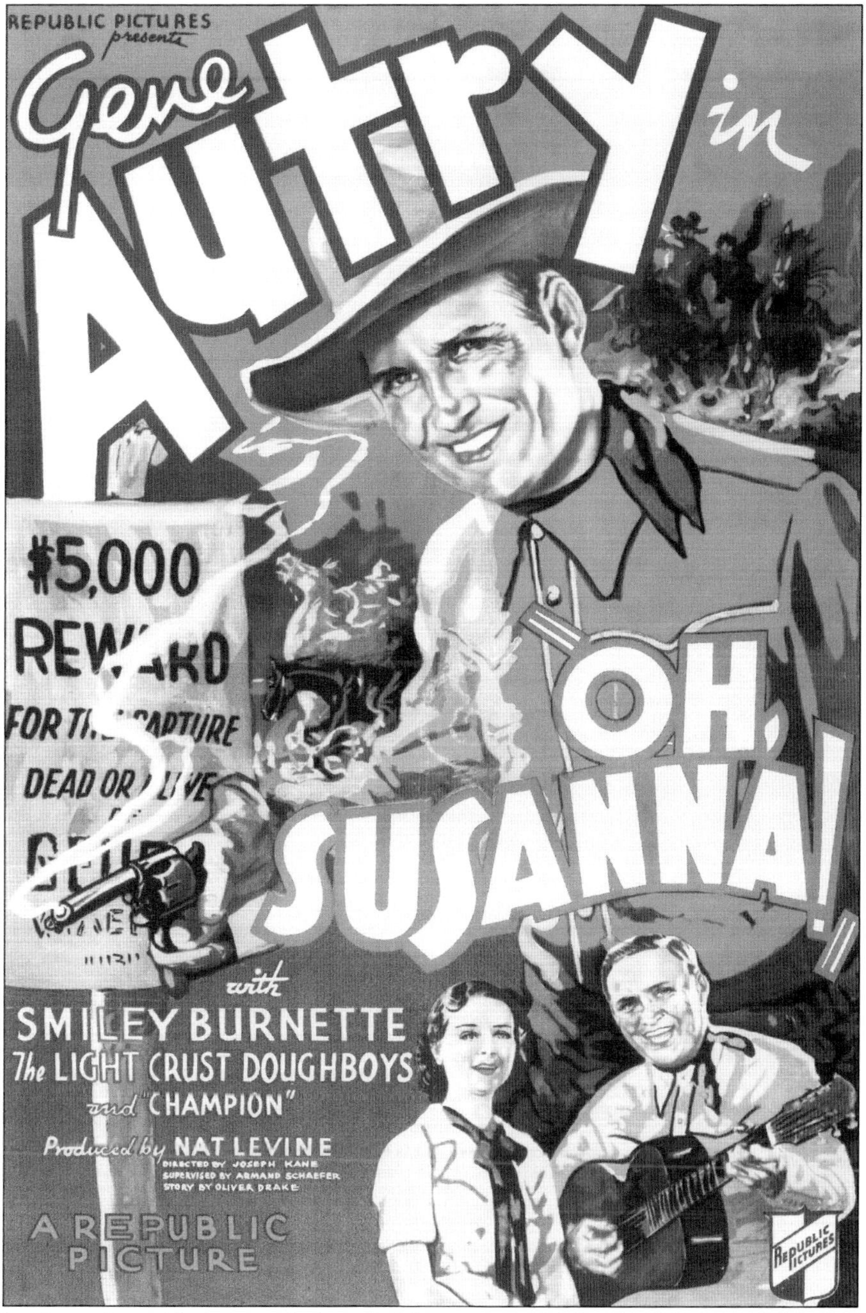


The Light Crust Doughboys traveled to California in 1936 for the filming of the Gene Autry Western *Oh, Susanna!* Milton Brown and His Musical Brownies had been set to play the band in the film, but Brown died after an automobile accident in Fort Worth. Banjo player Marvin "Smokey" Montgomery recalled taking some ribbing as a Texan who could not ride a horse. In truth, he was an Iowan who had been in the Lone Star State less than two years. The Doughboys appeared in another Autry film, *The Big Show*, shot that same year in Dallas during the Texas Centennial. This was one of the few films to feature both Autry and Roy Rogers, who appeared as a member of the Sons of the Pioneers. (Courtesy of the 508 Park Collection.)

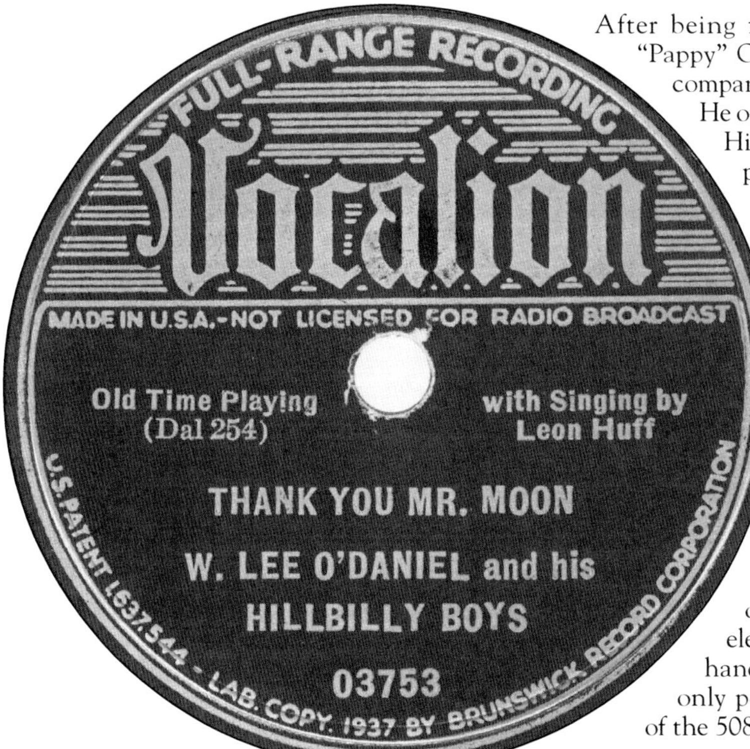


After being fired from Burrus Mill, "Pappy" O'Daniel formed his own company to make Hillbilly Flour. He organized another band, the Hillbilly Boys, to promote this product and his political career. The group recorded "Thank You Mr. Moon" and "I Can't Give You Anything But Love" on June 11, 1937. It is often erroneously reported that the Doughboys appeared at O'Daniel political events—an understandable error, since some of the same musicians played in both bands at various times. O'Daniel became governor of Texas in 1938 and was elected a US senator in 1941, handing Lyndon Johnson his only political defeat. (Courtesy of the 508 Park Collection.)

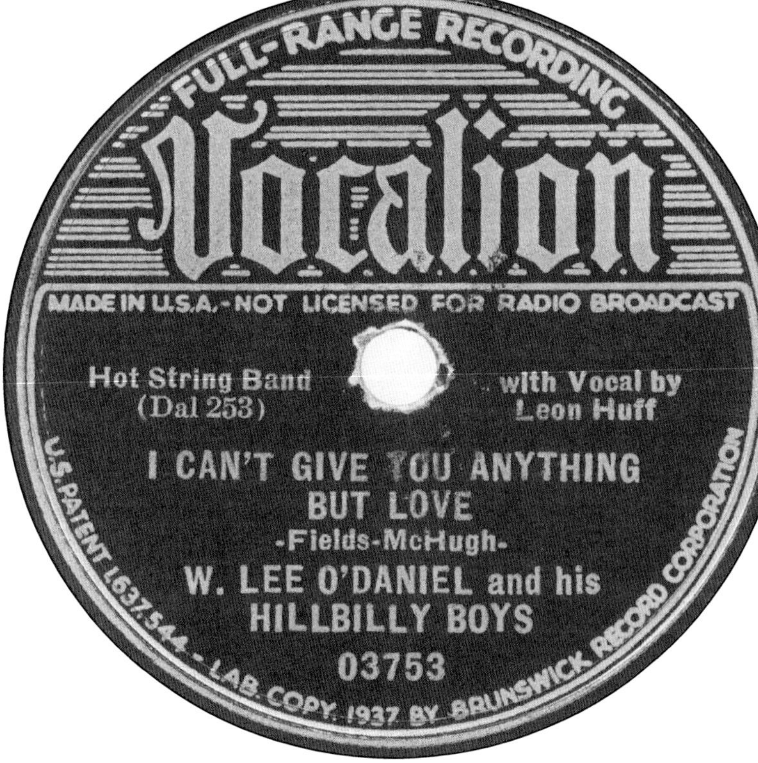

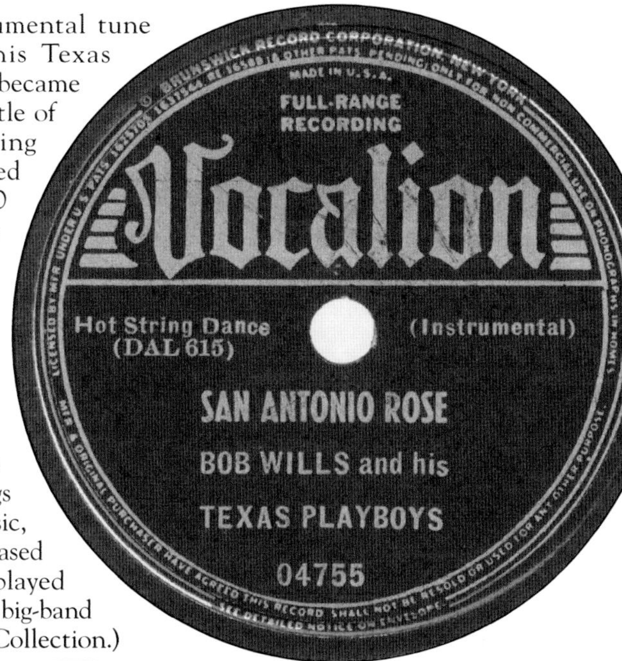


"San Antonio Rose," an instrumental tune recorded by Bob Wills and his Texas Playboys on November 28, 1938, became Wills's signature tune and the title of a biography of the Western swing bandleader. The song experienced a huge surge of popularity in 1940 when Wills recorded a version with lyrics called "New San Antonio Rose." It was covered by a number of other artists, including Bing Crosby. The flip side of the original instrumental tune, "The Convict and the Rose," is a sad tale of a prisoner receiving a letter and a rose from his sweetheart on the eve of his execution. The two songs illustrate the range of Wills's music, particularly that of his great Tulsa-based pre–World War II band, which played everything from country weepers to big-band swing. (Courtesy of the 508 Park Collection.)

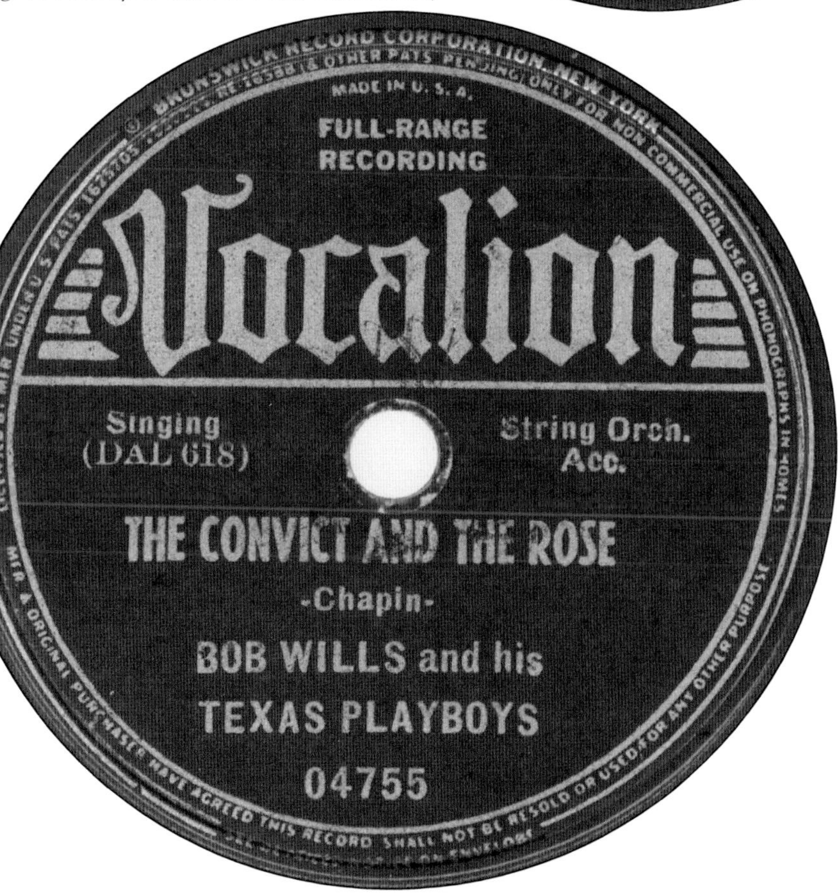

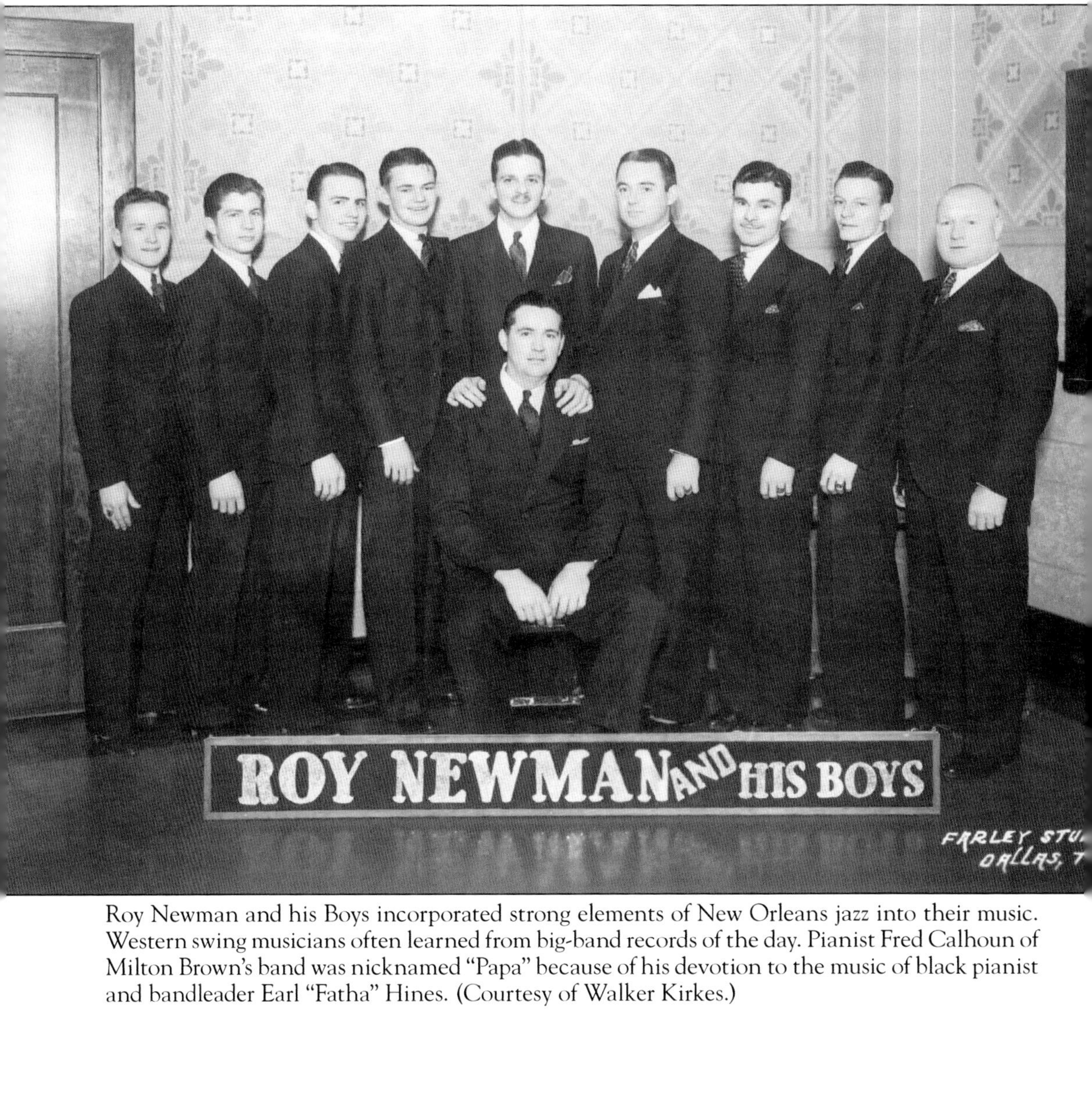


Roy Newman and his Boys incorporated strong elements of New Orleans jazz into their music. Western swing musicians often learned from big-band records of the day. Pianist Fred Calhoun of Milton Brown's band was nicknamed "Papa" because of his devotion to the music of black pianist and bandleader Earl "Fatha" Hines. (Courtesy of Walker Kirkes.)

Newman's band was featured on radio station WRR's *Noontime Varieties* program. Unlike the Playboys and the Doughboys, Newman's group played little country music, sticking to a jazzier sound. Newman rarely soloed on piano, preferring to remain part of the rhythm section, but he hired players who could "take off" with hot, improvised solos. The band on these two songs, recorded on June 14, 1937, included acclaimed fiddler Cecil Brower and electric steel guitar innovator Bob Dunn, who was a member of Milton Brown's band until Brown's death following a 1936 car accident. (Both, courtesy of the 508 Park Collection.)

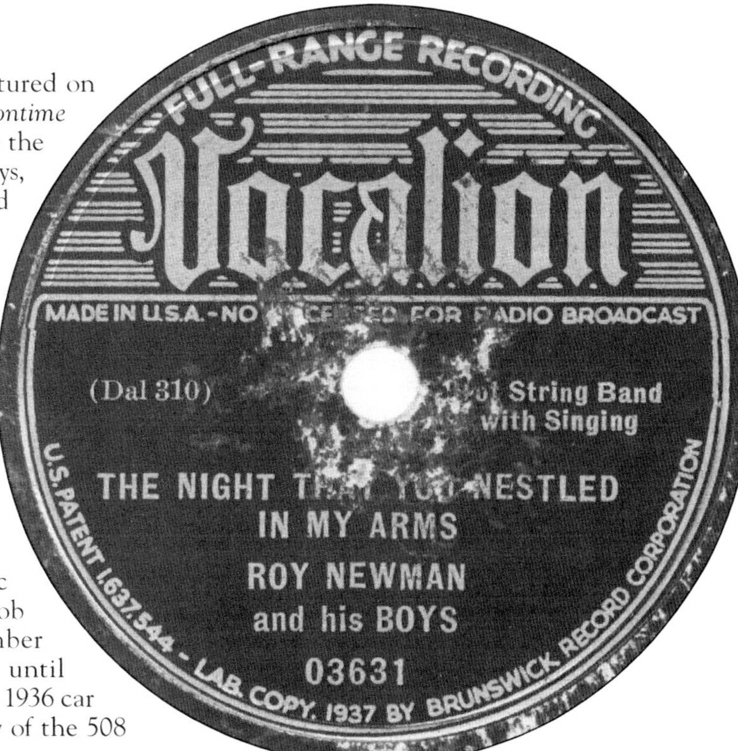


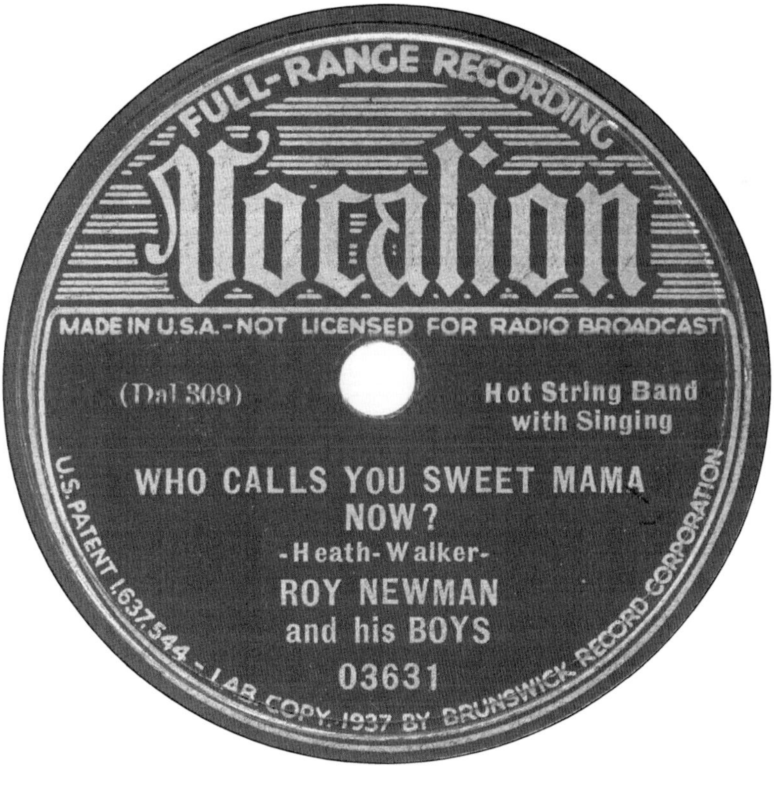

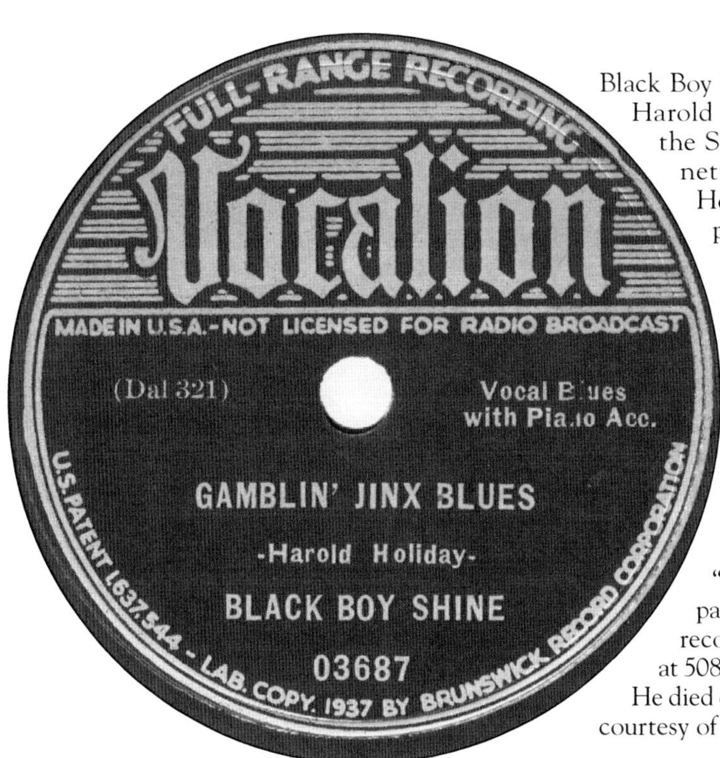


Black Boy Shine, whose real name was Harold Holiday, was a member of the Santa Fe Group, an informal network of pianists based in Houston's Fourth Ward who played in the joints along the Santa Fe Railroad tracks. The group included Robert Shaw, who was rediscovered and recorded years later while living in Austin. Shine sang and played piano on a number of sides made in Fort Worth, San Antonio, and Dallas, and he recorded with singer Bernice Edwards. "Gamblin' Jinx Blues" and "Business Woman Blues," paired on a Vocalion single, were recorded at Shine's final sessions, at 508 Park, on June 15 and 15, 1937. He died of tuberculosis in 1948. (Both, courtesy of the 508 Park Collection.)

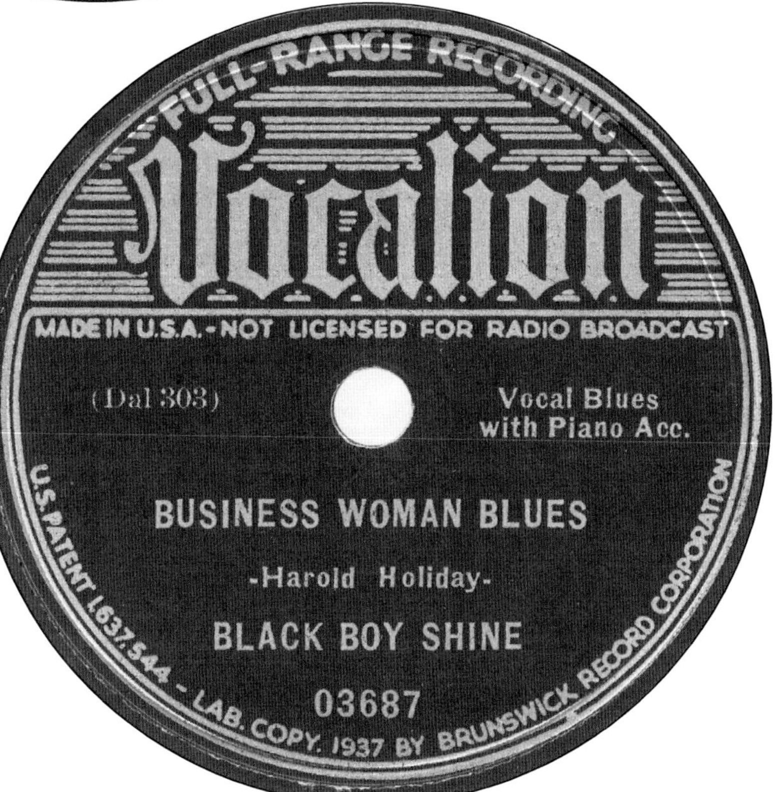

Among musicians who recorded at 508 Park were exponents of a Texas-Mexican working-class dance music called *conjunto,* whose lead instrument was the diatonic button accordion imported by German and other European immigrants. Accordionist Lolo Cavazos, born in northern Mexico in 1906, was a pioneer of this sound. On these records, he is accompanied by José Almeida on *bajo sexto,* a 12-string guitar used as a rhythm instrument. "La Chaparrita" (Short Woman) is a polka, while "El Rayo" (Ray or Lightning) is a waltz (*vals* in Spanish). After the outbreak of the 1910 revolution, Mexicans flooded into Texas, establishing communities such as Dallas's Little Mexico and increasing the market for their music on record. (Both, courtesy of the 508 Park Collection.)

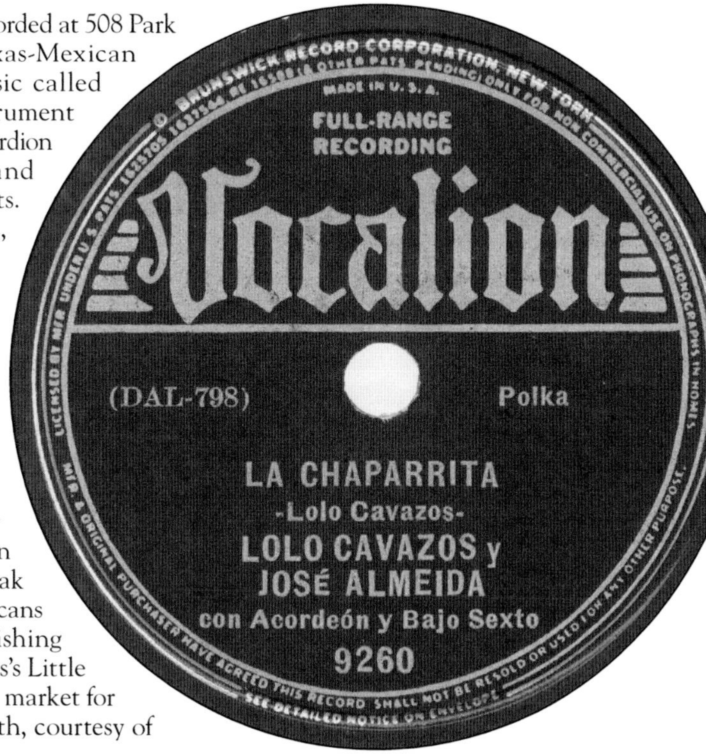


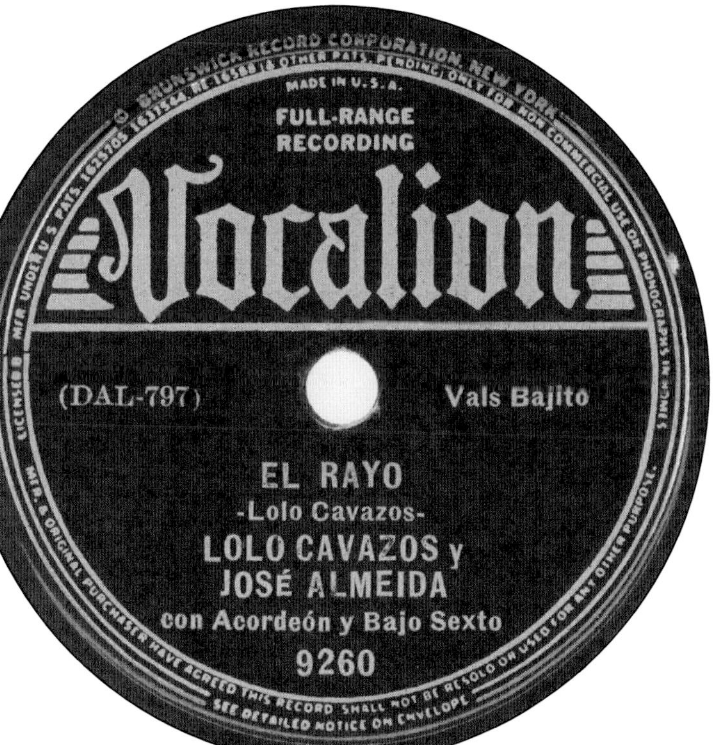

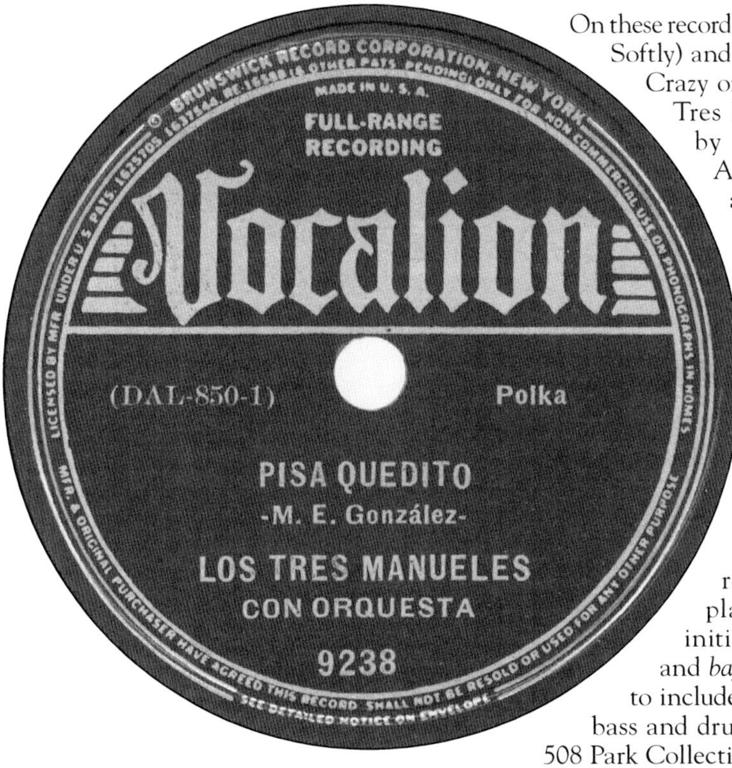


On these recordings, "Pisa Quedito" (Walking Softly) and "No Te Chifles" (Don't Go Crazy on Me), the vocal group Los Tres Manueles is accompanied by an *orquesta* (orchestra). Among Mexican Americans at that time, *conjunto* was considered the music of the uneducated lower class, while *orquesta* music was generally favored by more prosperous and better-educated people. Both *conjuntos* and *orquestas* played for dancing, however, and their repertoires overlapped. The polka and schottische (*schottis* in Spanish) represented here were also played by *conjuntos*, which initially consisted of accordion and *bajo sexto*, but later expanded to include other instruments, such as bass and drums. (Both, courtesy of the 508 Park Collection.)

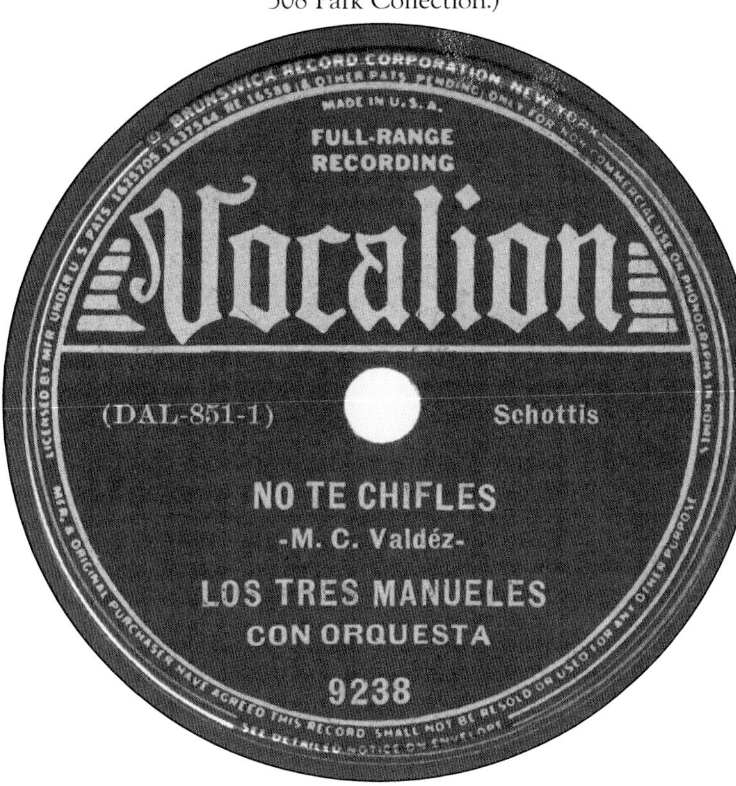

# Three

# Big "D" Jamboree

For almost two decades, the Sportatorium, a metal wrestling arena in a run-down industrial area south of downtown Dallas, rang with the sounds of a Saturday night extravaganza called the *Big "D" Jamboree*.

The *Jamboree* was born amid the burst of prosperity, optimism, and creative energy that followed World War II. Americans had money in their pockets. Country music was surging in popularity, and a new amplified sound drew fans to record stores and honky-tonks. In 1947, nightclub owner Slim McDonald and country music deejays Al Turner and "Uncle Gus" Foster began renting the Sportatorium for a Saturday night show that was first called the *Texas State Barn Dance* and then the *Lone Star Barn Dance*. McDonald's and Foster's involvement was short-lived, and by early 1949, the program, retitled the *Big "D" Jamboree*, was in the hands of wrestling promoter Ed McLemore, who would run it until its demise in 1966.

During its heyday, the *Jamboree* provided a showcase for performers ranging from local and regional favorites such as Bill Callahan, Riley Crabtree, and Orville Couch, to national figures. It played a major role in the careers of Sonny James, Hank Locklin, and Hank Snow. The Maddox Brothers and Rose and Ernest Tubb often graced the converted wrestling ring that served as a stage. One of the house bands was the venerable and versatile Light Crust Doughboys, appearing under a couple of different names. The show was broadcast over Dallas radio station KRLD and had some local television and national radio exposure as well.

The *Jamboree* also embraced the wild new music that came to be known as rockabilly and rock 'n' roll, though not without some backstage tension. Elvis Presley appeared several times, as did the exciting but erratic Gene Vincent and the fiery, versatile Wanda Jackson. Carl Perkins was a regular for a time. Local favorites such as Ronnie Dawson and the Belew Twins had a large following.

Efforts to revive the *Jamboree* in the early 1970s fizzled; its time had passed. But what a time it was.

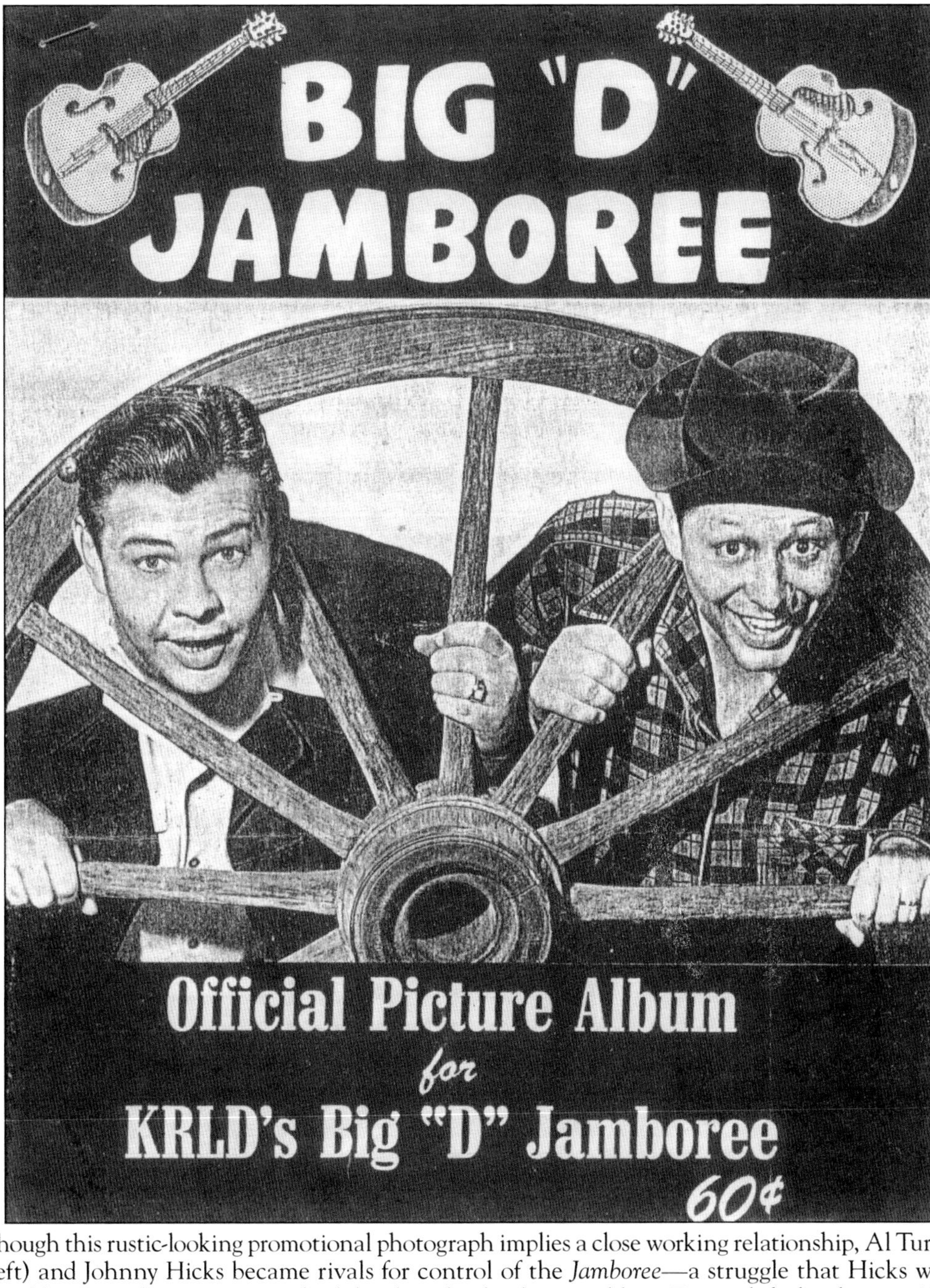


Though this rustic-looking promotional photograph implies a close working relationship, Al Turner (left) and Johnny Hicks became rivals for control of the *Jamboree*—a struggle that Hicks won, possibly in part because Turner had developed a drinking problem. Turner left the show in 1954 but returned four years later and created tension by pushing for a return to its country origins and away from rock 'n' roll. Hicks's history with the *Jamboree* was stormy as well; he was ambivalent about the new music, clashed with promoter and Sportatorium owner Ed McLemore, and walked out several times before leaving for good in 1959. McLemore subsequently hired Horace Logan, who for many years had been the producer and emcee for the rival *Louisiana Hayride* and apparently was the first to use the iconic line "Elvis has left the building." (Courtesy of David Dennard.)

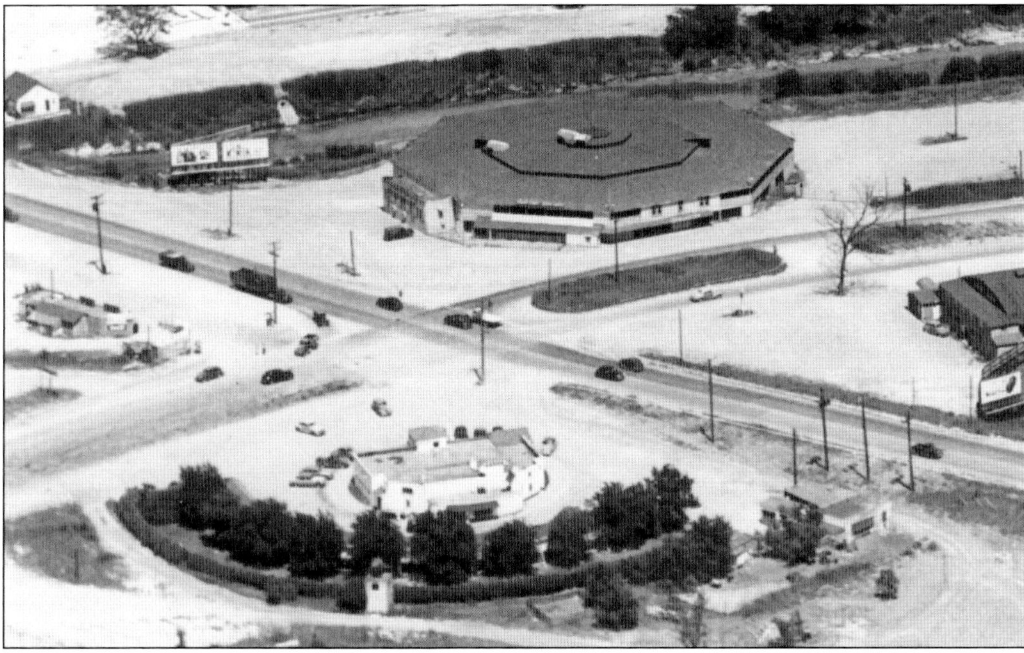

The *Big "D" Jamboree*, originally called the *Texas State Barn Dance*, began in 1947 in the Sportatorium, a wrestling arena at Industrial Boulevard and Cadiz Street, south of downtown Dallas. The building had been constructed in 1935 by businessman Bill Cox, who wanted to capitalize on the Texas Centennial the following year. Cox presented weekly wrestling matches and sometimes brought musical events to the octagonal metal building as well. (Courtesy of David Dennard.)

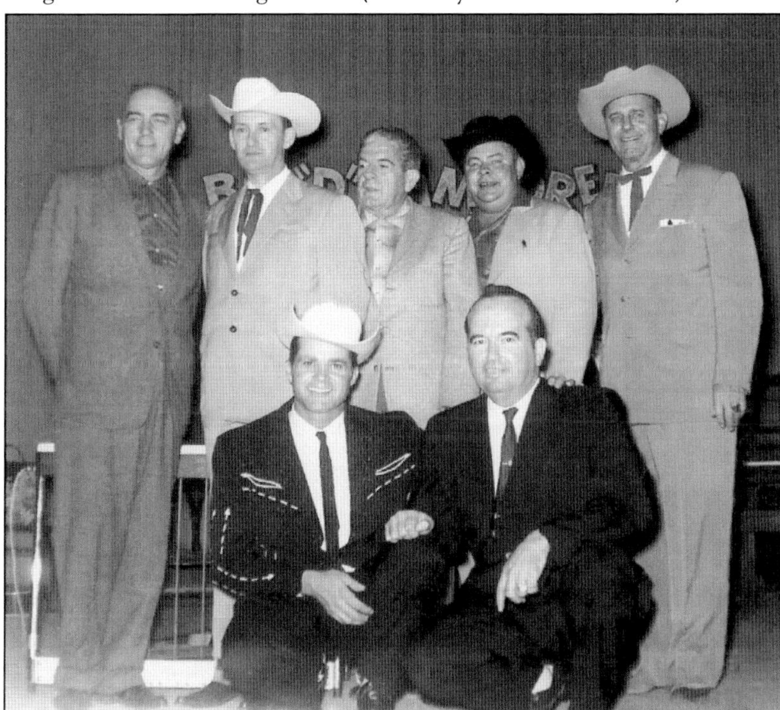

Ed McLemore moved into promoting wrestling and the music show that became the *Big "D" Jamboree*. Shown here in 1961 are, from left to right, (kneeling) singer Tony Douglas and musician and songwriter Tillman Franks; (standing) *Jamboree* emcee Horace Logan, performer Lawton Williams, McLemore, and emcees Al Turner and Parker Willson. (Courtesy of David Dennard.)

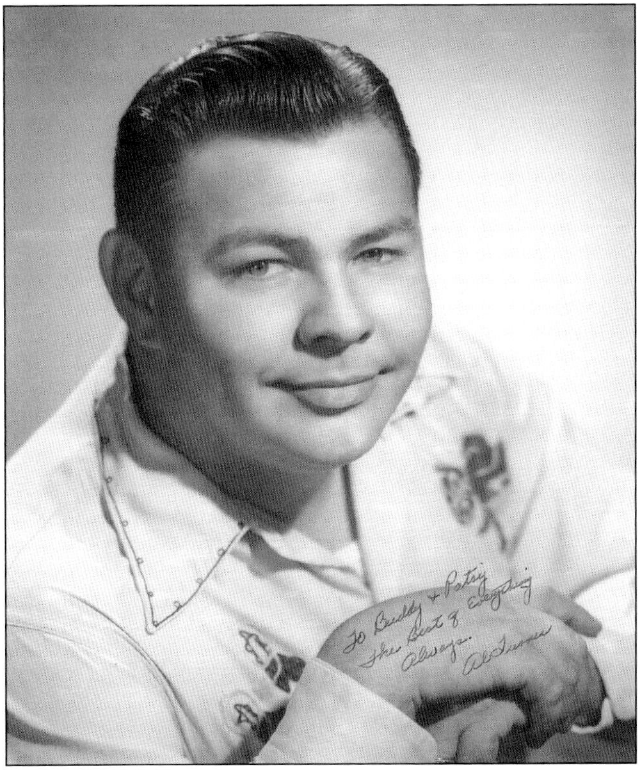

"Big" Al Turner was a disc jockey for Dallas radio station WFAA when he was involved in the creation of the *Texas State Barn Dance*, along with nightclub owner Slim McDonald and another radio personality, "Uncle Gus" Foster. Ed McLemore soon parted company with McDonald and Foster and assigned Turner a larger role, including booking the acts and emceeing the show. (Courtesy of David Dennard.)

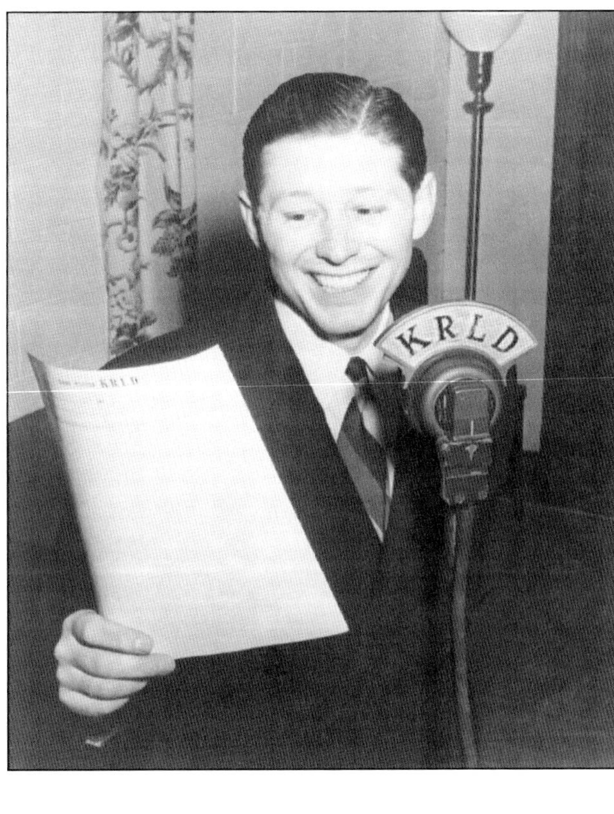


KRLD disc jockey Johnny Hicks became part of the *Lone Star Barn Dance* in late 1948 when the show moved back to his station from WFAA. Early in 1949, the name was changed again, to the *Big "D" Jamboree*. Not long before his death in 1997, Hicks told an interviewer that the new name was his idea: "It was quite euphonious and it stuck." (Courtesy of David Dennard.)

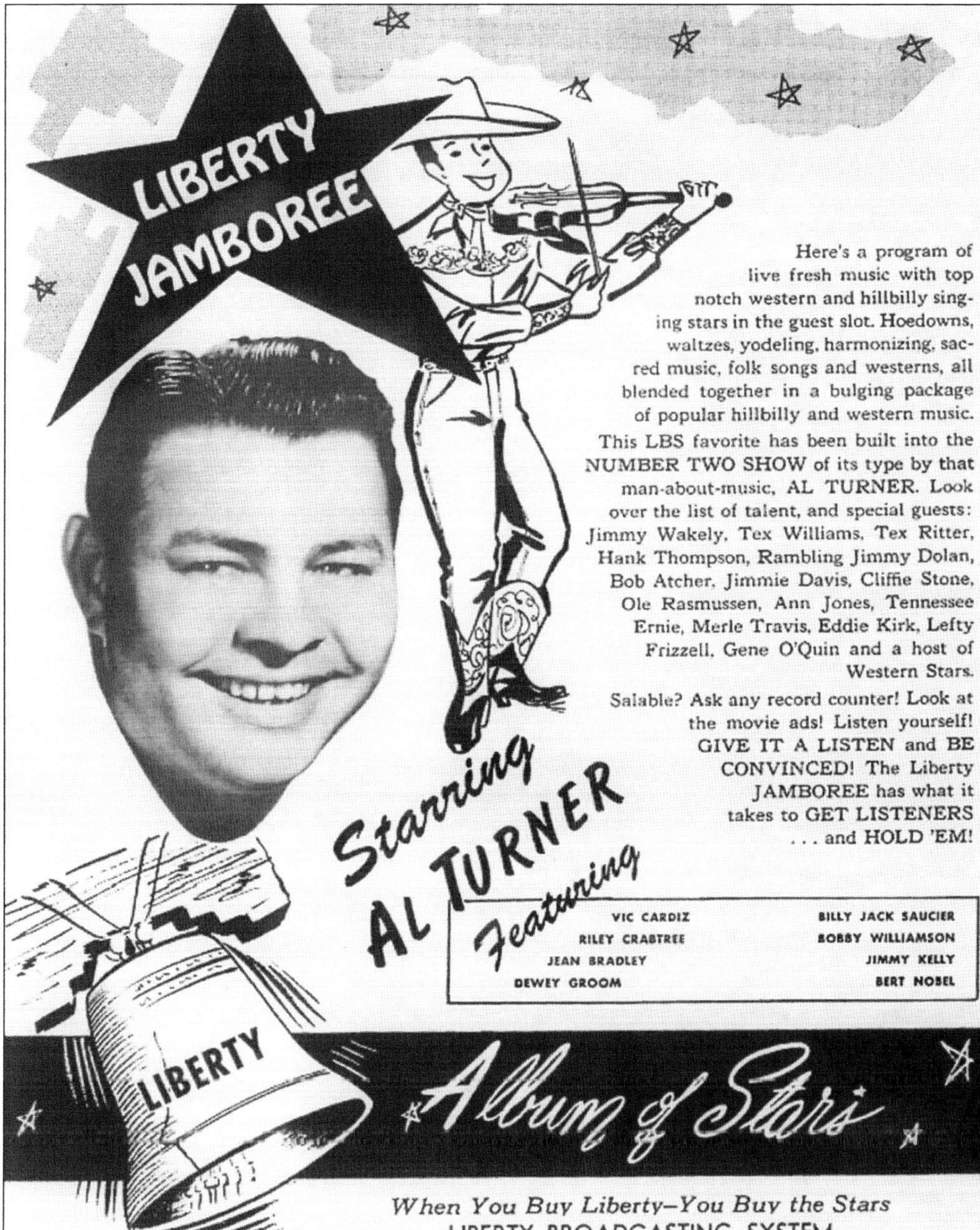


Among Al Turner's accomplishments was launching the *Liberty Jamboree*, an afternoon version of the *Big "D" Jamboree* broadcast on Dallas radio station KLIF. He also brokered a syndication deal with the Liberty Broadcasting Network, which called it the *Big T Jamboree*, probably to stress its identification with Texas rather than merely with Dallas. (Courtesy of David Dennard.)

# Spike Jones Visits "Liberty Jamboree"

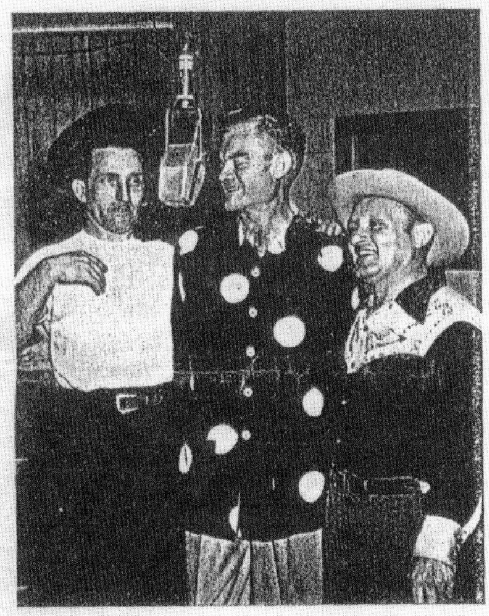

**Bill Callahan — Spike Jones — Joe Callahan**

The Callahan Corn and the Jones Corn get together and there's enough for the whole Liberty Jamboree gang. Spike is nearly a hillbilly but finds it hard to keep up with the Callahans, Favorite comics at Big "D"

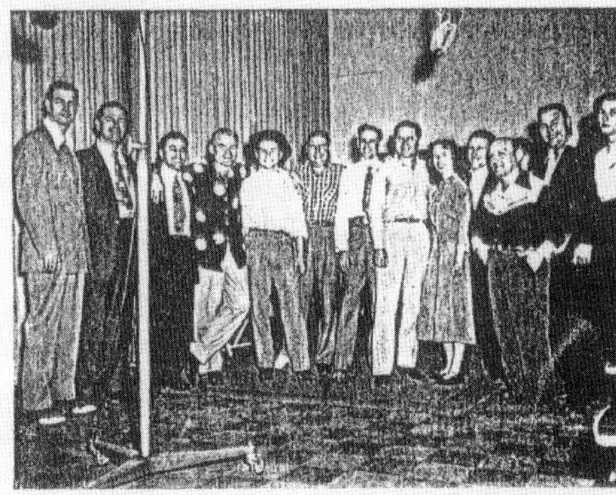

**Liberty Jamboree Gang**

Hank Thompson, Jim Beck, Dave Montrose, Spike Jones, Leon Rhoades, Buddy Griffin, Bobby Williamson, Dewey Groom, Betty Lou Lobb, Bill Callahan, Joe Callahan, Al Turner, and Louise Rowe, sister to Famous 7 Rowe Brothers. The Liberty Jamboree is heard over the Liberty network of more than one hundred stations every weekday from 4 to 5 P. M.

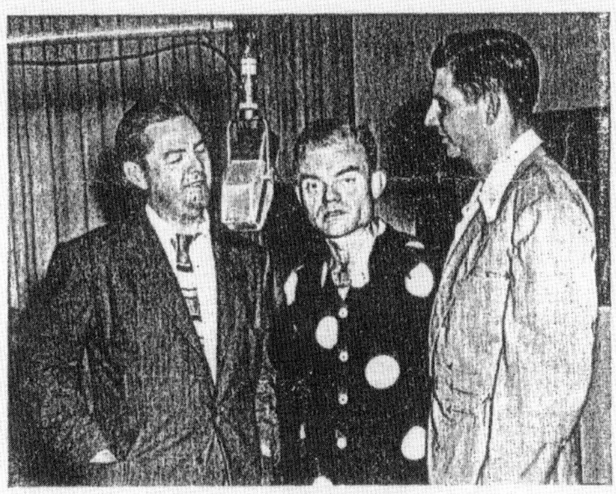

**Three Fast Talkers**

Jim Beck, Spike Jones, and Hank Thompson. Jim is selling Spike on the merits of the Jamboree. Hank seems to agree with everything, but it all seems to leave Spike a little bewildered, or confused, or something.

Among the guest stars who dropped by the *Liberty Jamboree* was satirical bandleader Spike Jones. In the photograph at upper left, Jones (center) is shown with the Callahan brothers, Bill (left) and Joe. At upper right, Jones poses with the *Liberty Jamboree* Gang. Shown are, from left to right, Hank Thompson, Jim Beck, Dave Montrose, Jones, Leon Rhodes, Buddy Griffin, Bobby Williamson, Dewey Groom, Betty Lou Lobb, Bill Callahan, Joe Callahan, Al Turner, and Louise Rowe. In the bottom photograph, Jones (center) poses with Jim Beck (left) and Hank Thompson. Beck worked for a radio station and announced wrestling matches in the Sportatorium, then opened a studio, where he recorded many of the performers and other artists of the time. (Courtesy of David Dennard.)

Walter and Homer Callahan became Joe and Bill when they moved to Dallas in the early 1940s, possibly to capitalize on the popularity of Joe and Bob Shelton. Bill Callahan was a multi-instrumentalist, singer, and clown. Joe sang harmony, played guitar, and served as straight man on corny jokes such as, "She's from Rotterdam. If she don't change her socks, she's gonna rot her damn feet off!" (Courtesy of David Dennard.)

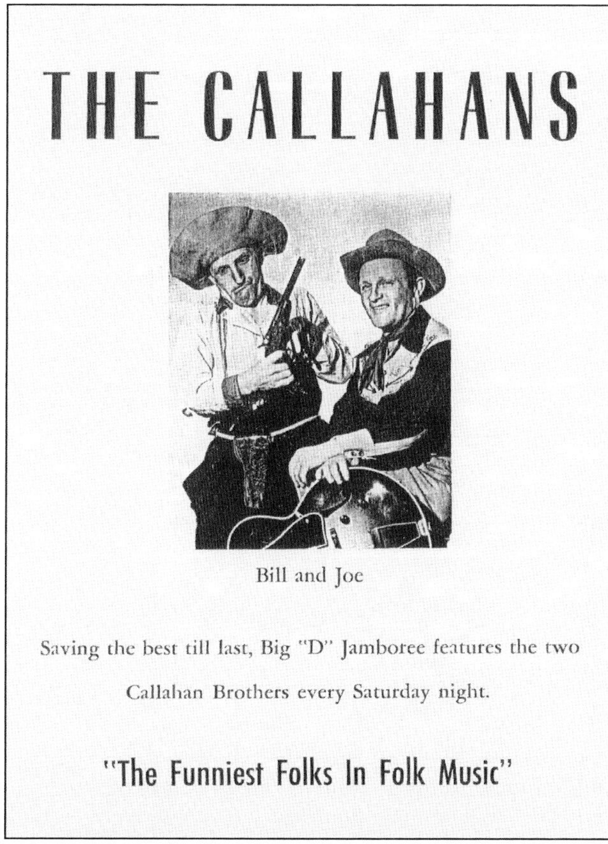


The Callahan brothers were featured in a saloon scene in the 1945 Jimmy Wakely film *Springtime in Texas*, performing "Old Joe Clark." The musicians shown here are, from left to right, Bill and Joe Callahan, Spud Goodale (guitar), Pat Patterson (accordion), Jerry Wolf (fiddle), and Rusty McDonald (guitar). The seated man looking away from the camera is unidentified. (Courtesy of David Dennard.)

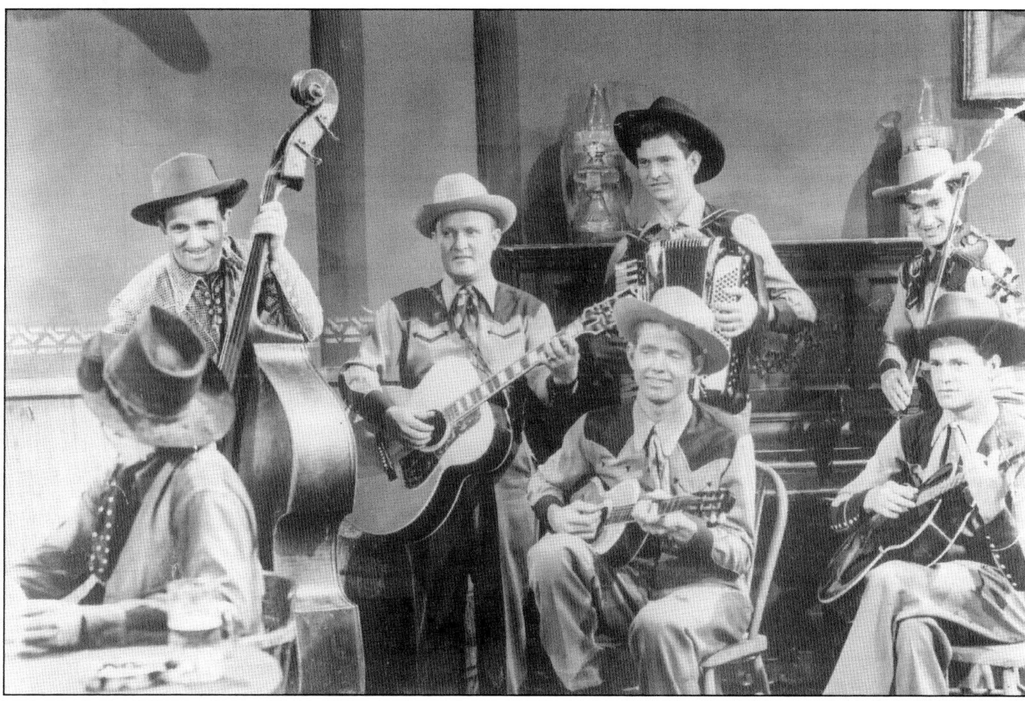

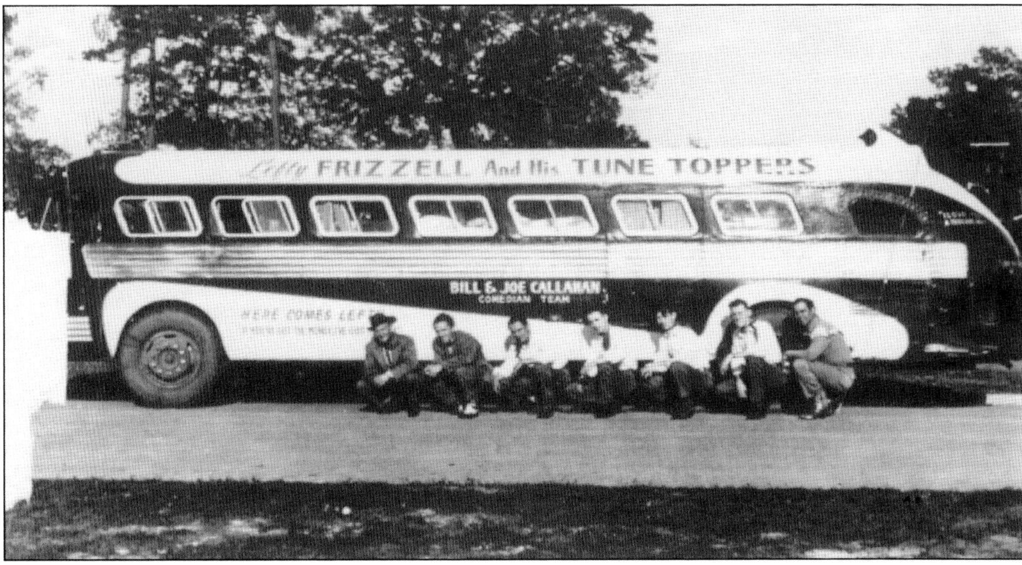


The Callahans toured with Lefty Frizzell, whom Bill also managed for a while, dealing with the honky-tonk singer's hard drinking, mood swings, and suicide threats. The 1955 photograph below shows Frizzell's band, from left to right, Joe Callahan, Pee Wee Reed, Bill Callahan, Jerry Desmond, Curley Chalker, Norman Stephens, Blacky Crawford, and Jimmy Benis. Joe Callahan periodically returned to North Carolina for extended visits and finally moved back there. Bill remained in Dallas, living in the same house in the Oak Cliff area. He worked in other professions, including photography, after his musical career faded. But he was always ready to entertain friends and strangers with comedy routines. Bill Callahan celebrated his 90th birthday before dying in 2002. (Courtesy of David Dennard.)

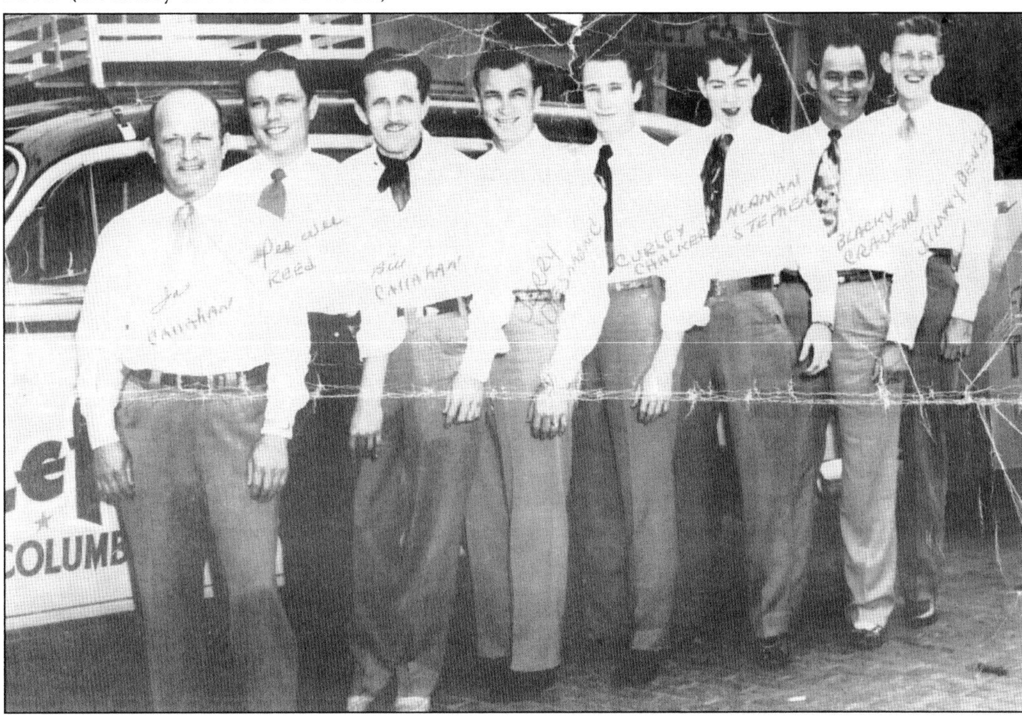

This cover of a Lefty Frizzell single features his first recording band. From left to right are Jimmy Kelley (steel guitar), Vic Candis (fiddle), Bobby Williamson (rhythm guitar and emcee), Buddy Griffin (bass), Leon Rhodes (lead guitar), and Frizzell. The photograph was taken in 1950 at the Ross Avenue studio owned by Jim Beck, who managed Frizzell and had a contentious relationship with the singer. (Courtesy of David Dennard.)

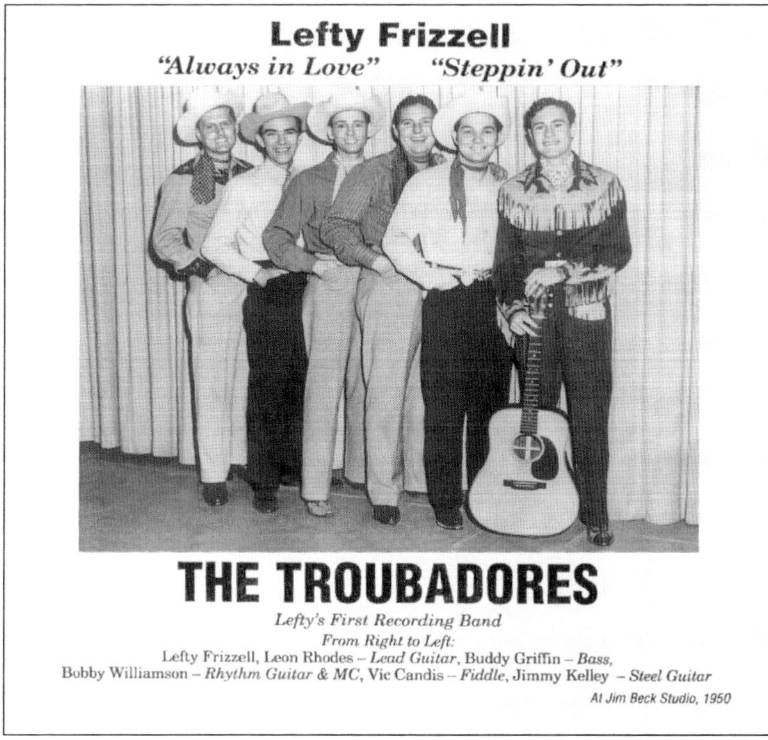


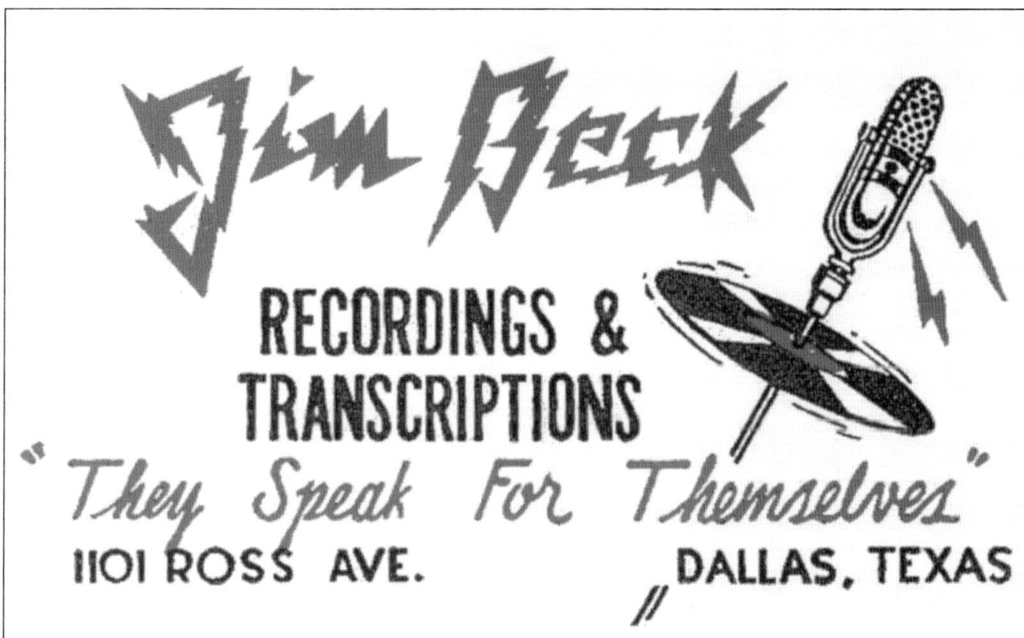


Jim Beck's studio became a magnet for talented musicians. Don Law, head of Columbia's country music division, used the studio extensively, and some say that Dallas, rather than Nashville, might have become the nation's hillbilly capital. Others consider that assertion far-fetched. At any rate, such a possibility was scotched when Beck, just 39, died in 1956 after using a toxic chemical to clean equipment in an unventilated room. (Courtesy of David Dennard.)

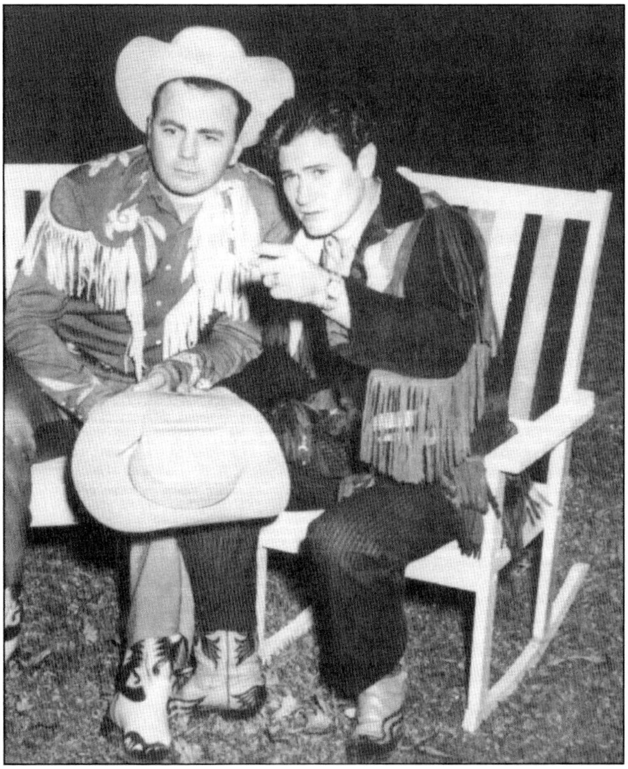

Lou Millet (left), a Baton Rouge, Louisiana, native, got a career boost when Lefty Frizzell (right) hired him. This led to a Columbia recording contract, but Millet's career fizzled. He cut some rockabilly classics for the Republic label and recorded the wonderfully titled "My Inlaws Made an Outlaw Out of Me." He remained musically active at least into the 1970s. (Courtesy of David Dennard.)

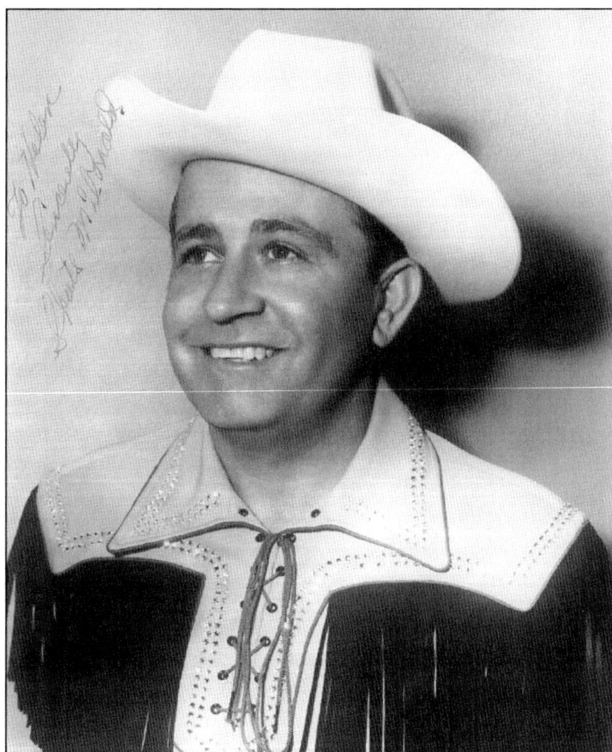

Skeets McDonald performed on the *Ozark Jubilee* and other "barn dance" shows in addition to the *Big "D" Jamboree*, and he became popular on the West Coast. McDonald had his biggest hit with "Don't Let the Stars Get in Your Eyes," which became his signature tune. He also waxed such rockabilly classics as "You Oughta See Grandma Rock." (Courtesy of David Dennard.)

In addition to recording with Lefty Frizzell, Bobby Williamson was among the early stars of the *Jamboree*. In 1952, he defected to the *Saturday Night Shindig* on WFAA. The stations were fierce rivals, and Williamson did not return to the *Jamboree* when the *Shindig* folded two years later, though he did make occasional appearances in the final years of *Big "D"* in the 1960s. (Courtesy of David Dennard.)

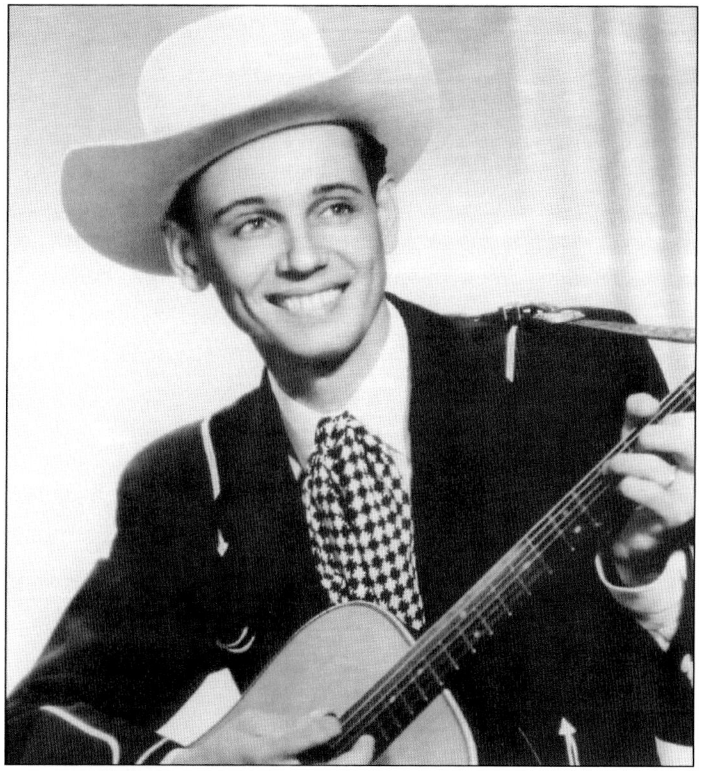

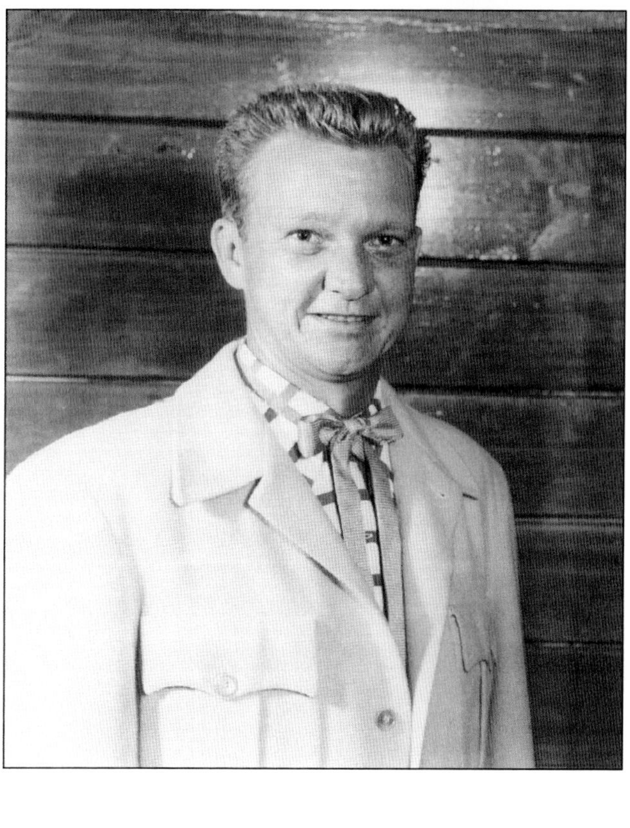

KRLD disc jockey Johnny Harper joined the *Jamboree* as an emcee in 1951 and became a producer when Al Turner departed in 1954. Harper stayed with the show until 1957, when he was replaced by former Light Crust Doughboys announcer Parker Willson. Harper also wrote songs, including "Little Girl Love," which proved to be an unfortunate choice for teenage Texas singer "Sunshine" Ruby Bateman. (Courtesy of David Dennard.)

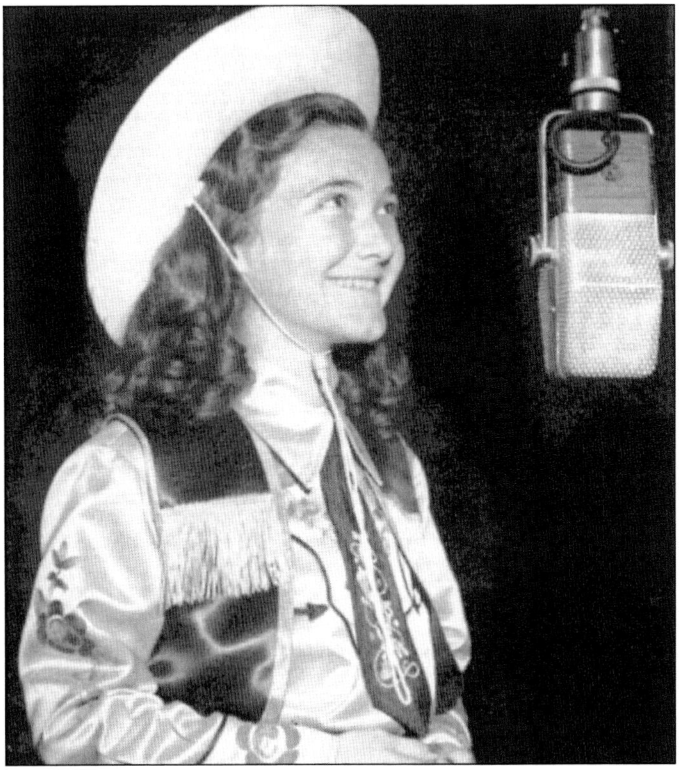

Sunshine Ruby was a childhood protégé of East Texas musicians the Shelton brothers, whose band, the Sunshine Boys, provided her nickname. She joined the *Jamboree* at 12, in 1952. But she chafed at RCA's choice of novelty material and at Ed McLemore's management. By 1956, she had abandoned music in favor of marriage and family, a decision she says she never regretted. (Courtesy of David Dennard.)

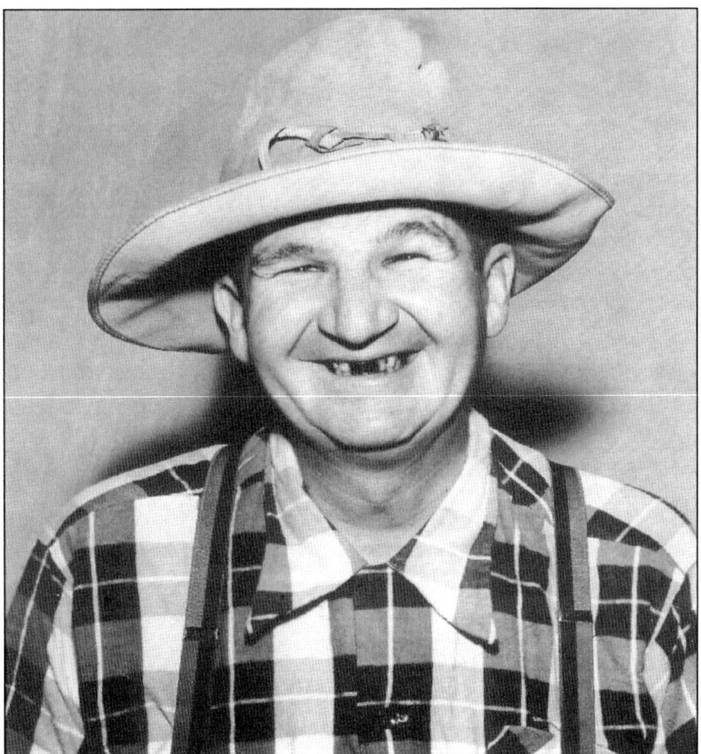

Comedian and musician Bob Shelton played in various bands with his brothers. One of these, the Lone Star Cowboys, made the first known recording of "Deep Elm Blues," in 1933. He became a personality on Dallas radio station WFAA and a regular on the early barn-dance versions of the *Big "D" Jamboree*, but left after the show moved back to rival KRLD. (Courtesy of David Dennard.)

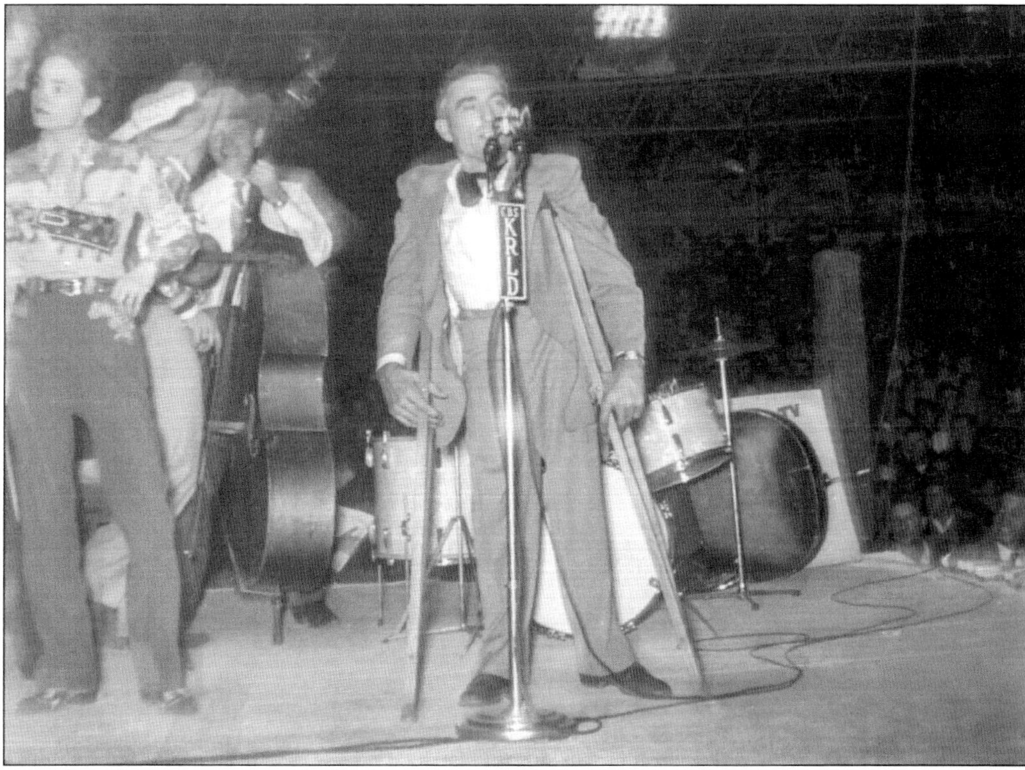


Riley Crabtree overcame polio to become a powerful and versatile singer. He began appearing on the *Texas State Barn Dance* in 1947 and became the most successful artist on Jesse Erickson's local Talent label. Crabtree's recording of "Shackles and Chains" landed him a contract with Columbia Records in 1950. The label dropped him after three years, but he continued to appear on the *Big "D" Jamboree* into the 1960s (Courtesy of David Dennard.)

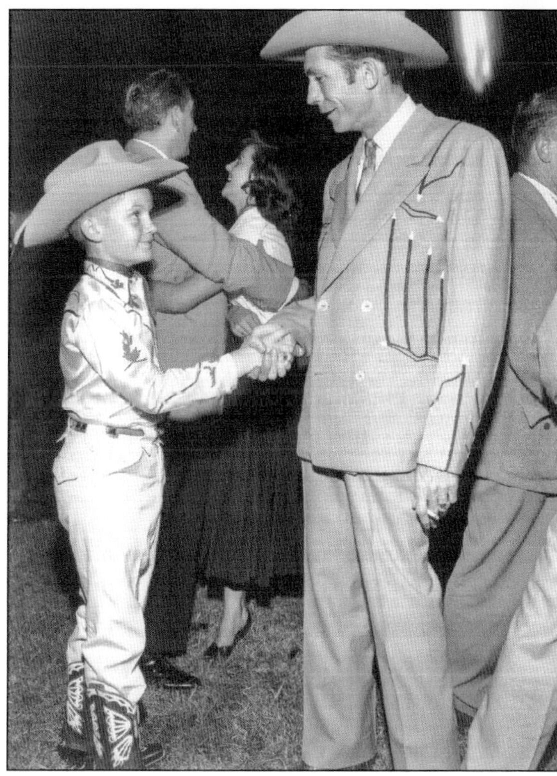

Hank Williams never appeared on the *Big "D" Jamboree*, but he performed on its predecessor, the *Lone Star Barn Dance*, in October 1948, in a show that also featured Bob Shelton. Williams, a brilliant country singer and songwriter known as the "hillbilly Shakespeare," is shown greeting a young fan on a return visit to Dallas in 1951. (Courtesy of David Dennard.)

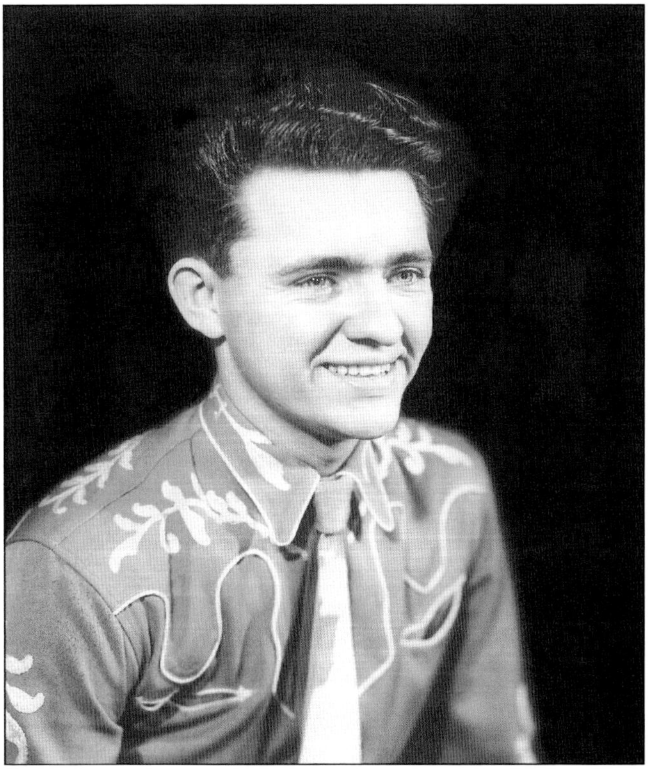

Talented fiddler and vocalist Billy Jack Saucier was 22 years old, but he had been playing professionally for almost 10 years when he performed as a member of the first *Jamboree* house band on the earliest-known surviving live recording of the show, in the fall of 1950. He later appeared as a featured performer. (Courtesy of David Dennard.)

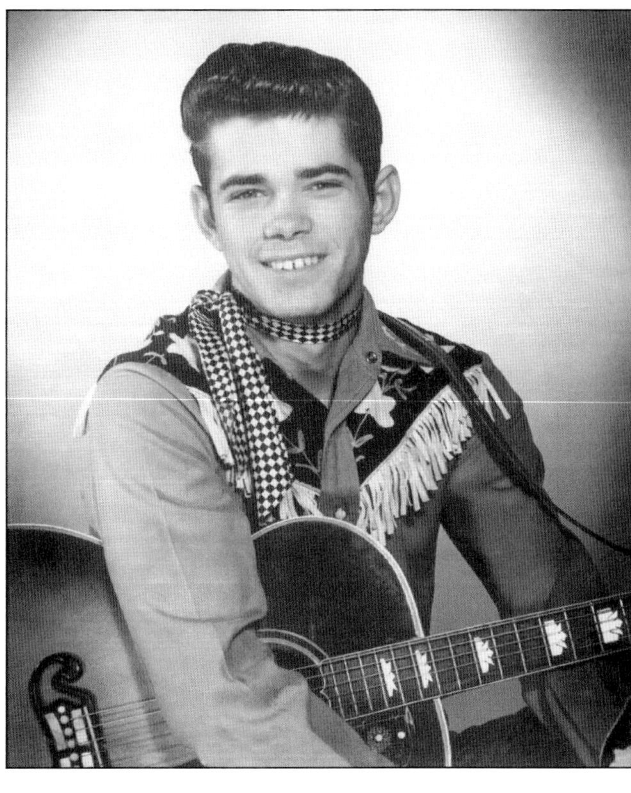

Jimmy Fautheree, a vocalist and Merle Travis–style guitarist, was performing on the *Jamboree* by the time he was 16, in 1950. He was soon wooed away by the rival *Louisiana Hayride*, signed a contract with Capitol Records in 1951, and later teamed up with another former *Jamboree* performer, "Country" Johnny Mathis, as Jimmy & Johnny. (Courtesy of David Dennard.)

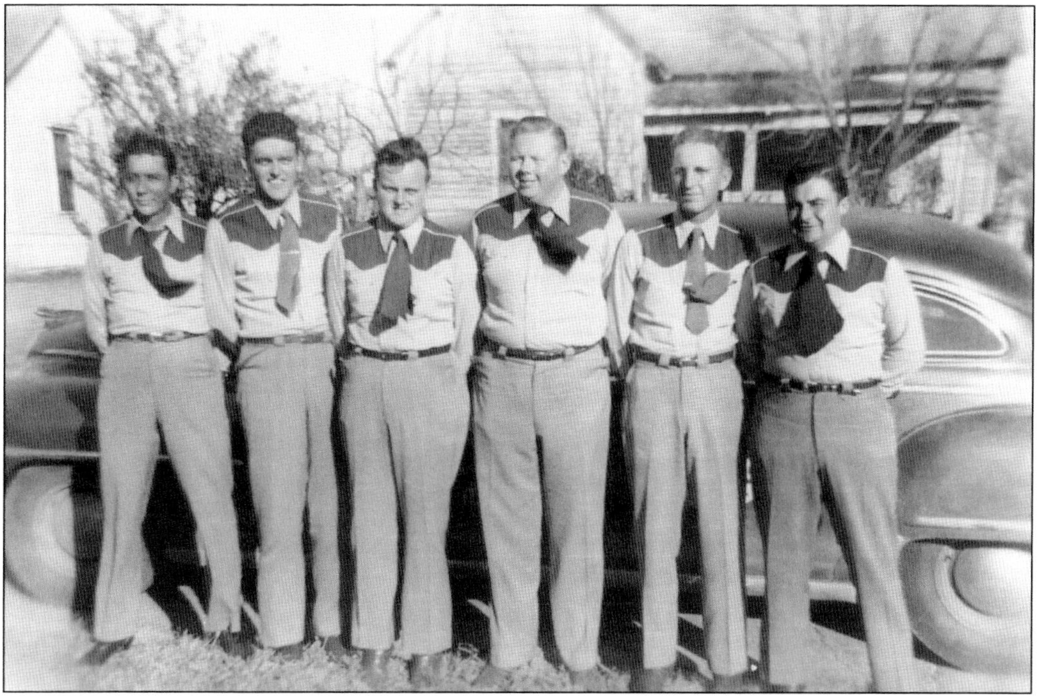

Jimmie Heap & the Melody Masters, a Central Texas band, appeared on the earliest known live recording of the *Big "D" Jamboree*, on October 21, 1950. Heap (fourth from left) formed the group soon after World War II, shaped it into a versatile show band, and kept it going until his death in a 1977 boating accident. (Courtesy of David Dennard.)

Fiddler Roy Wiley starred in the early days of the *Jamboree*. He recorded in 1948 for the Talent label in Dallas with his group, the Range Ramblers. Despite the band's name, Wiley was strongly influenced by Roy Acuff, and the group played in the style of Acuff's band, the Smoky Mountain Boys. (Courtesy of David Dennard.)

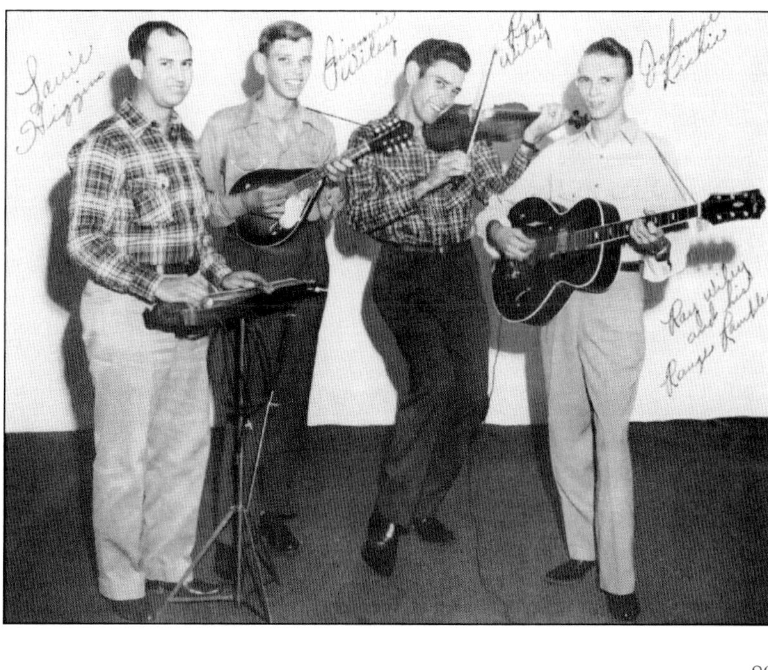

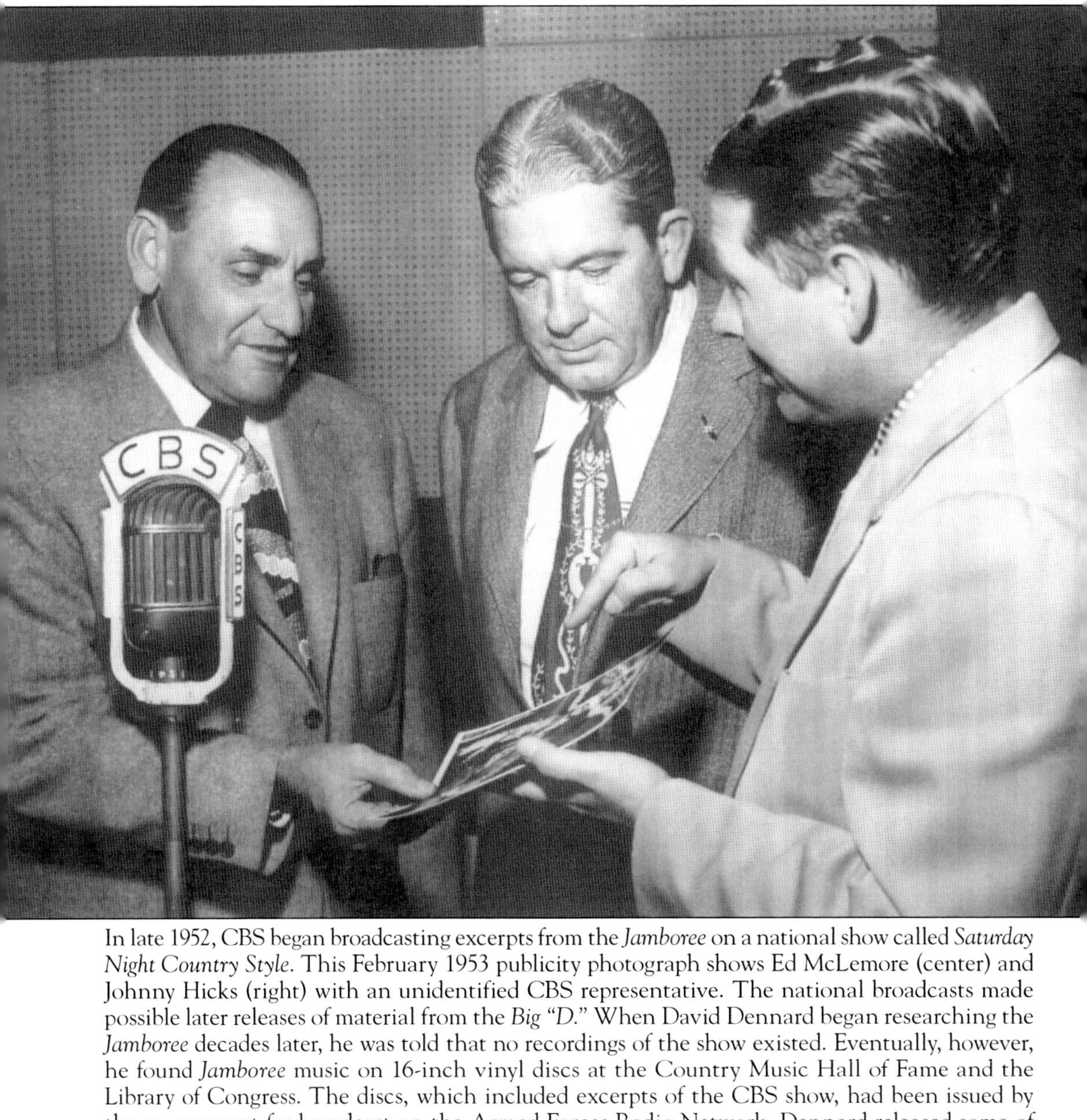


In late 1952, CBS began broadcasting excerpts from the *Jamboree* on a national show called *Saturday Night Country Style*. This February 1953 publicity photograph shows Ed McLemore (center) and Johnny Hicks (right) with an unidentified CBS representative. The national broadcasts made possible later releases of material from the *Big "D."* When David Dennard began researching the *Jamboree* decades later, he was told that no recordings of the show existed. Eventually, however, he found *Jamboree* music on 16-inch vinyl discs at the Country Music Hall of Fame and the Library of Congress. The discs, which included excerpts of the CBS show, had been issued by the government for broadcast on the Armed Forces Radio Network. Dennard released some of this music on his Dragon Street label, and a much larger selection made possible a Bear Family eight-CD box set that appeared in 2013. (Courtesy of David Dennard.)

These photographs of two unidentified young musicians highlight the *Jamboree*'s association with both local station KRLD and CBS. The national network may have been involved in the Dallas show's shift back to an emphasis on country music in the late 1950s, after its flirtation with rockabilly and rock 'n' roll. There was no going back, though, and changing times eroded the *Jamboree*'s popularity. KRLD dropped it in 1960, and it was briefly affiliated with another local station, KBOX. In the 1960s, as the *Jamboree* struggled to survive, it put greater emphasis on bringing in national figures, including Johnny Cash, Marty Robbins, George Jones, Patsy Cline, Ray Price, Roy Orbison, Ernest Tubb, Faron Young, Roger Miller, and Sonny James, who had gotten his start on the Sportatorium stage. (Courtesy of David Dennard.)

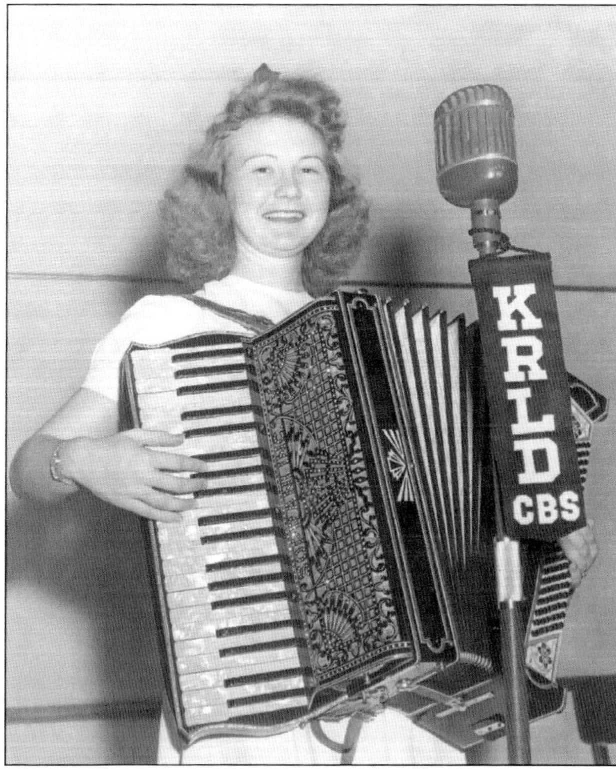


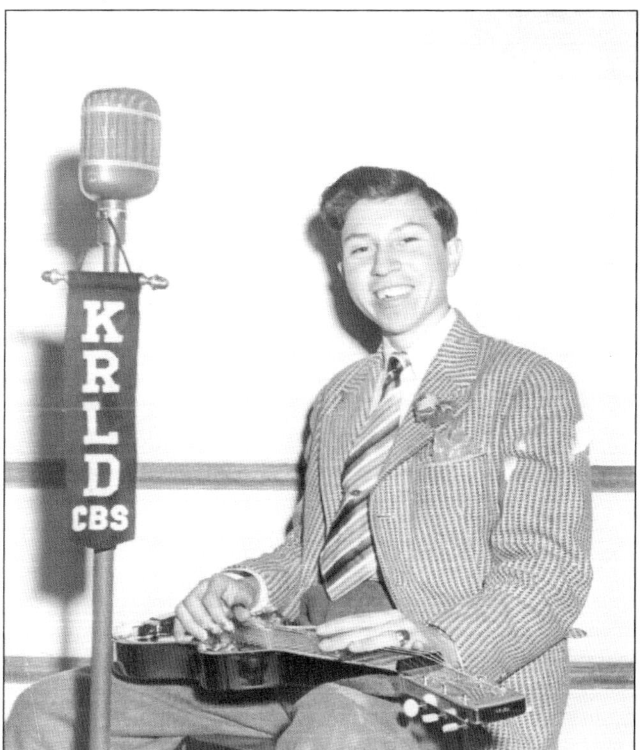

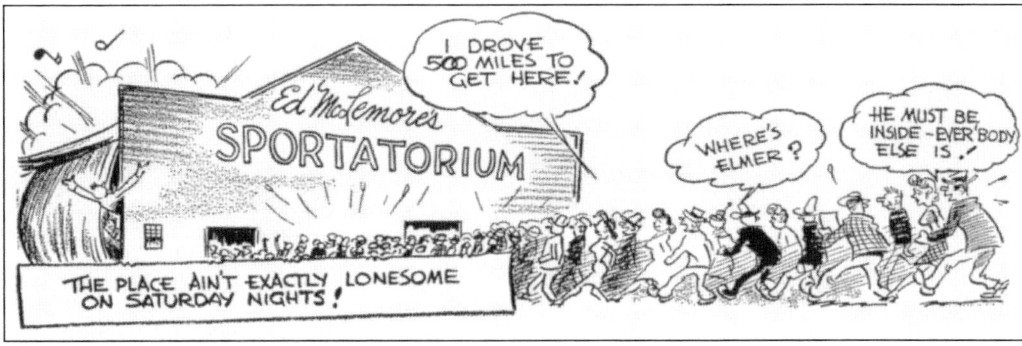


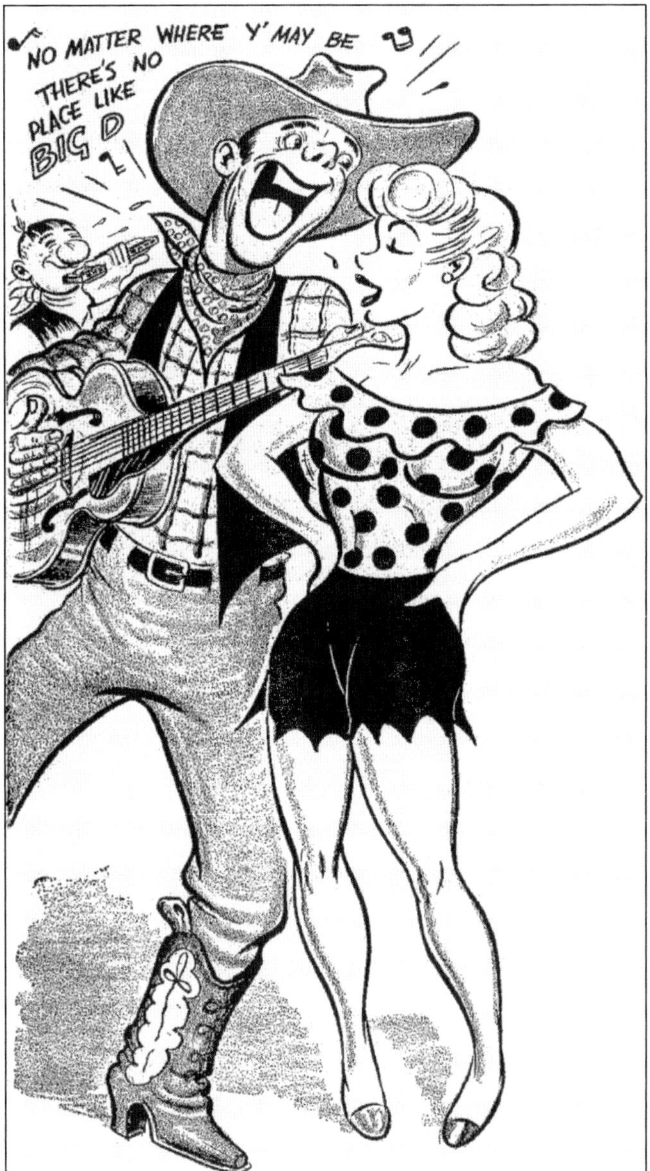


The *Big "D" Jamboree* initially ran rather plain, text-only advertisements in the local newspapers, the *Morning News* and the *Times Herald*. The cartoon format was an innovation of Ed Watt, who became Ed McLemore's right-hand man in 1953. Watt handled advertising, booking, and promotion for both the wrestling and musical sides of McLemore's operation. He put together tours that sometimes included performers from other shows, including the *Grand Ole Opry* and *Louisiana Hayride*. Displaying his own flair for showmanship, Watt appeared onstage in buckskin clothes and a coonskin cap at the height of the Davy Crockett craze, inspired by the Disney television series. The *Jamboree* ended in 1966, and McLemore died two years later, but Watt continued to promote wrestling in the Sportatorium until 1989. (Courtesy of David Dennard.)

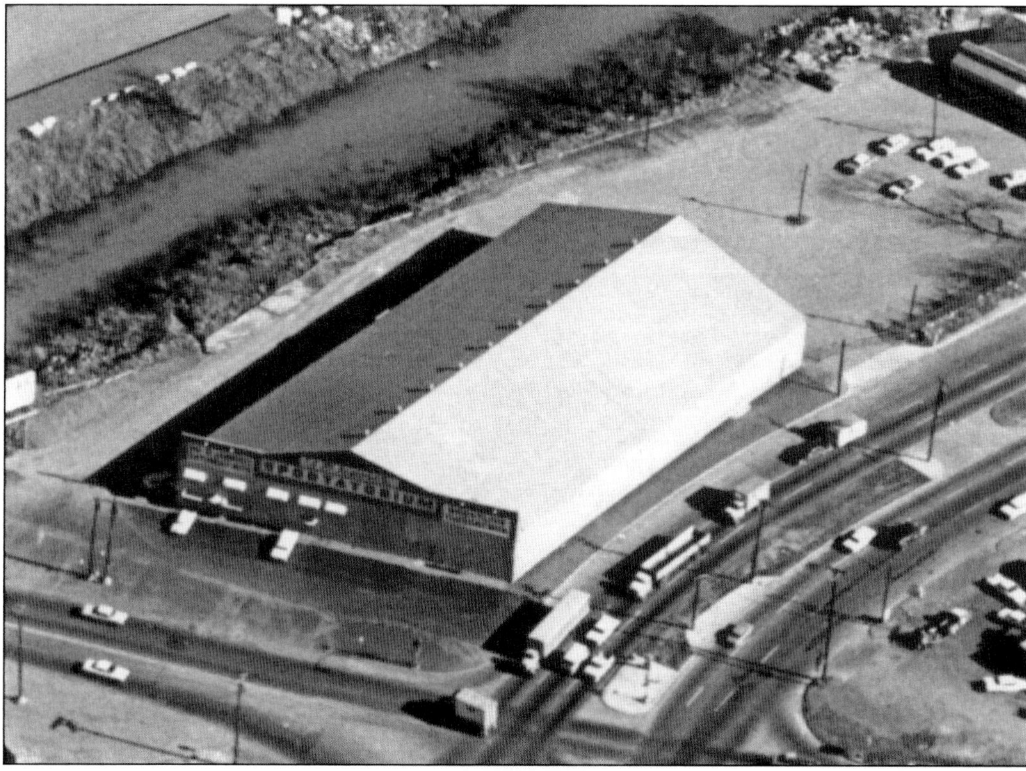

After a 1953 arson fire that may have been set on orders of a rival wrestling promoter, the original arena was replaced by the "million-dollar Sportatorium." Only the offices were air-conditioned; the audience made do with large fans and evaporative "swamp coolers." Rockabilly performer Ronnie Dawson said the place smelled of popcorn, stale beer, and the nearby Trinity River. (Courtesy of David Dennard.)

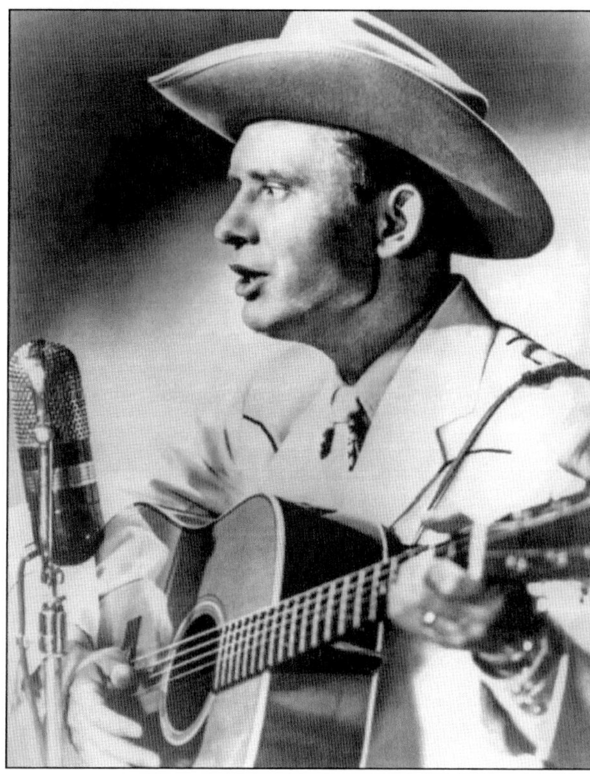

Blind singer and songwriter Leon Payne became a regular *Big "D"* performer in 1956. Best known for penning such classic country songs as "Lost Highway" and "I Love You Because," Payne was a versatile musician who played several instruments, including trombone, and had once been a member of Bob Wills's band. He died in 1969, at just 52 years of age. (Courtesy of David Dennard.)

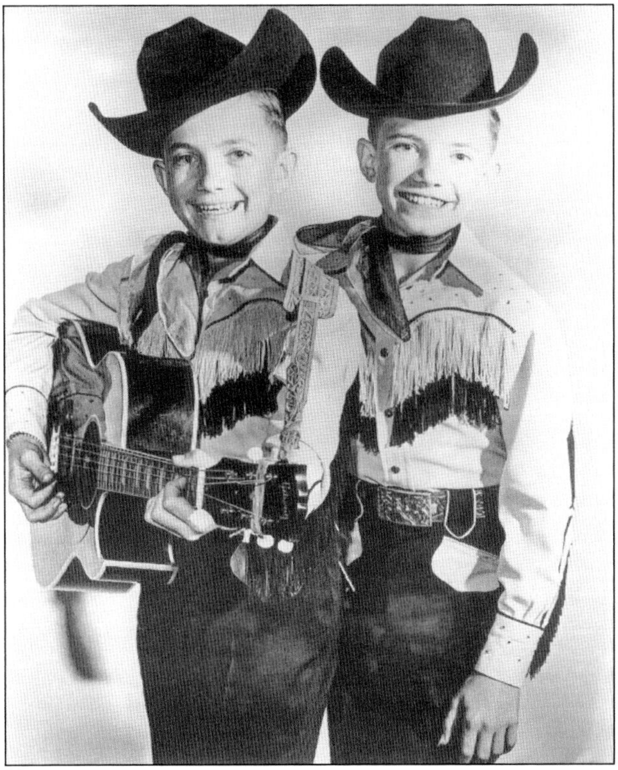

Twins Benny (left) and Bobby Belew, from Greenville, Texas, east of Dallas, joined the *Jamboree* cast in 1953, when they were just 13. They were managed by Ed McLemore. Though they were dynamic performers whom producer Johnny Hicks described as "showstoppers," they may have suffered by comparison to the Everly Brothers, whose material they sometimes performed. (Courtesy of David Dennard.)

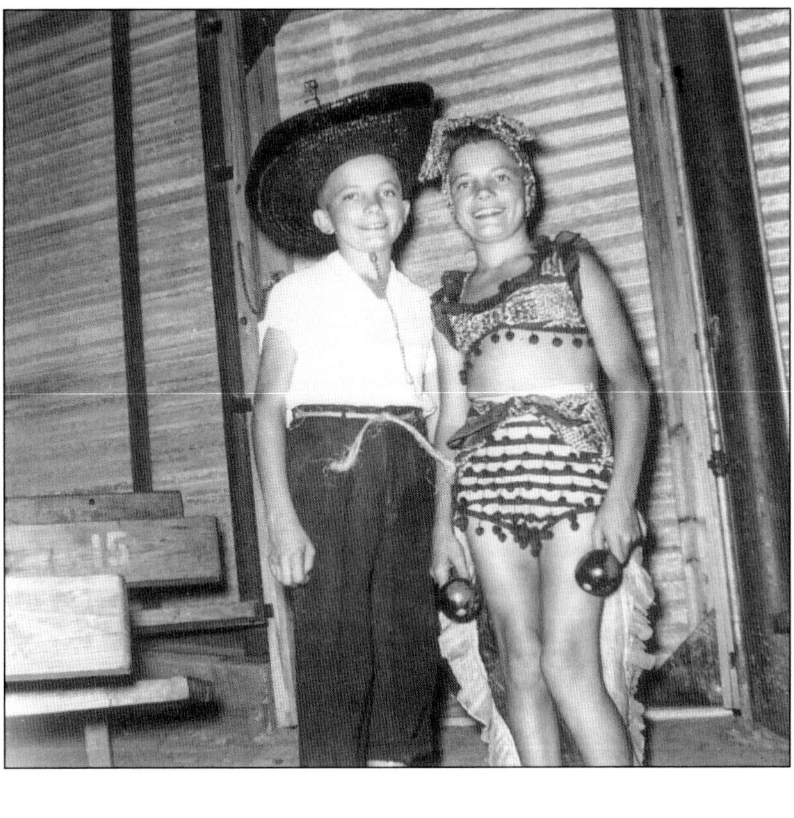

The Belew twins performed comedy material as well, sometimes in drag, which may have contributed to their reputation as nothing more than a novelty act. They appeared in the 1950s camp classic *Rock Baby Rock It!*, shot in Dallas. Their performance, though somewhat hammy, provides a rare opportunity to see them in action. (Courtesy of David Dennard.)

In the late 1950s, the Belews married twins Norma Sue and Linda Lou Graham, who apparently took a dim view of their husbands' musical careers. The Belews soon abandoned music. They made a final performance with their sister Carolyn in a 40th-anniversary *Big "D"* reunion in the late 1980s. Both died a few years later, in their early 50s. (Courtesy of David Dennard.)

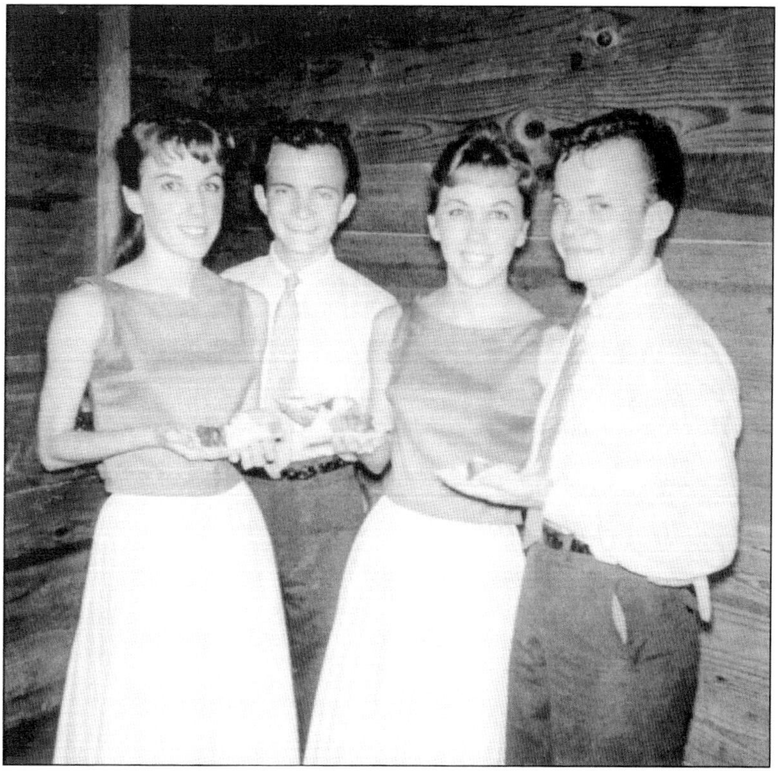

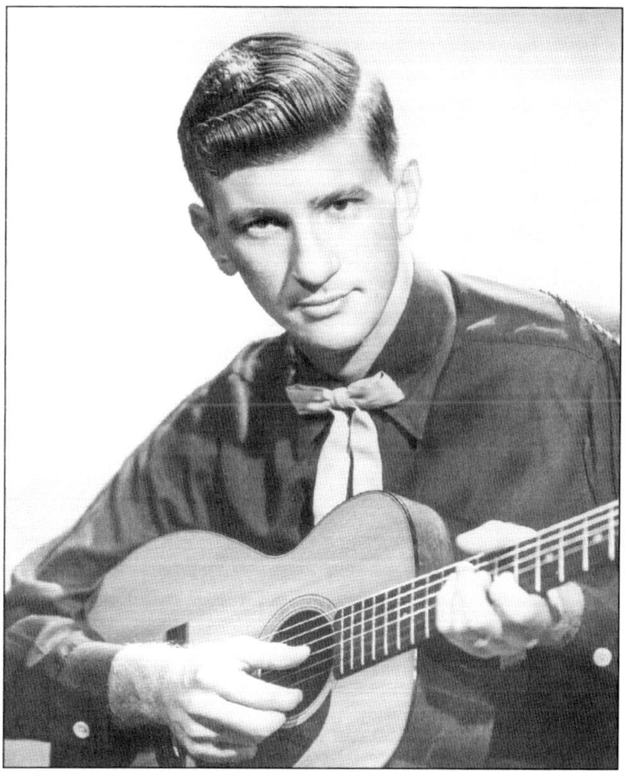

Singer and songwriter Mitchell Torok was a *Jamboree* regular off and on in the late 1950s and early 1960s when he lived in Dallas. Torok also performed on the *Louisiana Hayride*. His song "Mexican Joe" was a hit for Jim Reeves, and Torok had hits of his own, including "Caribbean," "Pledge of Love," and "Pink Chiffon." His career, however, never lived up to its early promise. (Courtesy of David Dennard.)

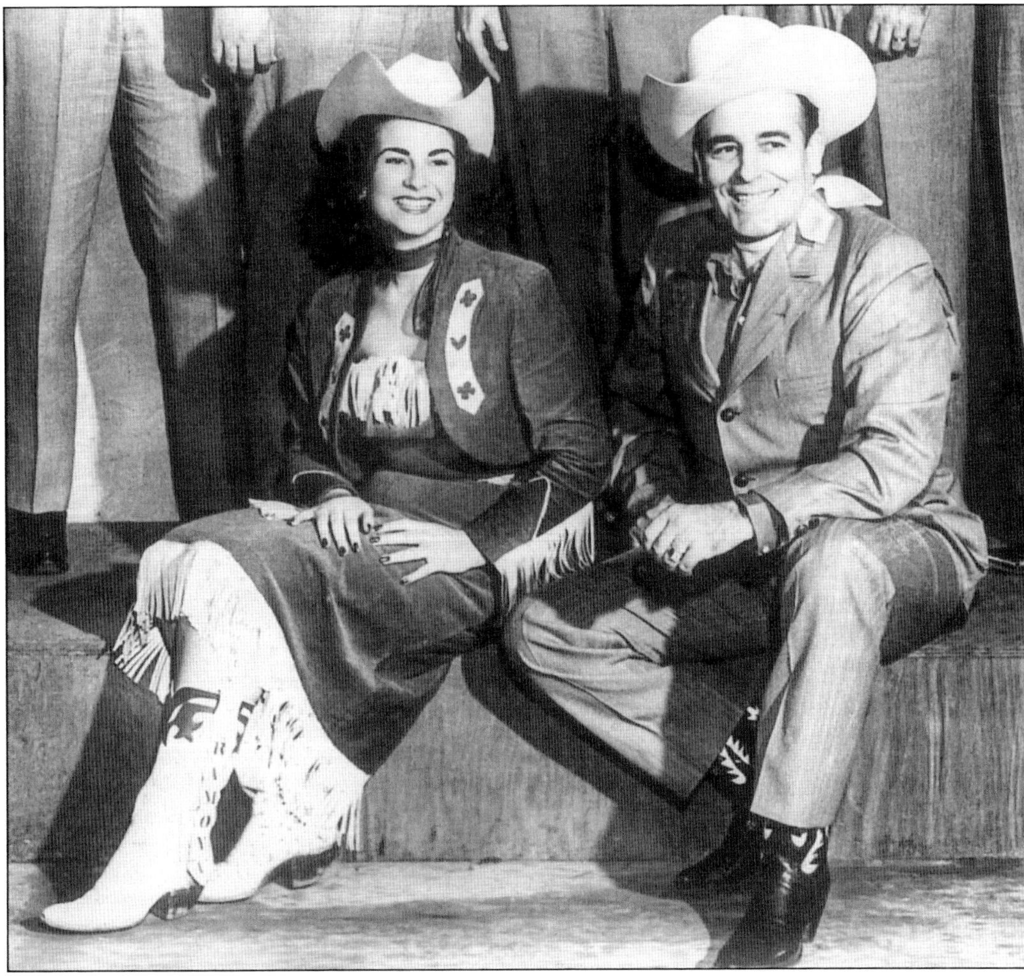

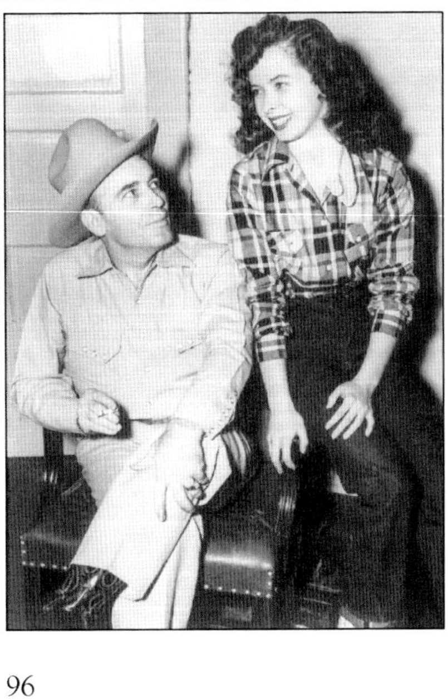

Western swing pioneer Bob Wills poses with vocalists Ramona Reed (above) and Betty Lou Lobb (left). Reed, an Oklahoma native, sang with Wills's band, the Texas Playboys, for a time. She and Wills made separate *Jamboree* appearances in late 1951. Lobb, who also hailed from Oklahoma, became the *Jamboree*'s first female star while still in her teens. Wills had returned to North Texas in 1950, hoping to retire from the road with proceeds from the Bob Wills Ranch House, down the street from the Sportatorium. But he was no businessman, and the place went bust. After Jack Ruby owned the massive venue, it was bought by bandleader Dewey Groom, who renamed it the Longhorn Ballroom and made it one of the premier country dance halls in Dallas. On Monday nights, Wilson Wren, one of Groom's employees, sometimes organized rhythm-and-blues concerts that featured performers such as B.B. King, Bobby "Blue" Bland, Millie Jackson, and Little Milton. (Courtesy of David Dennard.)

This March 21, 1953, *Big "D"* program book features Hank Locklin, a singer and songwriter best known for his hits "Please Help Me, I'm Falling," "Send Me the Pillow That You Dream On," and "Geisha Girl." Locklin returned to perform on the *Jamboree* when his schedule permitted. He joined the *Grand Ole Opry* in 1960 and remained a member of the Nashville institution until he died in 2009, at 91. (Courtesy of David Dennard.)

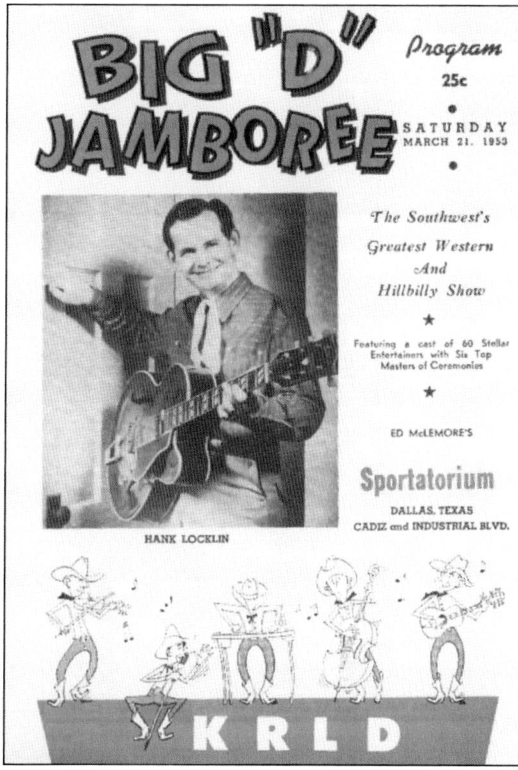


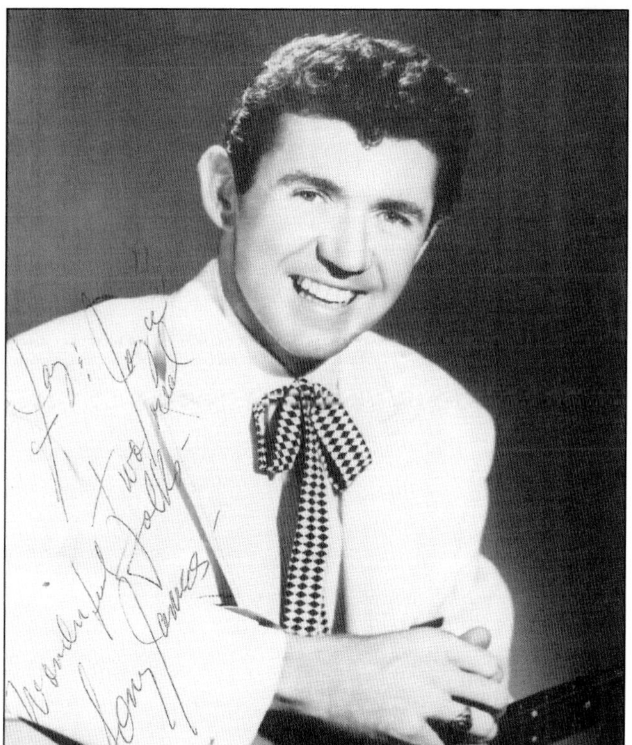

Sonny James, born James Hugh Loden in 1929, became a versatile musician and singer who played fiddle in Bobby Williamson's band before striking out on his own. He performed on WFAA's *Saturday Night Shindig* until it folded in 1954, then joined the *Jamboree* and signed a management contract with Ed McLemore. After "Young Love" catapulted him to stardom in 1957, James enjoyed hits into the 1980s. (Courtesy of David Dennard.)

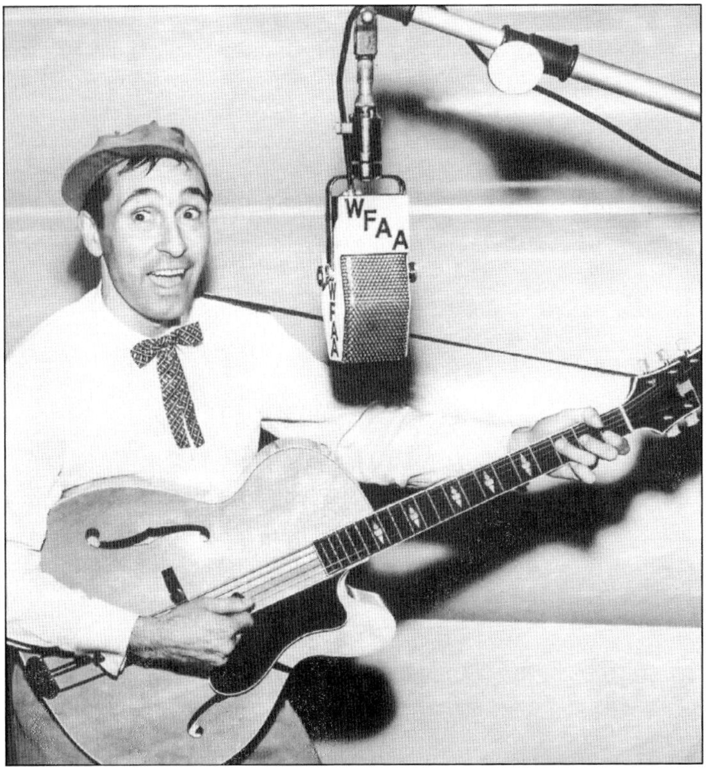


Neal Jones played guitar on a 1955 Sonny James session at Jim Beck's Dallas studio and appeared on the *Jamboree* in 1961. As indicated in this photograph, he was also featured on the rival *Saturday Night Shindig* on WFAA. He billed himself as the Tywopp Tornado and apparently did comic material as well as playing and singing. (Courtesy of David Dennard.)

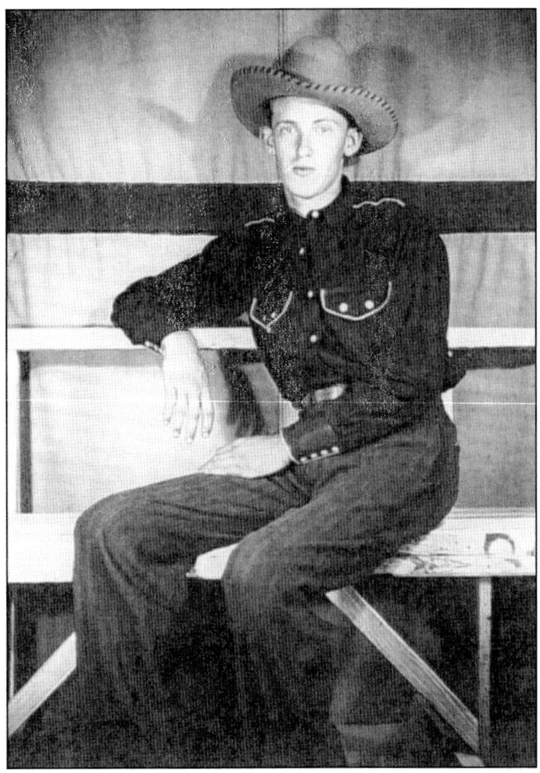

Lawton Williams is perhaps best known for the songs he wrote, including "Fraulein" and "Farewell Party," but he played a vital role in the *Big "D" Jamboree*, especially in its last years, when he performed and emceed. Williams also hosted a television show and worked as a deejay and program director of KCUL, then Fort Worth's top country radio station. He died in 2007, at 85. (Courtesy of David Dennard.)

A 1956 program book heralding the 11th anniversary of the *Big "D" Jamboree* was misleading. The show had actually begun not in 1945 but in 1947. But the promoters garnered publicity by celebrating the 10th anniversary in 1955 and followed up with the 11th the next year. (Courtesy of David Dennard.)

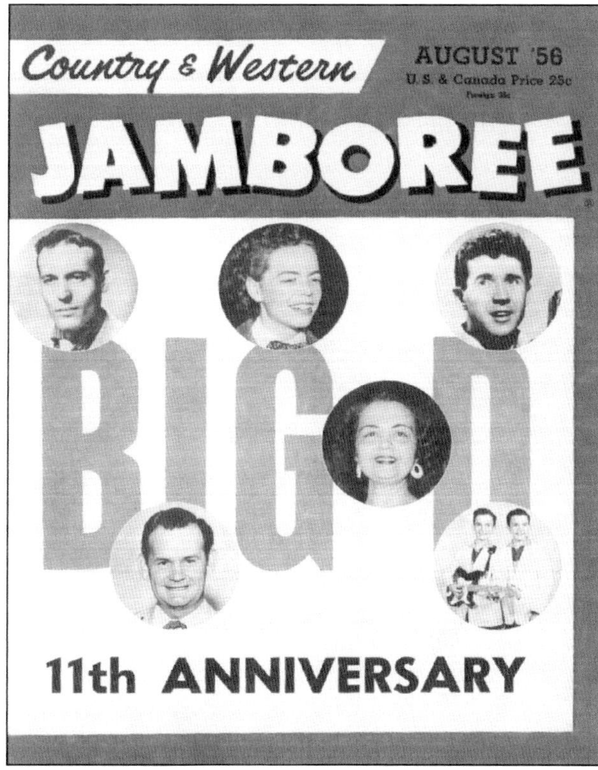


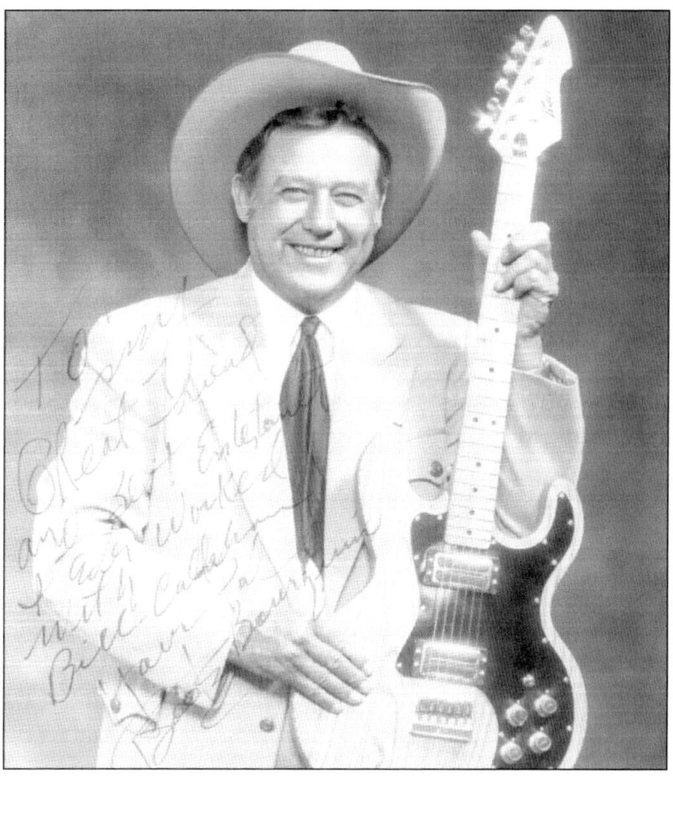

Boots Bourquin inscribed this photograph to his friend Bill Callahan. Bourquin led a hillbilly band, Boots and His Buddies, that performed on the *Texas State Barn Dance* and recorded for the local Talent label. Years later, as reported by *Dallas Observer* writer Robert Wilonsky, Bourquin loved to hold court at the Luby's Cafeteria in Casa Linda Plaza in East Dallas. (Courtesy of David Dennard.)

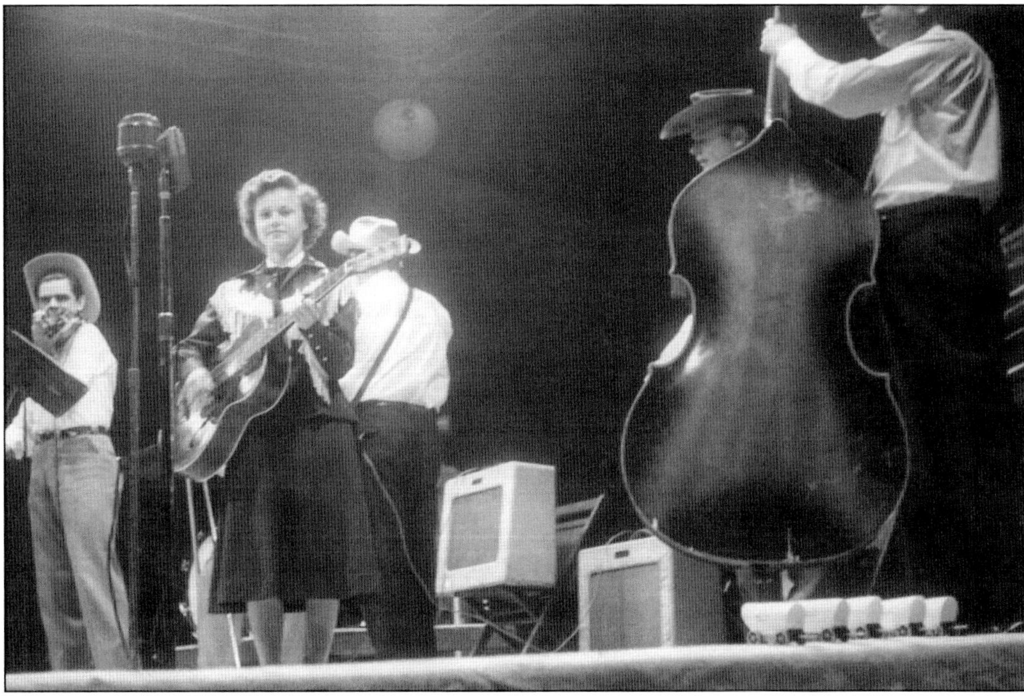

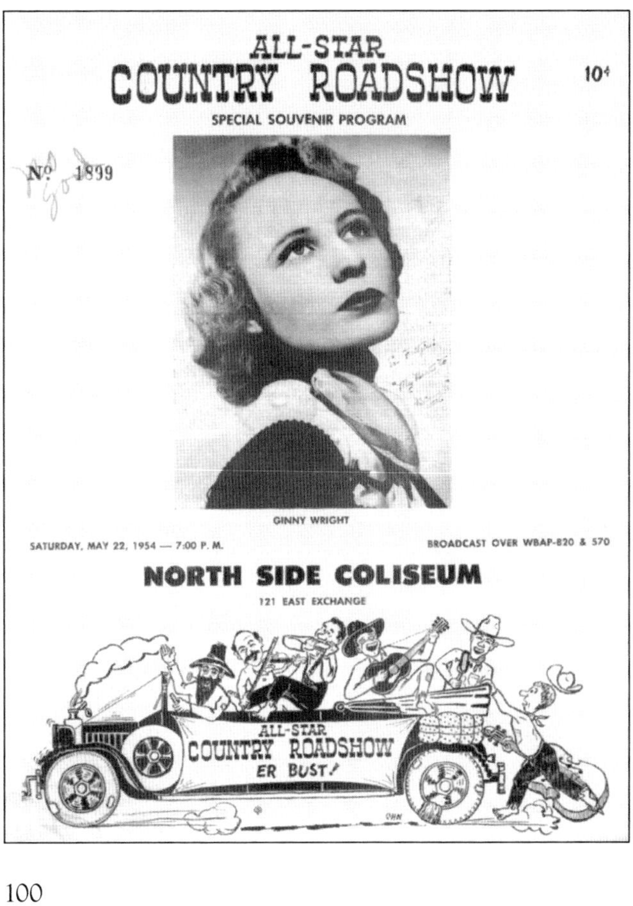


Helen Hall (above) joined the *Big "D" Jamboree* in October 1954 after a physical confrontation with a fellow performer led to her departure from the rival *All-Star Country Roadshow*, held in Fort Worth's North Side Coliseum. Despite her diminutive size and youthful appearance, Hall was a 27-year-old married woman with a child, and she possessed a powerful voice and stage presence. She turned down an offer from the *Louisiana Hayride* because of the travel involved, left the *Jamboree* within a few years, and quit performing about 1960, though she later made several comeback attempts. Another *Roadshow* regular, shown on the promotional literature on the left, was Ginny Wright, a Georgia native who later scored top 10 country hits in duets with Jim Reeves and Tom Tall. (Courtesy of David Dennard.)

Many felt that Helen Hall, shown in a newspaper photograph on the right, had the talent as a singer and songwriter to be a national star. Elmer Snodgrass, talent director of radio station WGGA in Gainesville, Georgia, inscribed the photograph below to Hall, calling her "my favorite gal singer." Her decision to leave the *Jamboree* and quit performing might have been influenced by family commitments and her involvement in a serious car crash that occurred on her return from an East Texas engagement. She was badly hurt and her fan club president was killed, and Hall was still on crutches when she returned to the *Jamboree* weeks later. (Courtesy of David Dennard.)

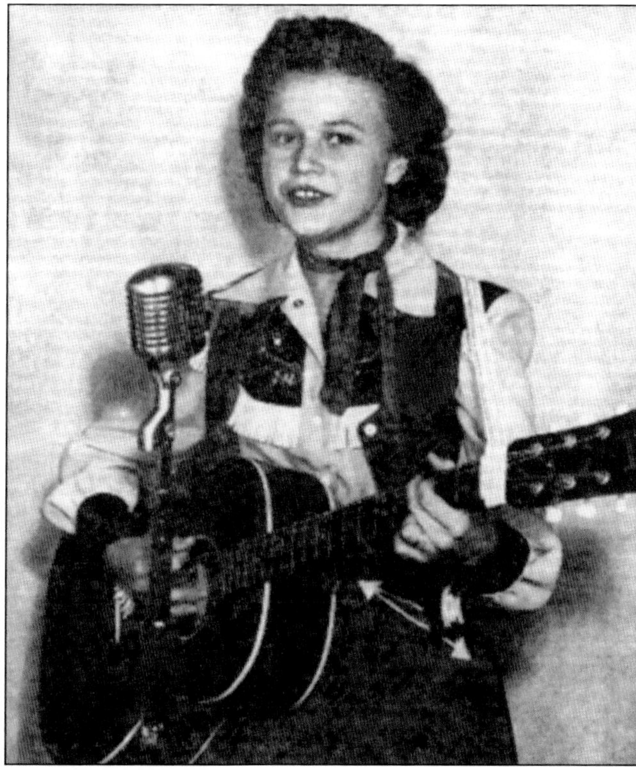

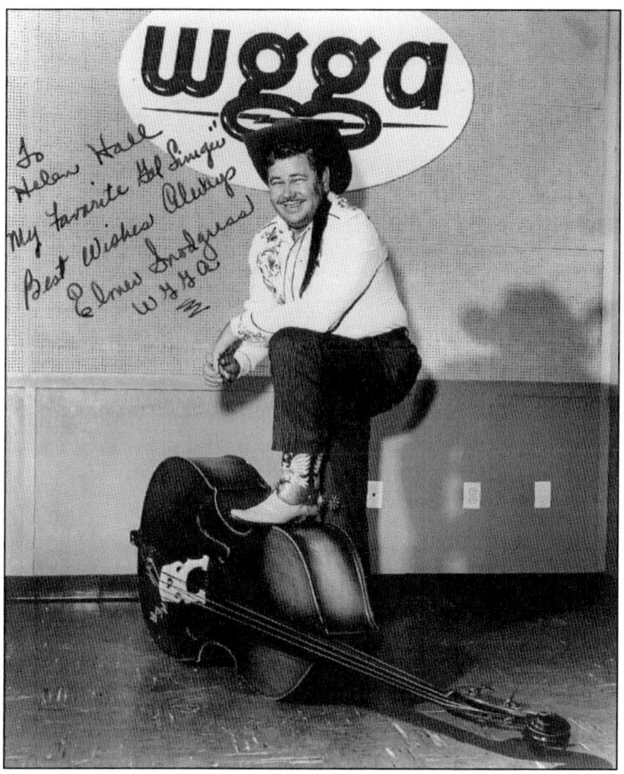

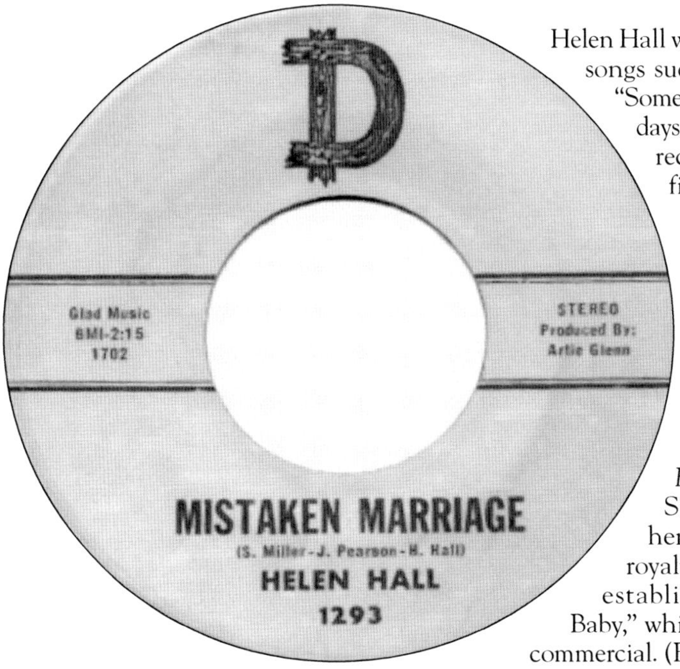


Helen Hall wrote and recorded classic country songs such as "Mistaken Marriage" and "Something Special" during her *Jamboree* days, and she made additional excellent records in the 1970s. But some of her finest recordings were made in the 1950s at her Fort Worth home, often with Charline Arthur on lead guitar and her husband, Jack Arthur, on bass. Writer Kevin Coffey found a tape reel with material from those sessions in the 1990s, and record producer David Dennard included some of the songs on *The Gals of the Big "D" Jamboree* on his Dragon Street label. A few years before her death in 2006, she received a royalty windfall after Dennard helped establish her authorship of "Hello, Baby," which had been used in a television commercial. (Both, courtesy of David Dennard.)

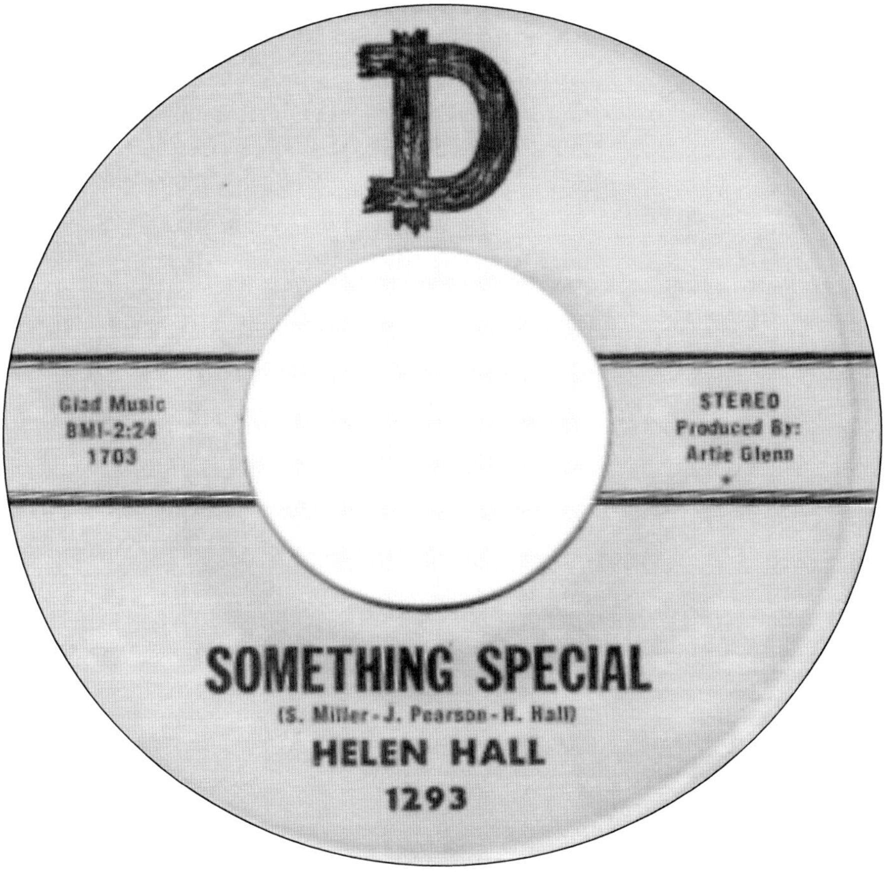

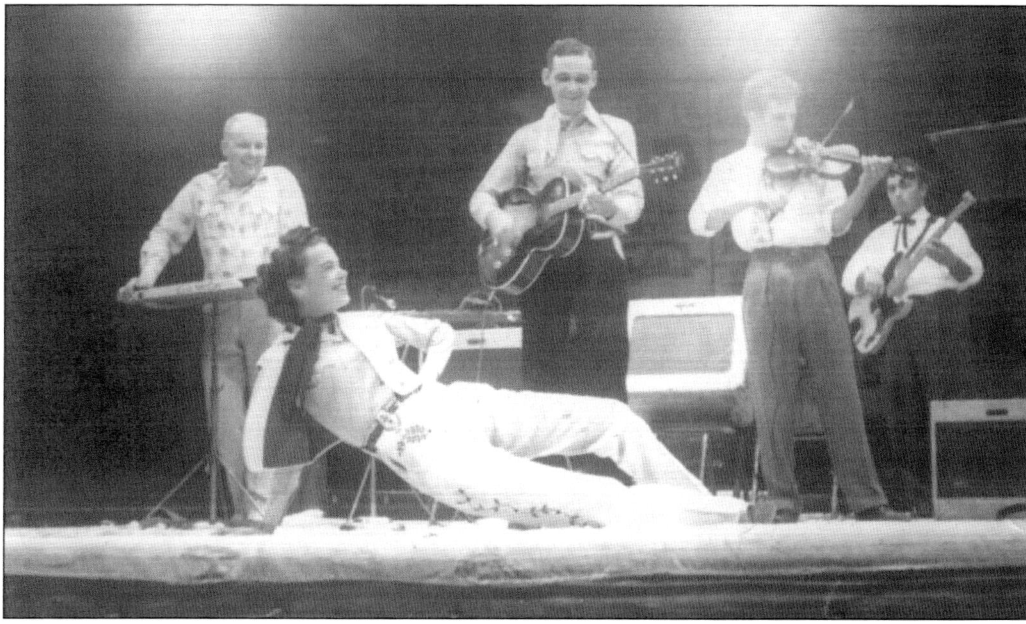

Charline Arthur delivers a dynamic mid-1950s performance on the *Big "D" Jamboree*, backed by, from left to right, George McCoy (steel guitar), Tex Raye (guitar), an unidentified fiddler, and her husband, Jack Arthur (bass). Arthur, whom Helen Hall called a Janis Joplin before her time, was outspoken to a fault, and her career faded into a long decline of small gigs and substance abuse before she died in 1987. (Courtesy of David Dennard.)

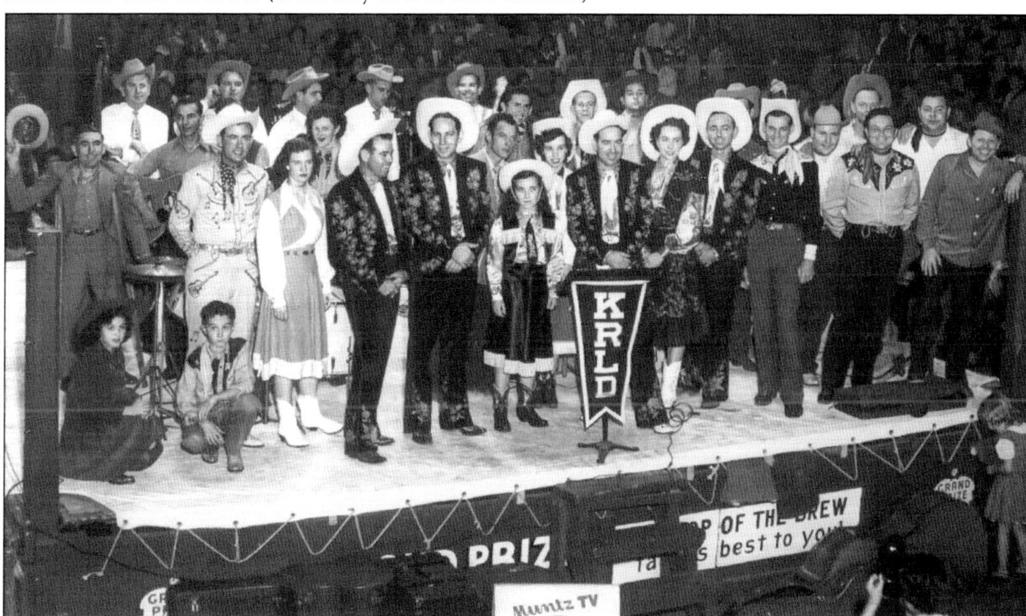


The Maddox Brothers and Rose are front and center in this photograph from the *Jamboree*'s 1950s heyday. Rose Maddox began performing with her brothers at age 11, after the family moved from Alabama to California during the Great Depression. The family band broke up in 1956, but Rose Maddox, known as the "Queen of Hillbilly Swing," continued her career and made appearances on the Dallas show through the mid-1960s. (Courtesy of David Dennard.)

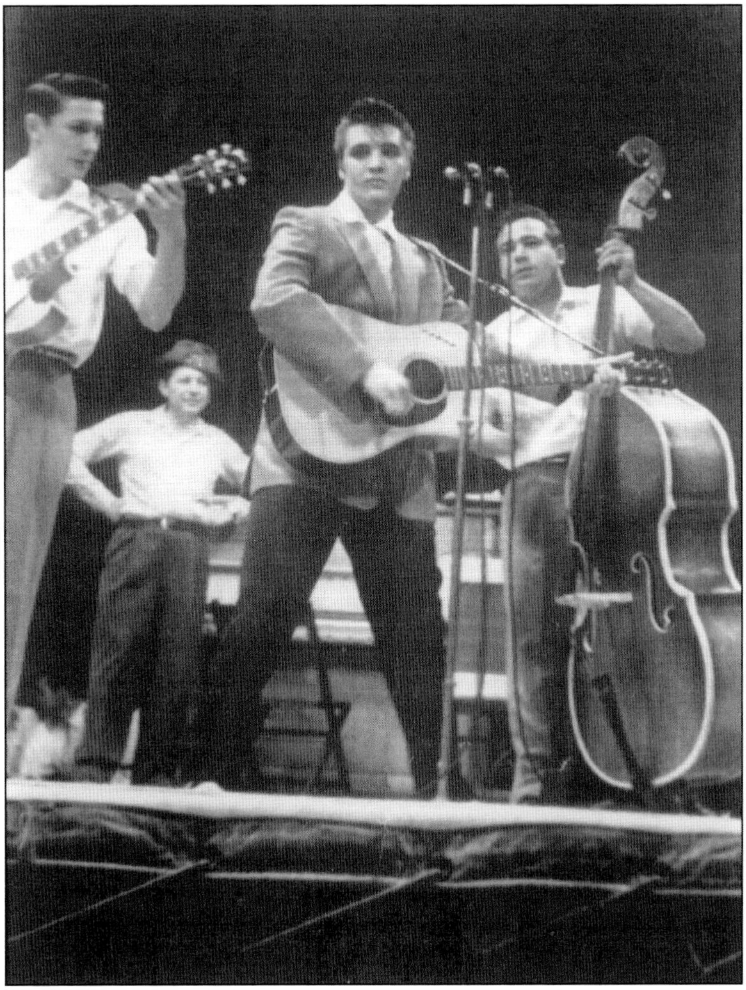

Left, Elvis Presley performs at the *Big "D" Jamboree* on June 18, 1955, with guitarist Scotty Moore and bassist Bill Black. In the background is emcee and producer Johnny Hicks, who seemed ambivalent about the presence of rock 'n' roll on the show. This was the third of four appearances Presley made on the *Jamboree* that year while also performing on the rival *Louisiana Hayride* in Shreveport. His debut, on April 16, 1955, was an explosive event that helped push the *Jamboree* from its country origins to more inclusiveness of rock 'n' roll. A "permit" issued by a Waco show promoter (below) entitles a fan to an hour with Elvis, "If she can catch him." (Courtesy of David Dennard.)

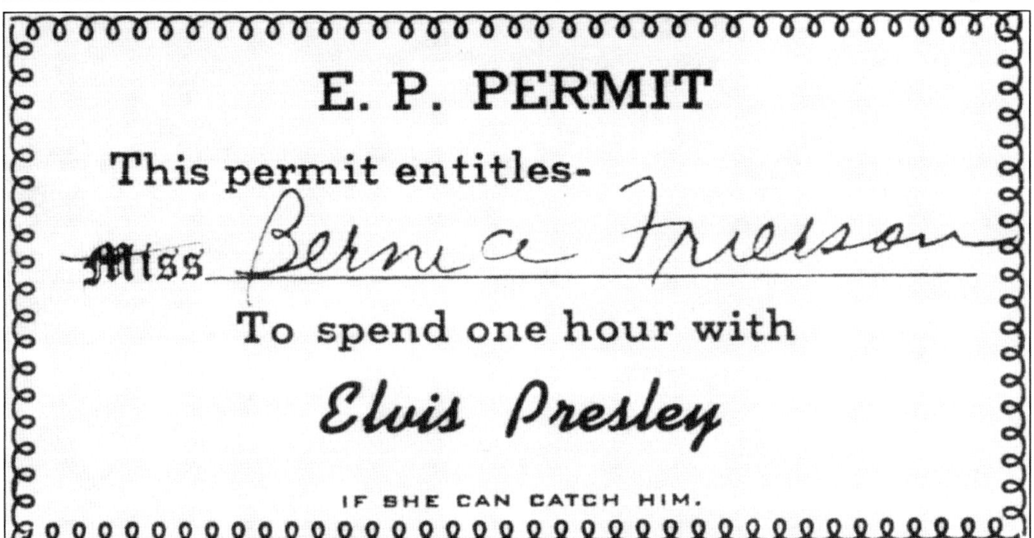

E. P. PERMIT

This permit entitles-

Miss ______________________

To spend one hour with

*Elvis Presley*

IF SHE CAN CATCH HIM.

A program heralds Presley's final *Jamboree* appearance, as a "special guest," on September 3, 1955. The show also featured the Belew Twins, Helen Hall, Jimmie Collie, and LaFawn Paul. Several key events in Presley's career followed soon after that appearance: Col. Tom Parker gained full control of the singer's business dealings; Presley was given top billing on the *Louisiana Hayride*; and he signed a contract with RCA Records. (Courtesy of David Dennard.)

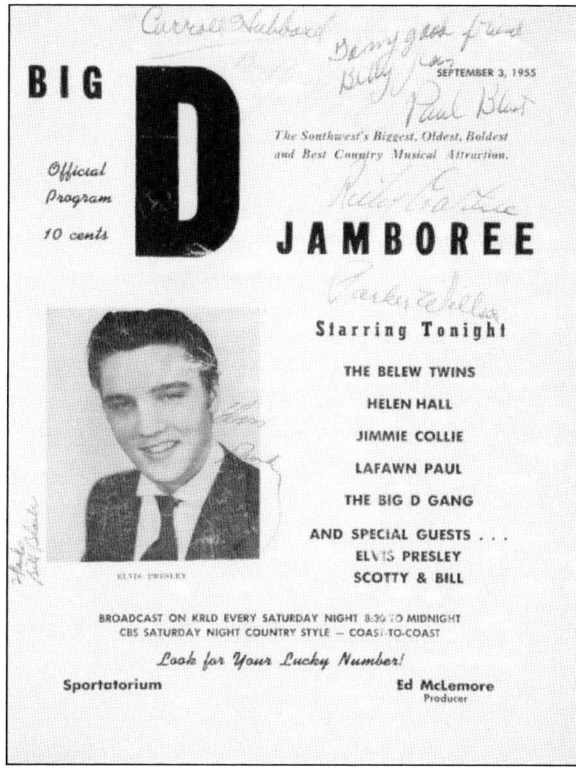


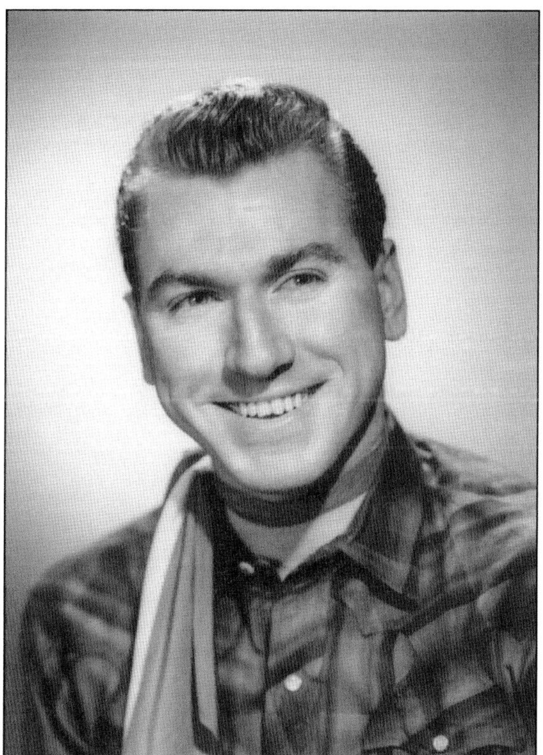

Dallas native Joe Poovey formed a country band when he was 12, and he soon became a *Jamboree* regular. After hearing Elvis Presley on the *Jamboree* in 1955, Poovey became a rockabilly performer known as "Groovy" Joe Poovey. He subsequently returned to country music and worked as a deejay, but his popularity among rockabilly fans in Europe sparked a career resurgence in the 1980s and 1990s. He died in 1998. (Courtesy of David Dennard.)

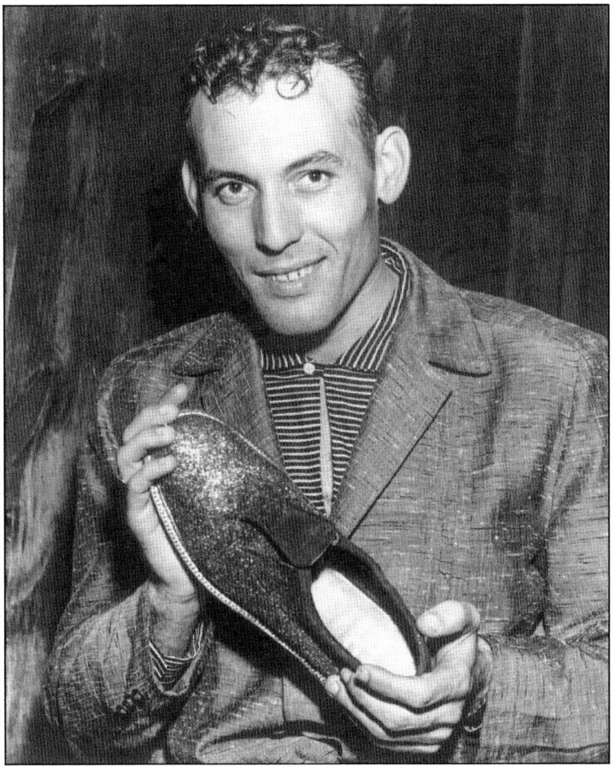

Sun Records artist Carl Perkins appeared frequently on the *Jamboree* after he had a hit with his song "Blue Suede Shoes." He had written the song on a grocery sack while living in public housing in Jackson, Tennessee. Perkins made eight appearances on the show in 1956, including one just weeks after a car crash that badly injured him and led to the death of his brother Jay. (Courtesy of David Dennard.)

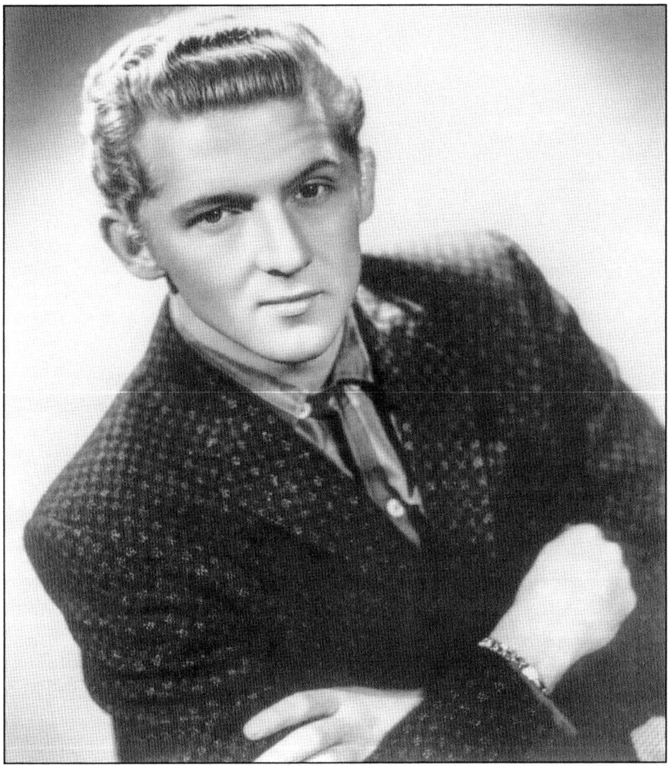

Piano pounder Jerry Lee Lewis made his first *Jamboree* appearance in March 1957 while riding his Sun hit "Whole Lotta Shakin' Goin' On." He continued to rock the Sportatorium in the ensuing years. The Ferriday, Louisiana, native was equally adept at rock 'n' roll and country. (Courtesy of David Dennard.)

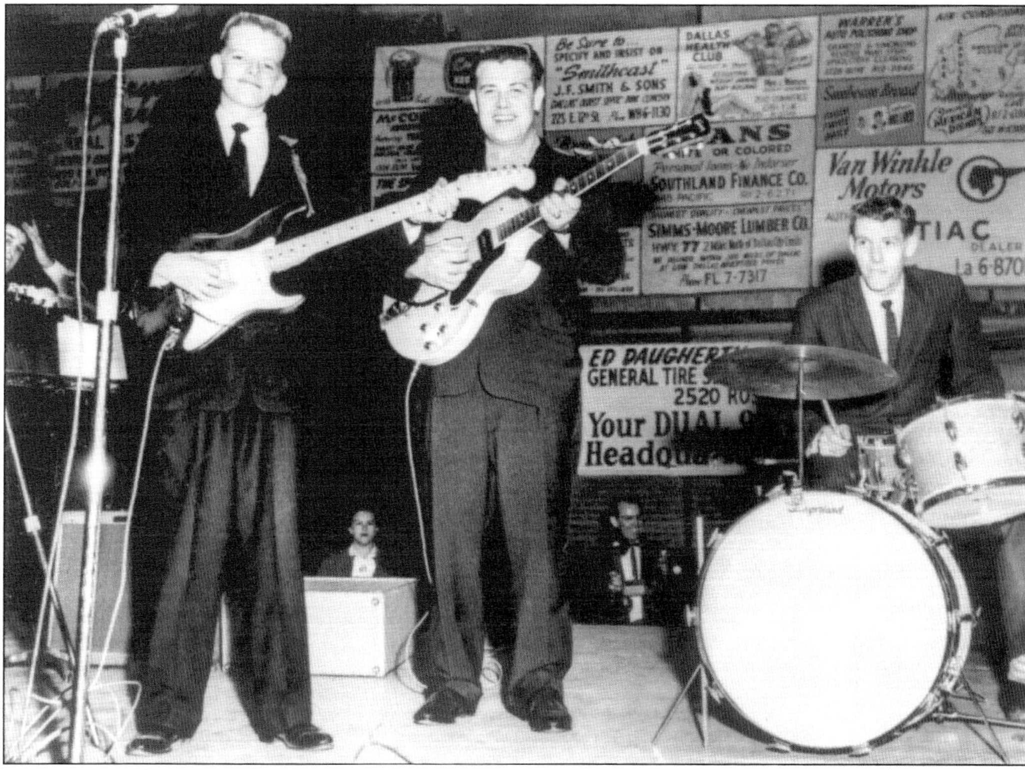


Dynamic rocker Ronnie Dawson (left) grew up in Waxahachie, south of Dallas. His father had led a band, and Dawson took to music at an early age. He originally billed himself as Ronnie D or Dee and performed with the band shown here, the D Men, which included the late guitarist Sam Wolaver (center). (Courtesy of David Dennard.)

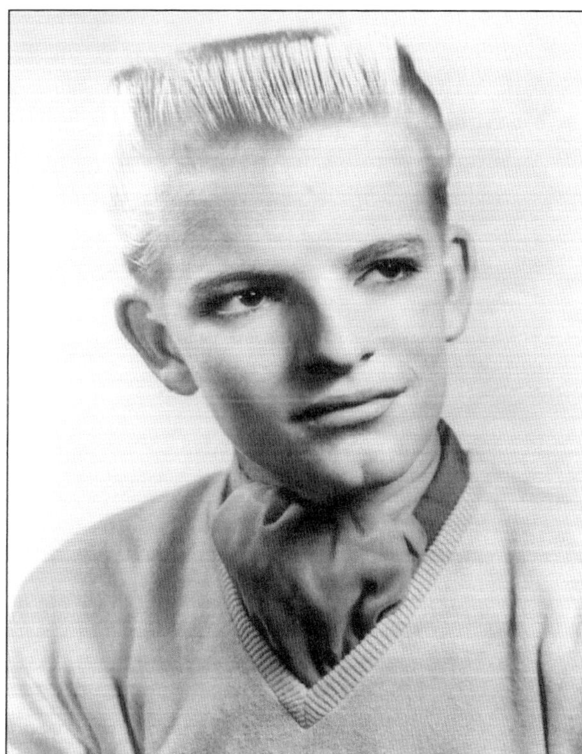

A promotional photograph heralds Ronnie Dawson's presence on the *Jamboree* and on Swan Records, whose owners included Dick Clark. Dawson's career stalled, in part due to backstage conflict between country and rock. He survived for years by playing in bands, including the Light Crust Doughboys, and doing session and commercial work. British rockabilly fans revived his career in the 1980s. The clean-living Dawson died of cancer in 2003. (Courtesy of David Dennard.)

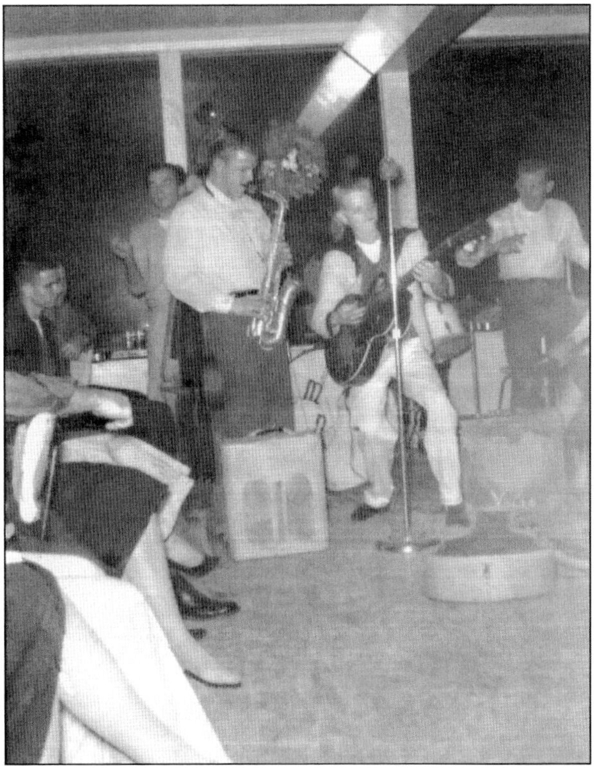

At left, Ronnie Dawson rocks out in a performance at Lake Waxahachie, near his hometown, in 1956. Dawson was then about 17. He formed his first band, the D Men, after getting a good response to a performance at his high school. Dawson and his bandmates became regulars on the *Big "D" Jamboree* after wining its talent contest 10 consecutive times. The show's promoter, Ed McLemore, became Dawson's manager, adding him to a stable that included Gene Vincent and Dale Hawkins. Big Al Turner stands behind Dawson during a *Jamboree* performance (below). Turner ignited backstage controversy when he returned in 1958 after a four-year absence, determined to roll back the calendar to the show's early days, before rockers such as Dawson became popular. (Courtesy of David Dennard.)

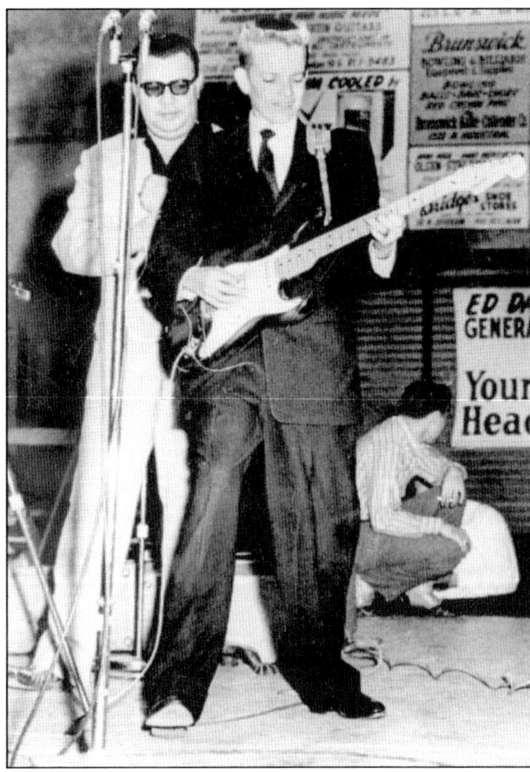

Weldon "Buddy" Walker was among the earliest performers on the show that became the *Big "D" Jamboree*, and he was the first artist to record for Jesse Erickson's Talent label. Walker's "Border Town Fiesta" became a regional hit, but his career fizzled and he reluctantly abandoned music for a career with the post office. Before his death in 2002, however, some of his music had been released on CD. (Courtesy of David Dennard.)

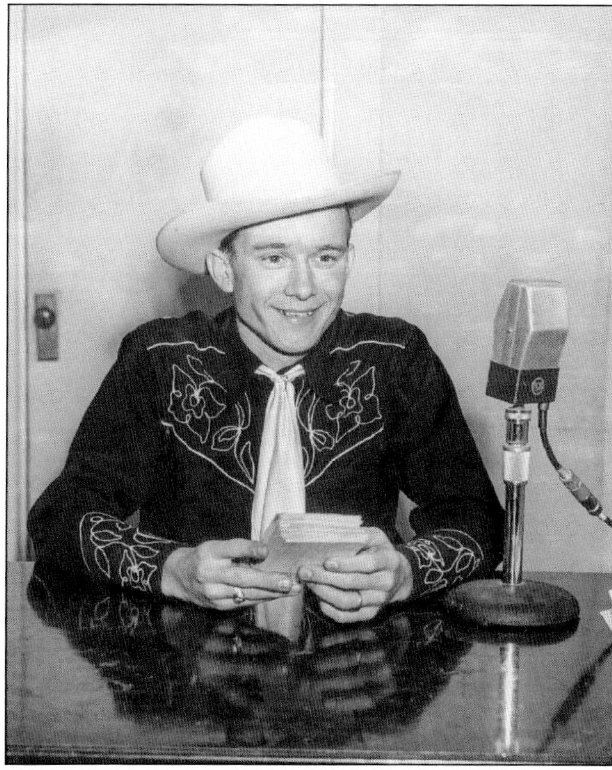

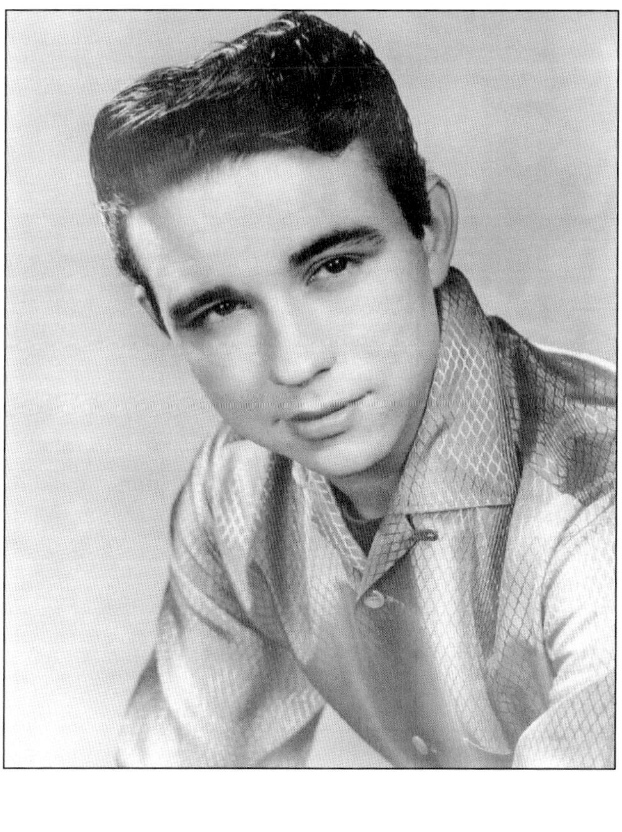

Growing up south of Fort Worth, Johnny Carroll led a country band that was also influenced by black music. He began appearing on the *Jamboree* in 1955, joined Decca Records, and recorded rockabilly classics such as "Crazy Crazy Lovin' " and "Wild, Wild Women." Ed McLemore managed Carroll, whose career stalled until the 1970s rockabilly revival. He died in 1995. (Courtesy of David Dennard.)

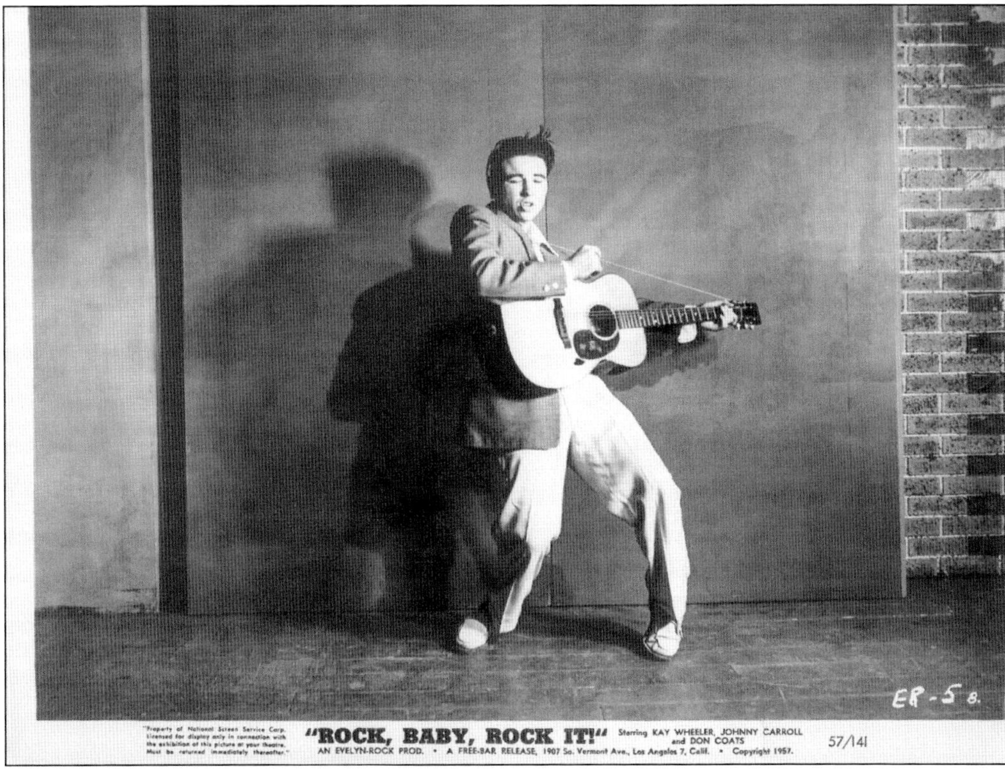


A lobby card touts Johnny Carroll's prominent role in *Rock Baby Rock It!*, a 1957 film shot in Dallas that *Dallas Observer* writer Matt Weitz called "a steaming bowl of celluloid queso." The movie was notoriously bad, but more than two-thirds of its 77-minute length is devoted to bands playing music, which makes it a historical document. (Courtesy of David Dennard.)

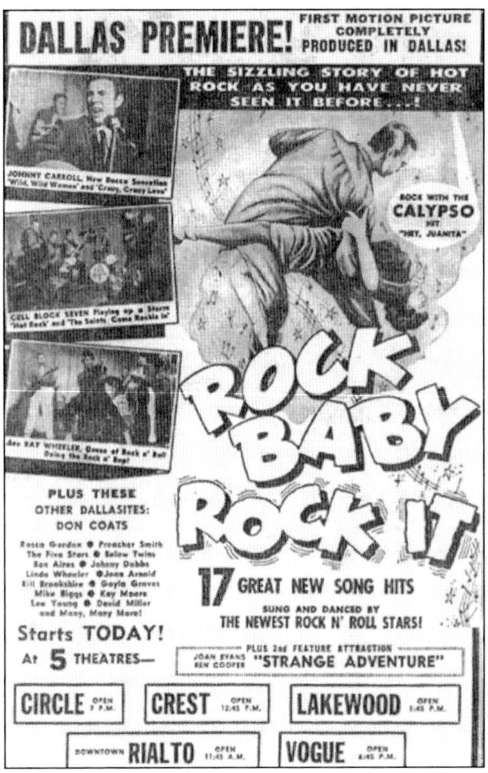


The overblown copy for a *Dallas Times Herald* advertisement hints at the original title of the film, *Hot Rocks*, which was deemed too racy, though the film features Johnny Carroll and his band, the Hot Rocks, performing a song called "Hot Rock." The advertisement's assertion that the film was the first completely produced in Dallas overlooks a series of African American features shot in and around the city in the 1940s. (Courtesy of David Dennard.)

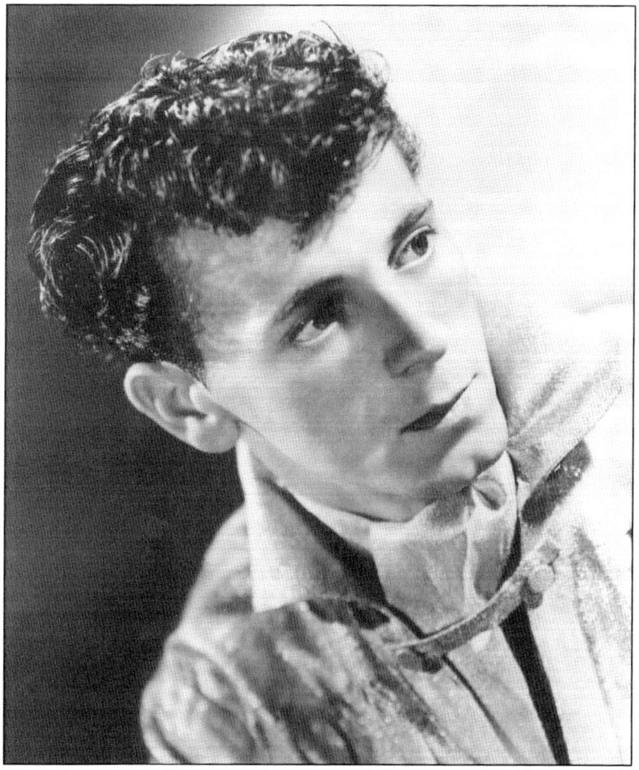

Hard-drinking rocker Gene Vincent, after scoring a huge hit with "Be Bop A Lula" in 1956, moved to Dallas and performed several times on the *Jamboree* while under Ed McLemore's management. He is shown on the right in a portrait and, below, with Darrell Glenn, who began performing on the show after his 1953 hit with "Crying in the Chapel," written by his father, Artie Glenn. (Courtesy of David Dennard.)

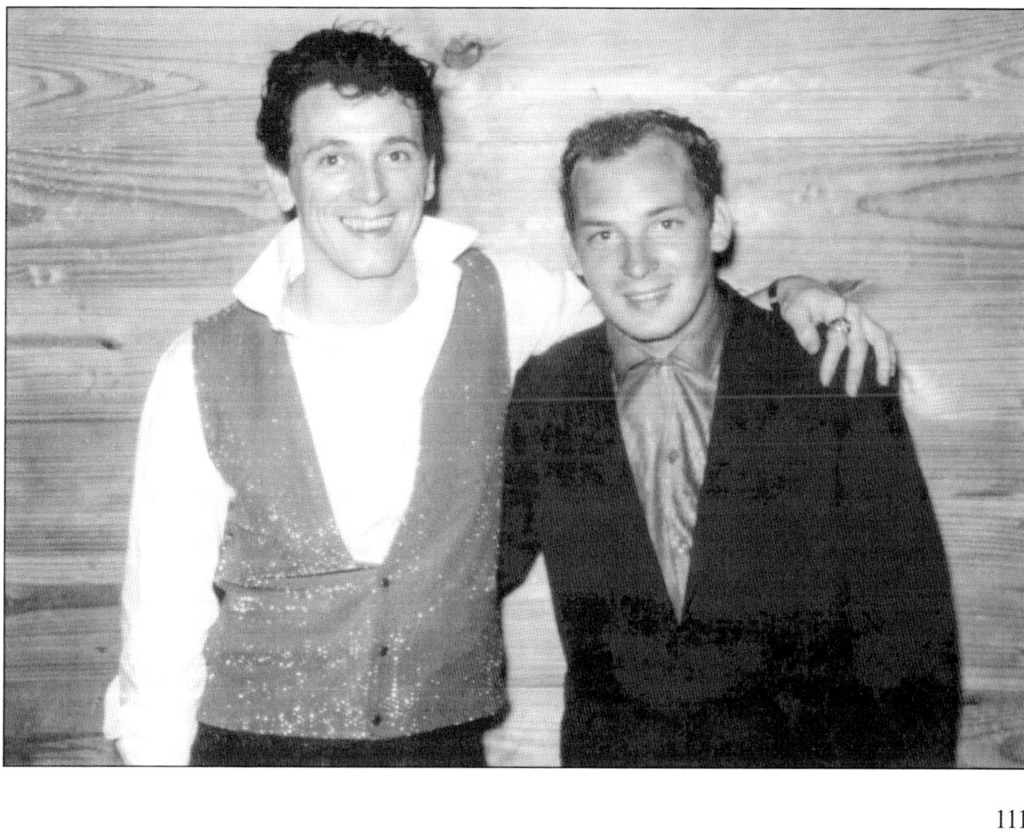

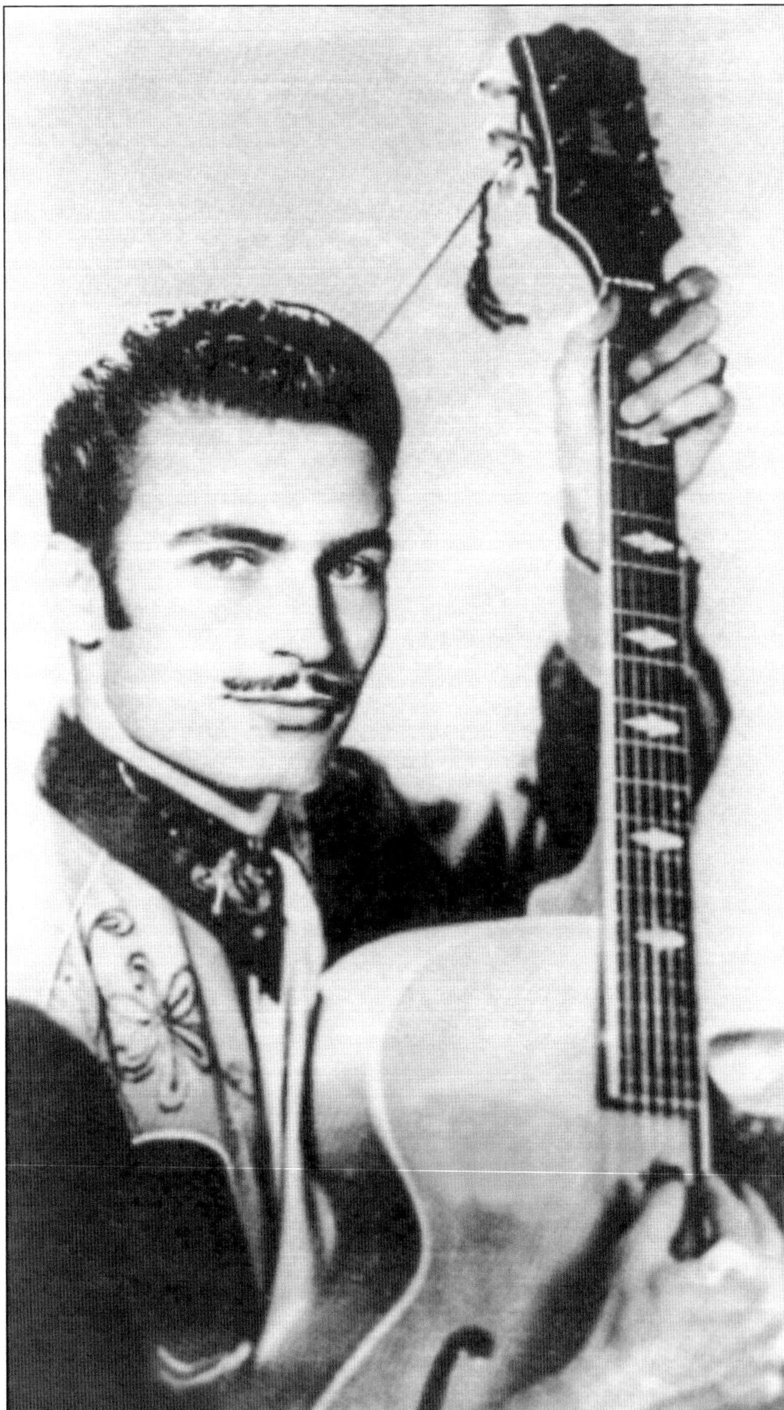

New Orleans–born country and rockabilly singer Werly Fairburn performed occasionally on the *Jamboree* in the late 1950s while also working as a regular on the *Louisiana Hayride* in Shreveport, where he lived. In the 1960s, he moved to California, where he continued to perform and to record on his own Milestone label. Fairburn died in 1985 at age 60. (Courtesy of David Dennard.)

Wanda Jackson performs on the *Jamboree* in 1960. The Oklahoma native was still in her teens when she was discovered by bandleader Hank Thompson, who sometimes appeared on *Big "D."* Though equally adept at rockabilly, Jackson seems to have stressed her country side starting in the late 1950s, as the show's emphasis shifted. She remained musically active in 2013, at 75, and her website proclaimed her the "Queen of Rock." (Courtesy of David Dennard.)

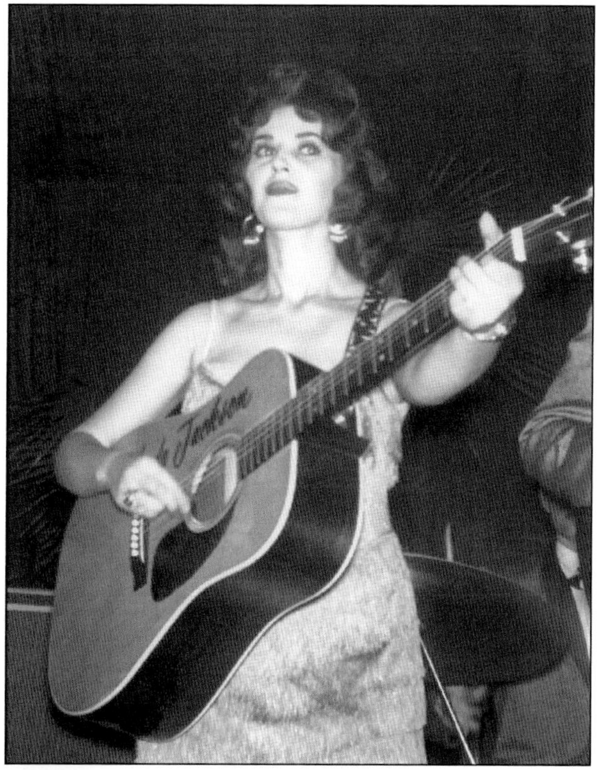

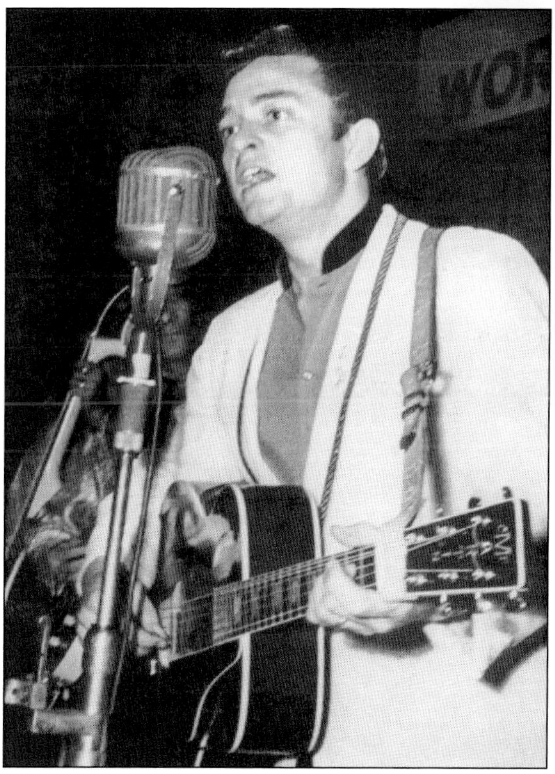

Johnny Cash was a popular performer on the *Jamboree* for a decade, and he probably held the attendance record, though Hank Snow also claimed that honor. Fellow performer Orville Couch recalled that in Cash's last appearance on the show, he came out as rain pounded the metal building and captured the audience with a line from one of his hits, "How high's the water, mama?" (Courtesy of David Dennard.)

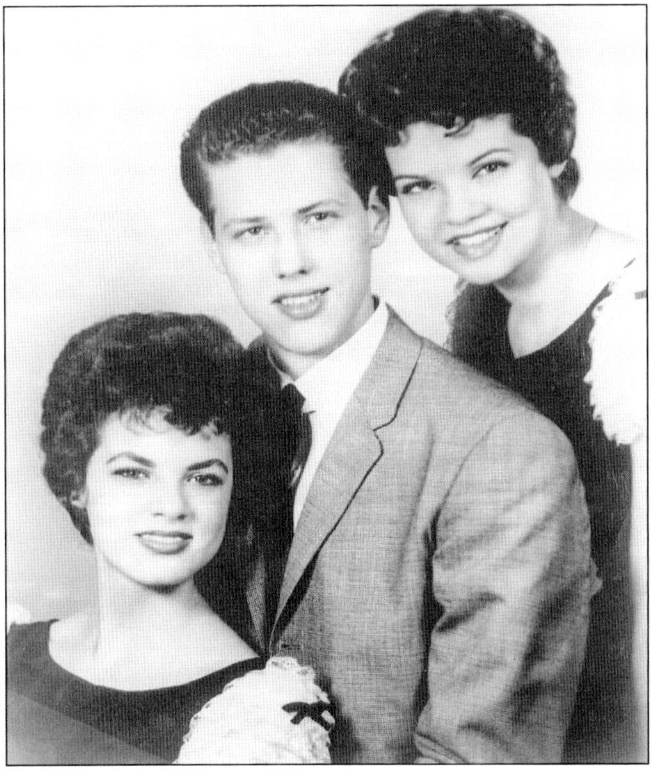

Siblings Judith "Judy" (left), Rick, and Robin Beaver joined the *Jamboree* about 1958, during the folk music boom. Their repertoire included songs such as "If I Had a Hammer" and the traditional ballad "Barbara Allen." Within a few years, however, the group split up over musical and personal differences. In 2013, only Judy Beaver survived, having become a successful painter and retired to Louisiana. (Courtesy of David Dennard.)

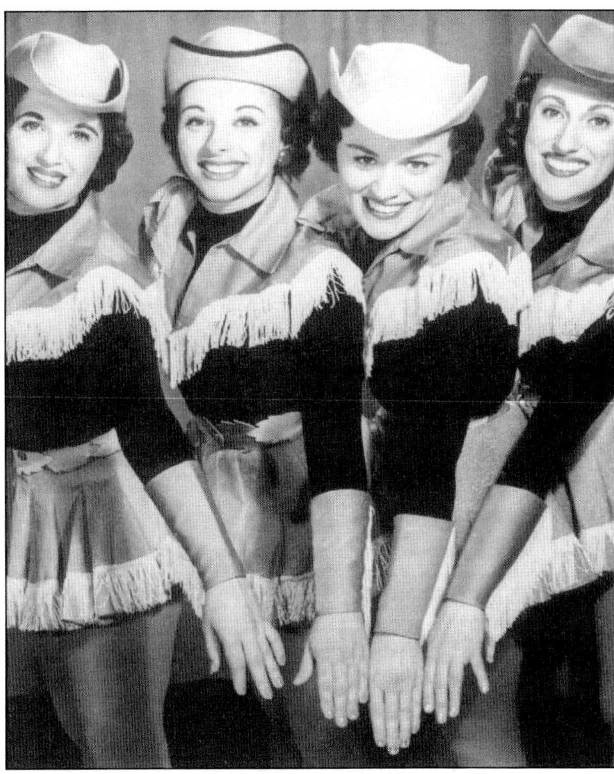

Esther "Abbie" Neal (second from left) and Her Ranch Girls made weekly appearances on the *WWVA Jamboree* in Wheeling, West Virginia, and were featured guests on the *Big "D" Jamboree*. Neal, born in Pennsylvania in 1918, got her nickname after working as a comedian, playing a character named Abigail Aloysius Paperwad. She died in 2004. (Courtesy of David Dennard.)

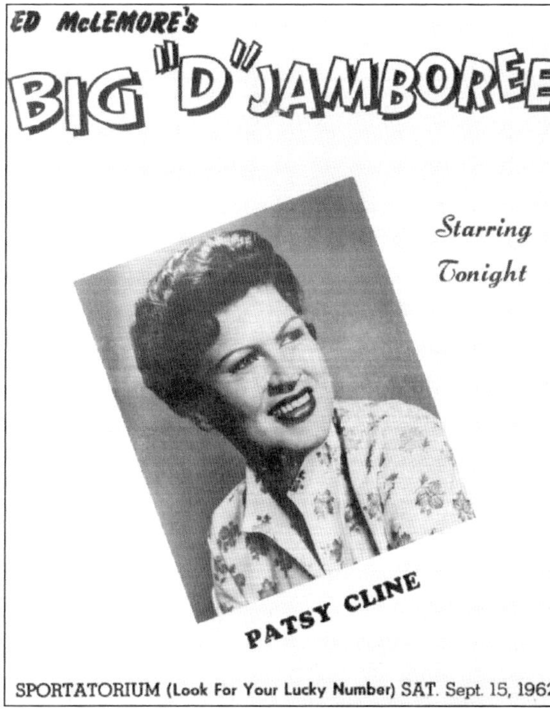


A September 15, 1962, program features star attraction Patsy Cline, a country music legend who was a regular on the *Grand Ole Opry* and made classic recordings of songs such as "Crazy" and "I Fall to Pieces." Cline was just 30 when she died in a plane crash the following year. The program cover also promotes a raffle ("Look For Your Lucky Number"). (Courtesy of David Dennard.)

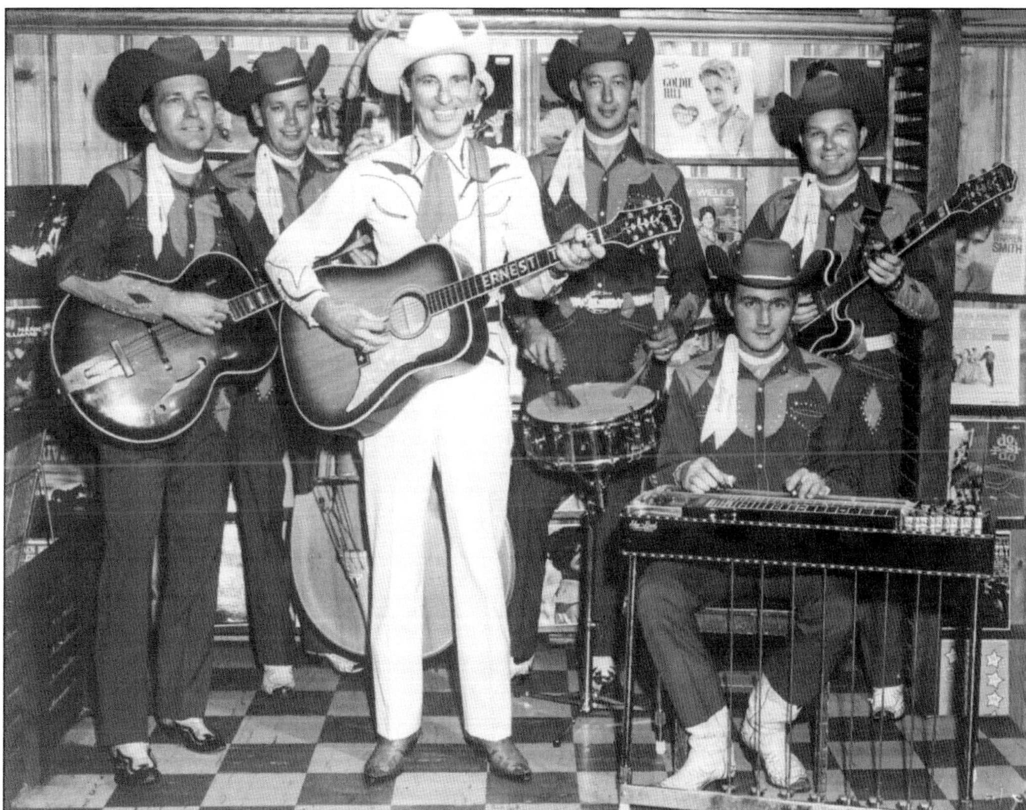

Texas-born Ernest Tubb (in white suit), another *Opry* member who performed on the *Big "D,"* is shown in the early 1960s with his band, the Texas Troubadours. The members are, from left to right, an unidentified guitarist, Jack Drake, Jack Greene (drums), Buddy Charleton (steel guitar), and Leon Rhodes (guitar). Best known for hits such as "I'm Walking the Floor Over You" and "Waltz Across Texas," Tubb died in 1984, at age 70. (Courtesy of David Dennard.)

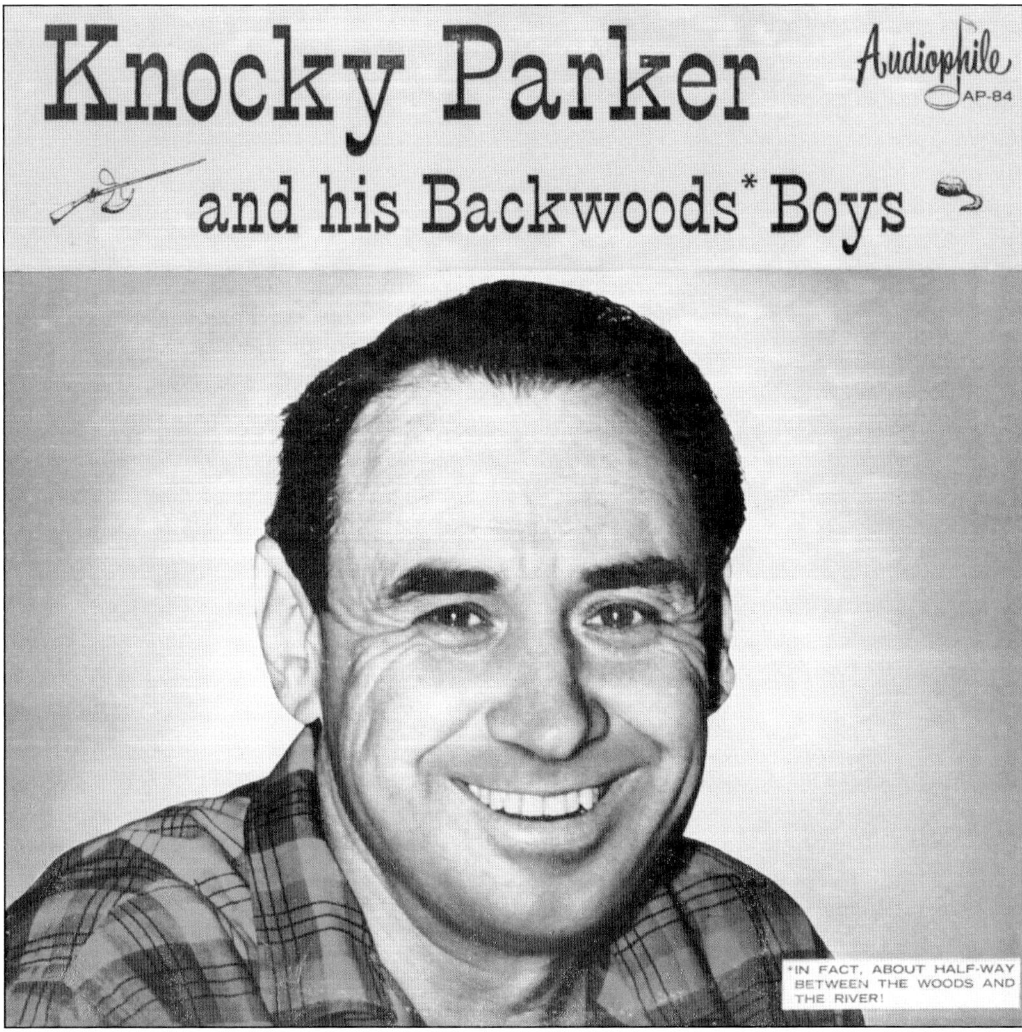


In the 1960s, pianist John W. "Knocky" Parker again teamed up with banjo player Marvin "Smokey" Montgomery, with whom he had played in the Light Crust Doughboys, to make this album. Personnel also included harmonica player Delbert McClinton, who became a popular rhythm-and-blues artist. It was fitting that the album featured a version of "Deep Elm Blues." As a child, Parker learned from African American barrelhouse pianists in Deep Ellum. "They were my first teachers," he said later, calling them "terrific musicians, really. . . . They saw that I liked them, and there was never any feeling of black and white at all." After his Western swing days, Parker became a professor of English but continued to play music and recorded the complete works of ragtime composer Scott Joplin. (Courtesy of Jay Brakefield.)

The material on Parker's album leans toward blues, reflecting the heavy African American influence on Western swing. Smokey Montgomery said that, when he met Knocky Parker in the mid-1930s, "He liked the blues. . . . Knocky played things like 'Honky Tonk Train,' which is on the blues, and all those things the black piano players were doing. Knocky could play them just as good as they could, and we played them on the air. We recorded them." Though Texas was rigidly segregated, blacks and whites listened to each other's music, and black and white musicians found ways to play together in settings such as late-night jam sessions at Fort Worth's black Jim Hotel. Pianist Fred "Papa" Calhoun recalled a gig in Whitney, Texas, when hundreds of blacks gathered outside. "They couldn't come in, but they had to listen," he said. (Both, courtesy of Jay Brakefield.)

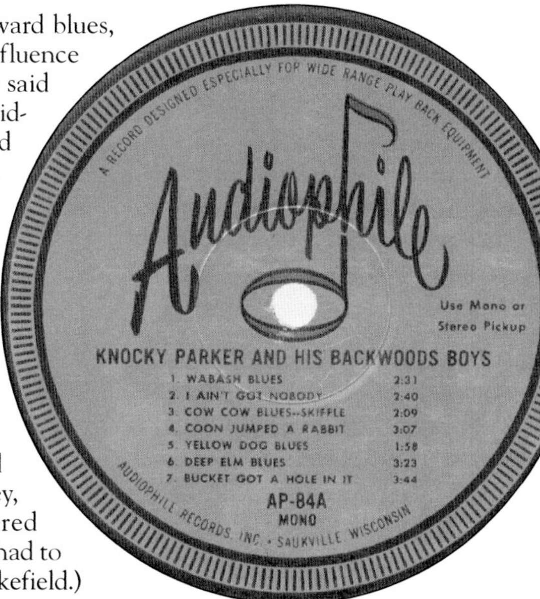


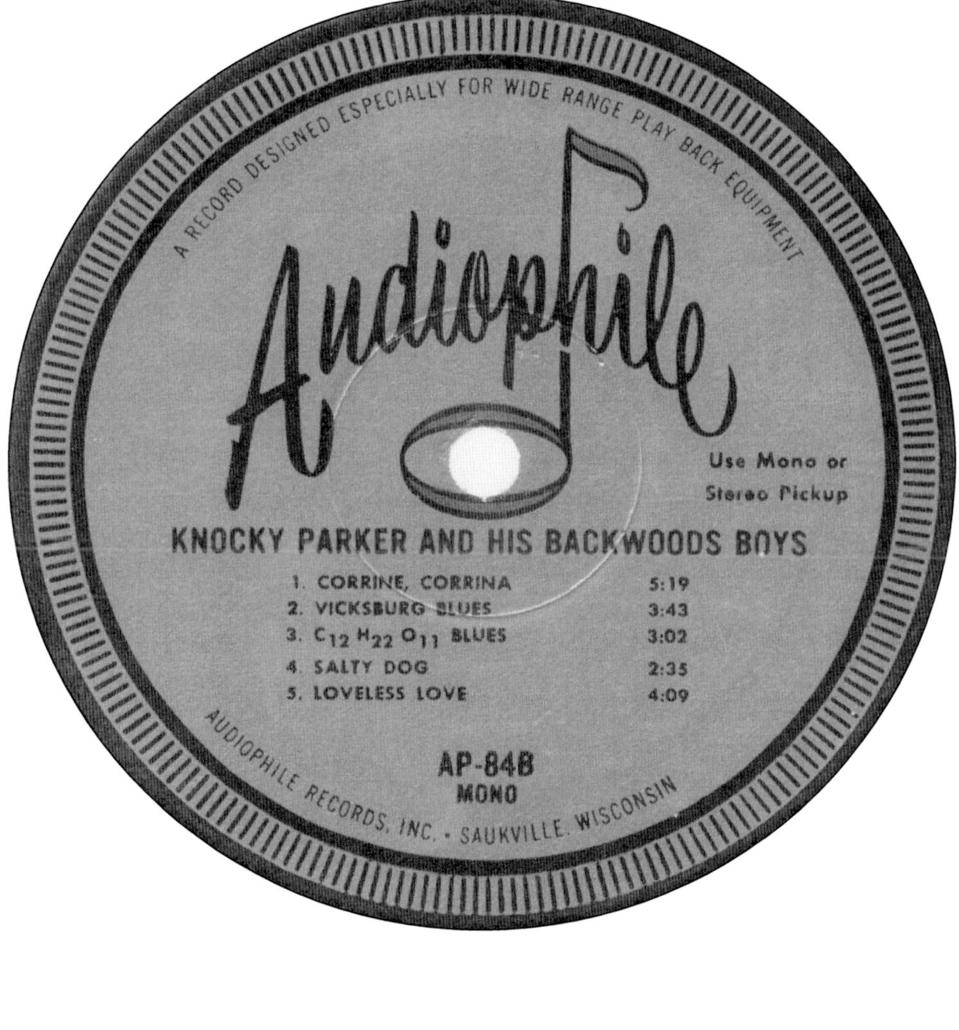

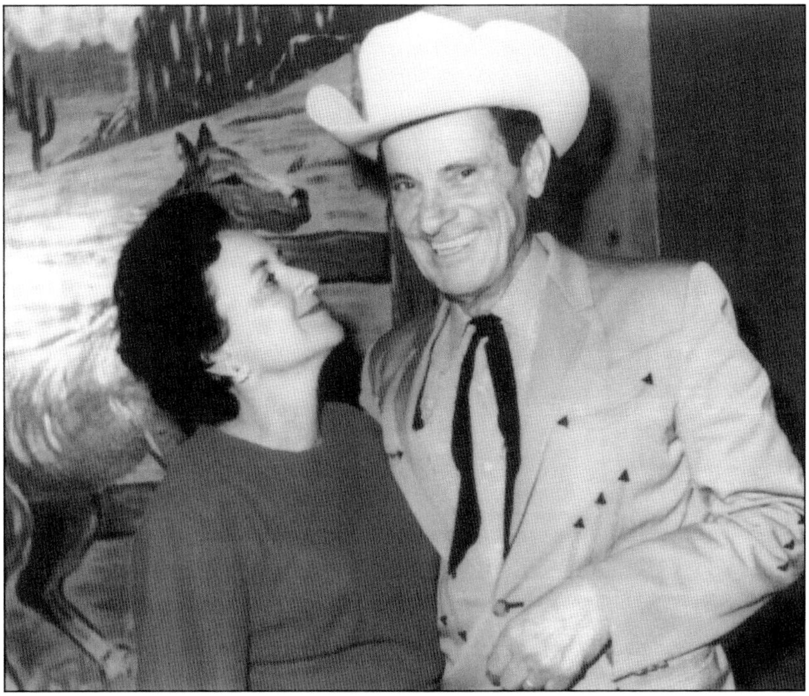

Ernest Tubb smiles with Mary Hallett, evidently a fan, in the 1960s. Tubb was a popular, accessible figure who was a fixture on the *Grand Ole Opry* for decades. He hosted the *Midnight Jamboree* radio program at the record store he owned just a few blocks from the Ryman Auditorium, the home of the *Opry* until 1974. (Courtesy of David Dennard.)

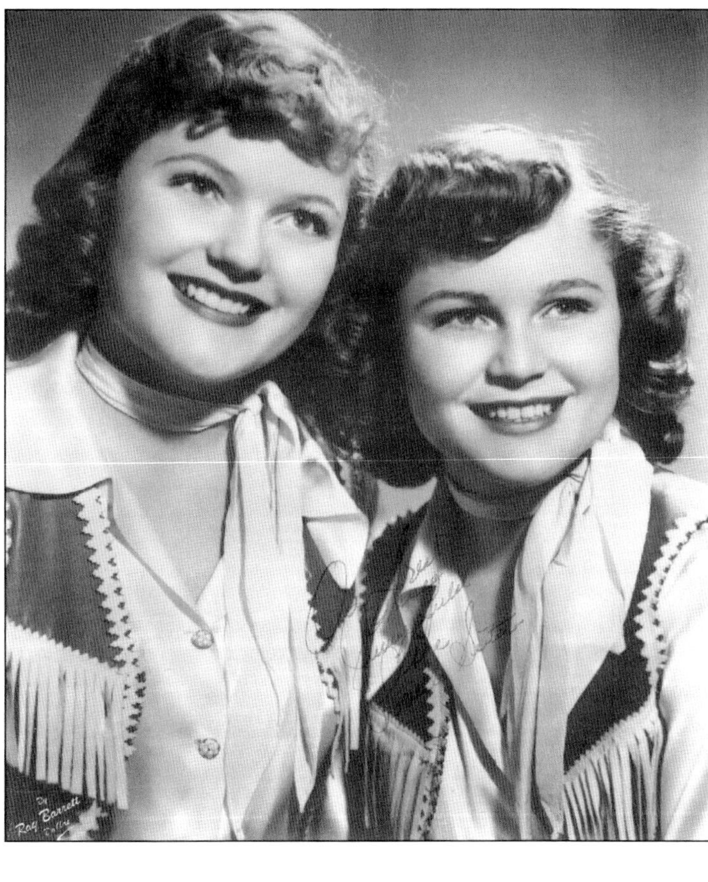

The Lovett Sisters, Charlotte and Colleen, began performing with their father's band as children. They were still in their teens when they sang on WFAA's *Saturday Night Shindig* and then on the *Big "D" Jamboree*. They performed on a Chicago radio show before embarking on solo careers. The sisters reunited as a duo in 2003. (Courtesy of David Dennard.)

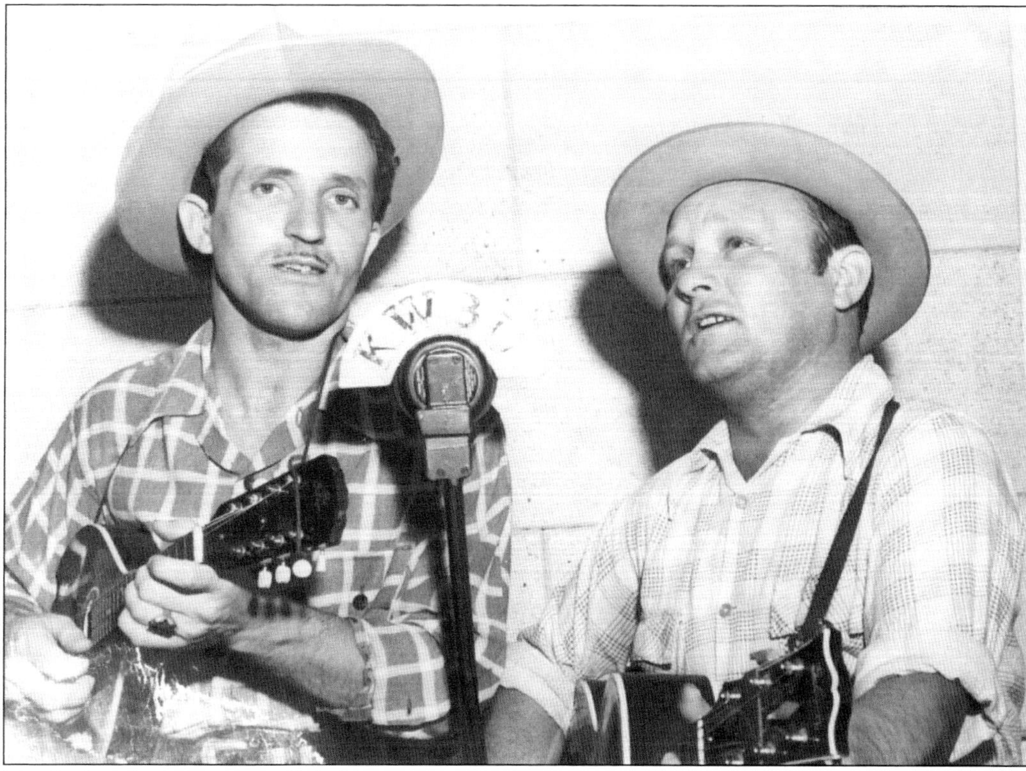

North Carolina natives Bill (left) and Joe Callahan made their first records in 1934 in New York City. Bill Callahan said in an interview late in his life that New Yorkers sometimes bought them food just to hear their unfamiliar Southern accents. The Callahans' repertoire ranged from sentimental country songs to blues. (Courtesy of David Dennard.)

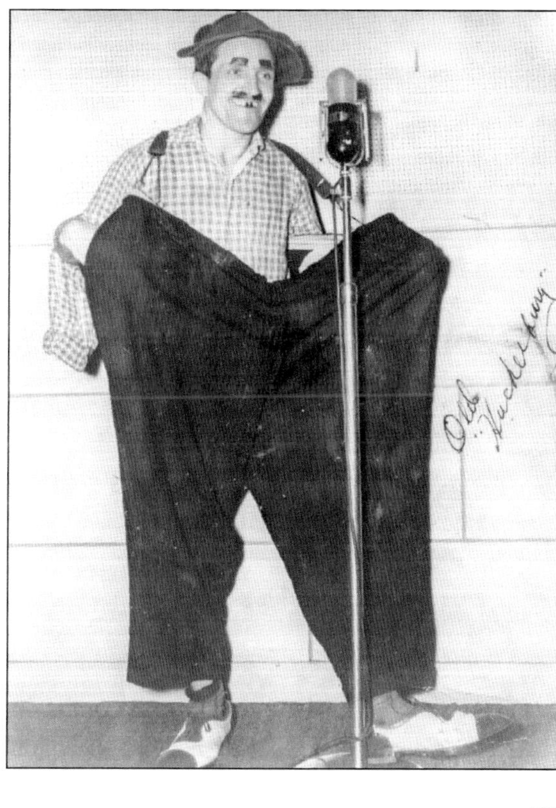

Bill Callahan was a ham who could wring laughs from the corniest material and would tell a joke at the drop of a hat. Years after he had retired from performing, he would launch into his act in almost any situation, even entertaining fellow patients in a doctor's waiting room. (Courtesy of David Dennard.)

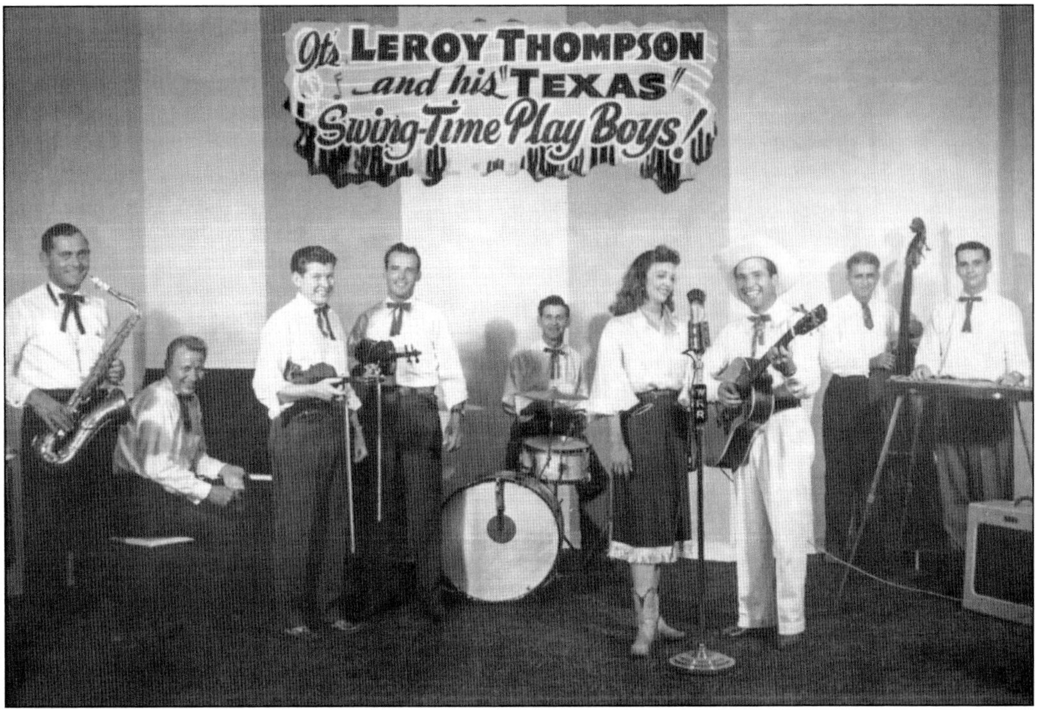


Country and Western swing performer Leroy Thompson (third from right, with hat and guitar) appeared on a November 13, 1954, show that also featured Gene O'Quin, Gabe Tucker, Buck Griffin, and Ted Rains. Elvis Presley's "That's All Right" had been released only four months before, and the *Jamboree* would soon have an identity crisis as it struggled to include the new rockabilly and rock 'n' roll music while hanging on to its more traditional audience. (Courtesy of David Dennard.)

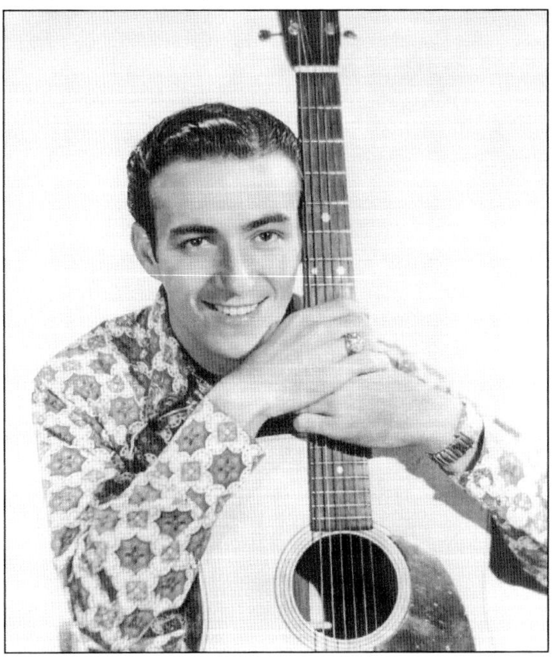

Faron Young was among *Grand Ole Opry* stars who appeared on the *Jamboree*. He performed a number of times between 1952 and 1966, the year the show closed. Young was among the first to record songs by Willie Nelson, and his version of the Texan's "Hello Walls" went to No. 1 on the country charts and broke into the top 20 on the pop charts in 1961. (Courtesy of David Dennard.)

*Big "D" Jamboree* emcee and producer Johnny Hicks made a number of records for Columbia in the early-to-middle 1950s. "The Sweetheart Waltz" was written with Smokey Montgomery, who led the *Jamboree* house band, called at various times the Country Gentlemen and the Texas Stompers. The band was essentially the Light Crust Doughboys, sometimes augmented by other musicians. Hicks was among a number of disc jockeys signed by Columbia with the expectation that this would ensure airplay for other artists. Hicks also sang on the *Jamboree*, but after his Columbia contract expired in 1955, he focused increasingly on songwriting and producing the weekly show at the Sportatorium. (Both, courtesy of Jay Brakefield.)

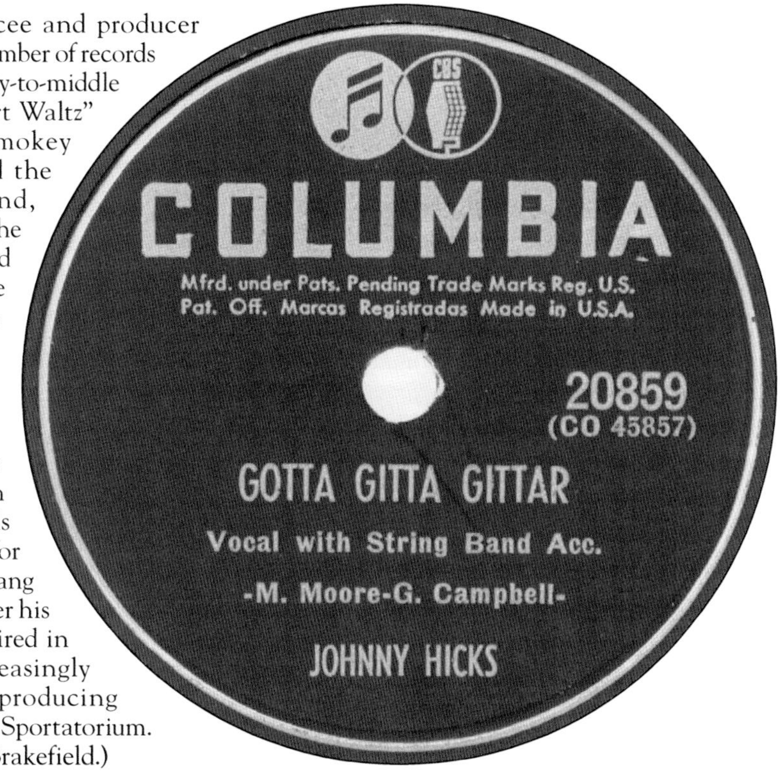


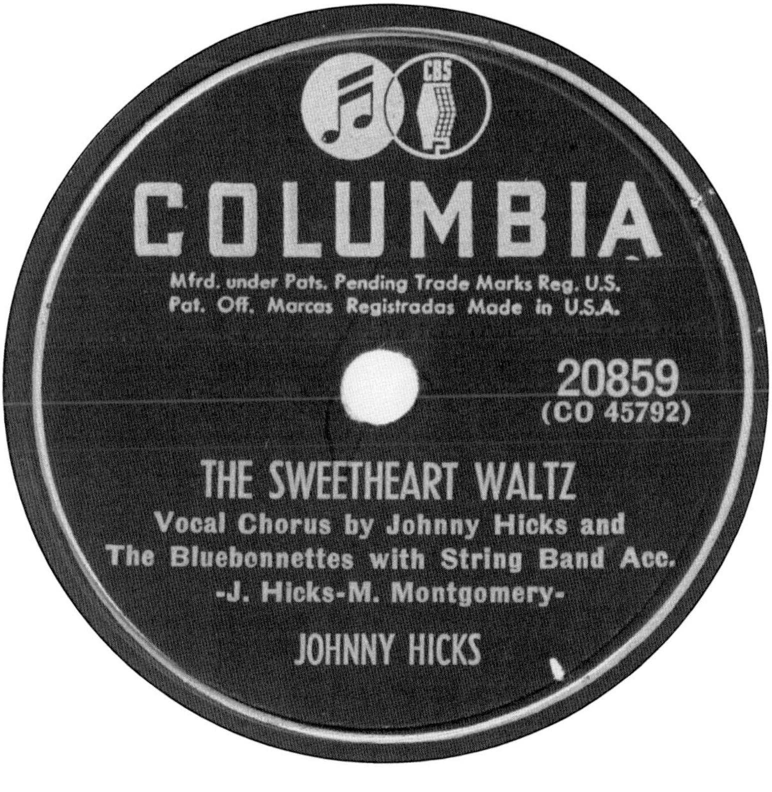

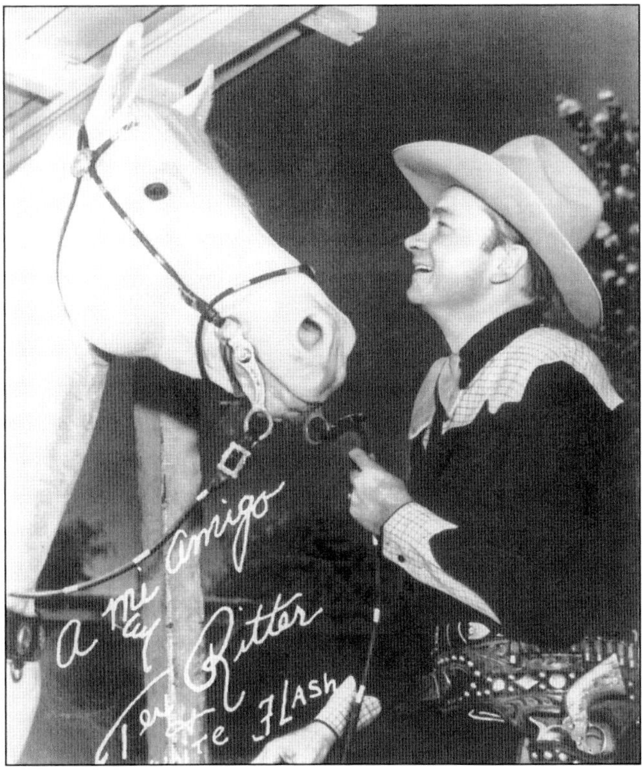

Cowboy singer and movie actor Tex Ritter appeared a number of times on the *Jamboree* and often brought along his horse, White Flash, when he performed. Bill Callahan recalled an occasion when the horse relieved himself onstage. The proceedings were halted for some time while the audience was convulsed with laughter. (Courtesy of David Dennard.)

Guitarist Chuck Jennings backs up an unidentified vocalist in the mid-to-late 1960s. Jennings was a formidable lead guitarist, singer, and songwriter. He remained active in music after the *Jamboree* folded, playing *Grand Ole Opry* package shows and working for a number of years with singer Boxcar Willie. (Courtesy of David Dennard.)

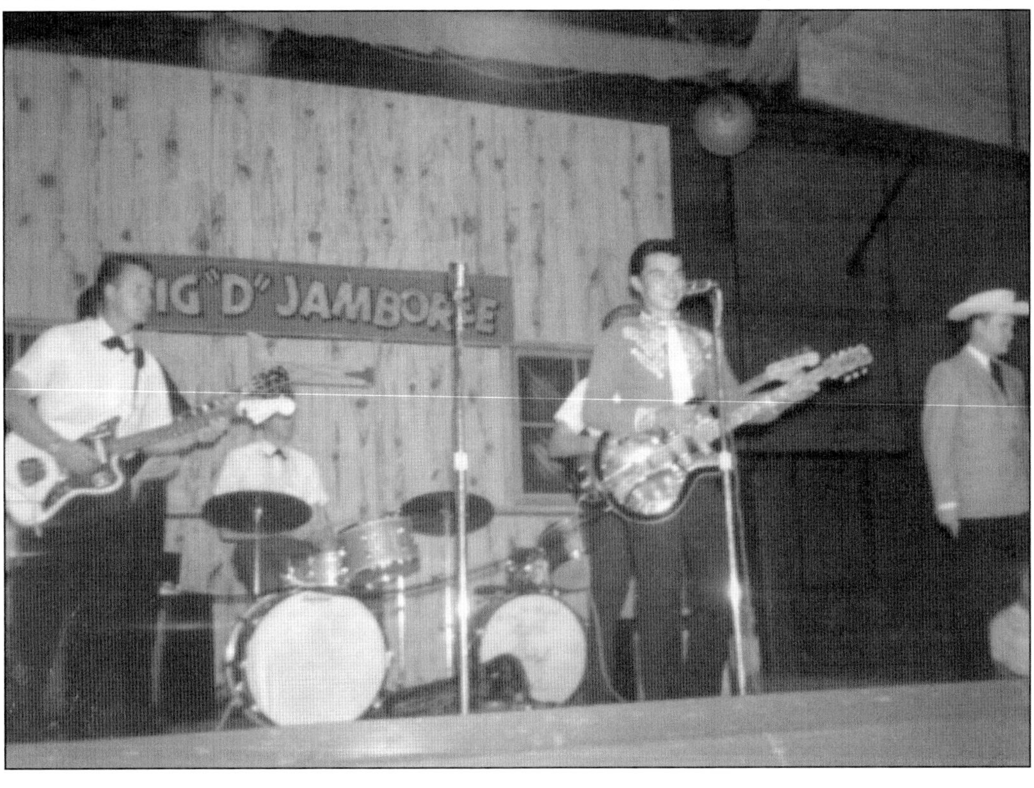

Ferlin Husky and Jean Shepard made a *Big "D"* appearance in September 1953 after their duet "A Dear John Letter" became a hit on both the country and pop charts. Both had illustrious careers and became members of the *Grand Ole Opry*. Husky died in 2011, at age 85. In 2013, Shepard was still performing at 79. (Courtesy of David Dennard.)

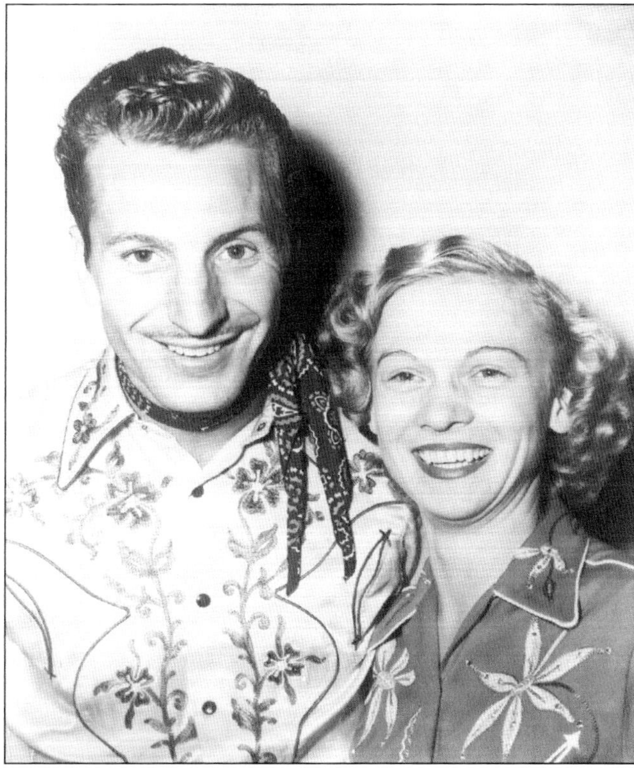

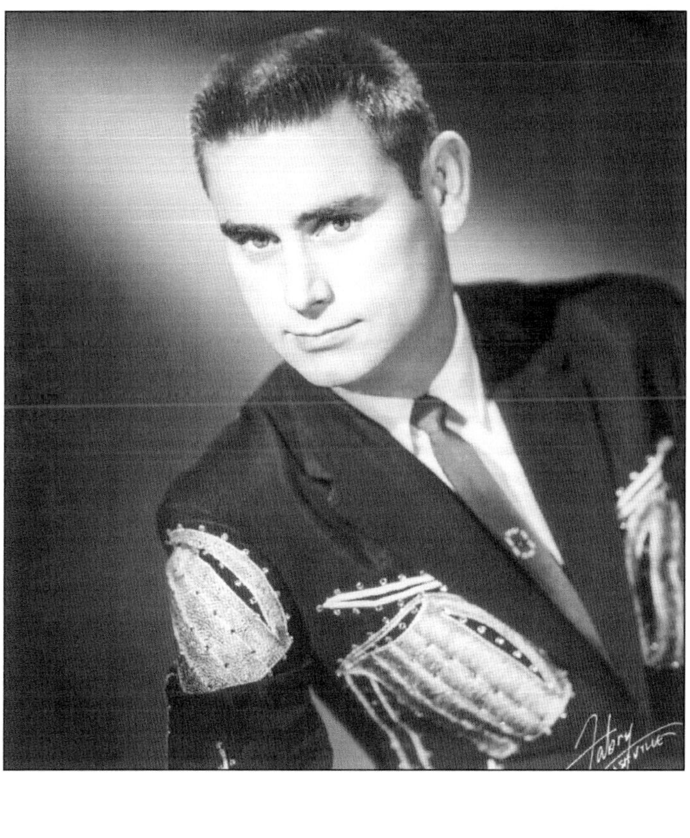

Singer George Jones, shown in the 1960s, performed regularly on the *Jamboree* for a decade, through its last year, 1966. He eventually overcame the propensity for drinking heavily and missing shows that threatened to eclipse his musical brilliance. After he died in April 2013, at age 81, his funeral drew, along with country music celebrities, Kid Rock, former first lady Laura Bush, CBS newsman Bob Schieffer, and Tennessee governor Bill Haslam. (Courtesy of David Dennard.)

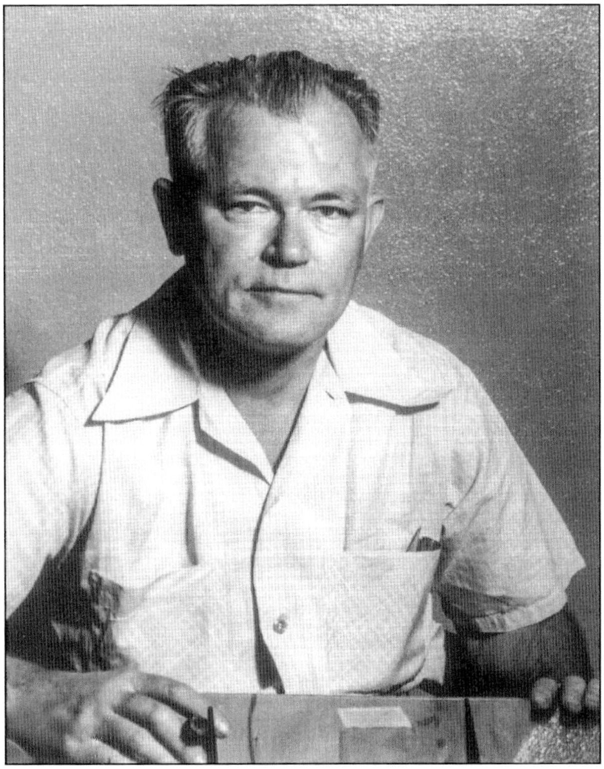

Harold W. "Pappy" Daily was a Houston record producer, music publisher, and promoter who recorded a number of *Big "D"* performers, including George Jones, Roger Miller, Frankie Miller, and Willie Nelson, on the Starday and D labels. Daily leased his hot D releases to Mercury Records for national distribution. His biggest hit was "Chantilly Lace" by the Big Bopper (J.P. Richardson) in 1958. Daily, aged 85, died in 1987. (Courtesy of David Dennard.)

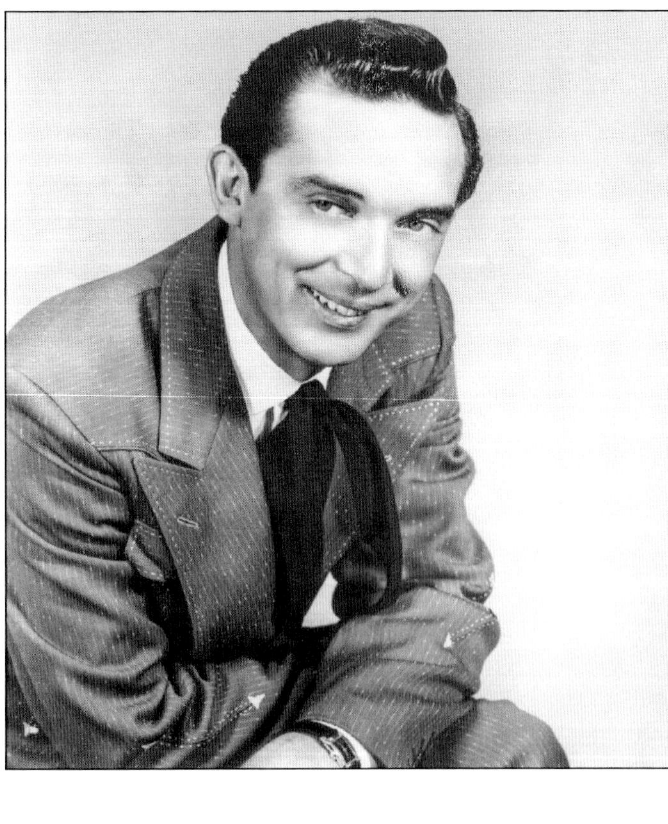

Ray Price was another national country star who made regular appearances on the *Jamboree*. Early in his career, Price recorded at Jim Beck's Dallas studio. Price once roomed with Hank Williams and emulated Williams's style, but he developed his own distinctive, smoother sound. He was inducted into the Country Music Hall of Fame in 1996 and continued to tour in his late 80s despite battling cancer. He died in December 2013. (Courtesy of David Dennard.)

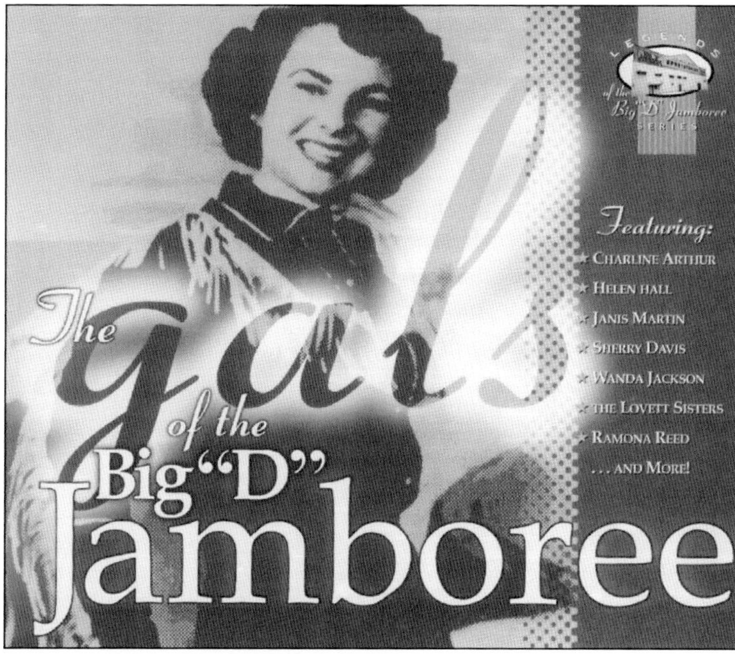


*The Gals of the Big "D" Jamboree*, released in 2001 on David Dennard's Dragon Street label, featured recordings by Helen Hall, Charline Arthur, the Lovett Sisters, Abbie Neal and Her Ranch Girls, Janis Martin, Pat Smith, Doreen Freeman, and Sherry Davis. (Courtesy of David Dennard.)

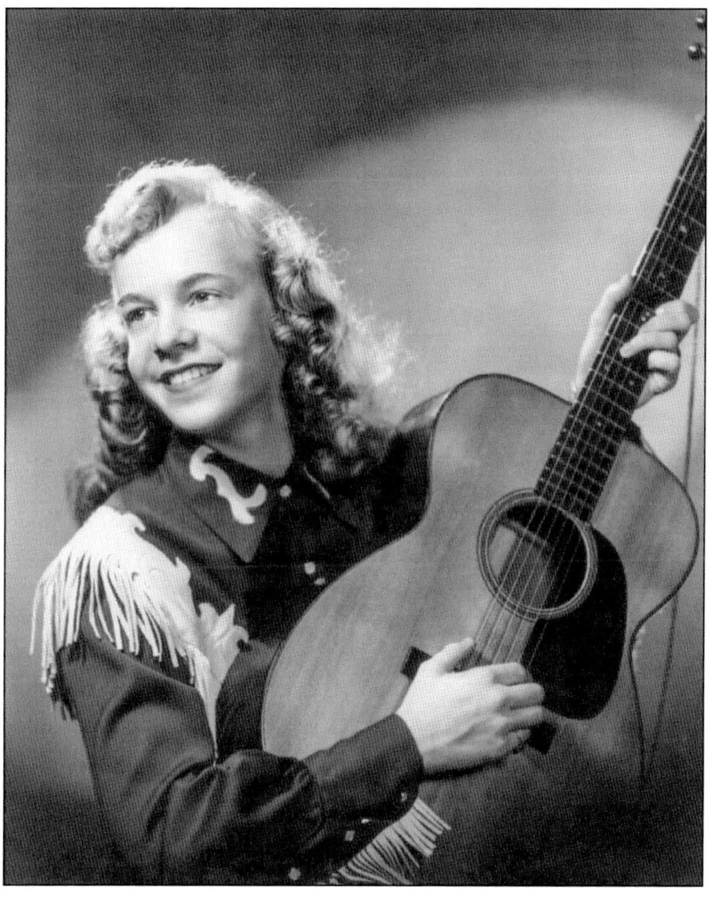

Janis Martin, among those featured on the *Gals* CD, was a country and rockabilly performer called the "female Elvis." She sang on Texas rocker Rosie Flores's 1995 CD *Rockabilly Filly*, and the two became friends. In 2007, just months before her death at 77, Martin made her final recordings. Due to Flores's unremitting fundraising efforts, these were released in 2012 as *The Blanco Sessions* on the Cow Island label. (Courtesy of David Dennard.)

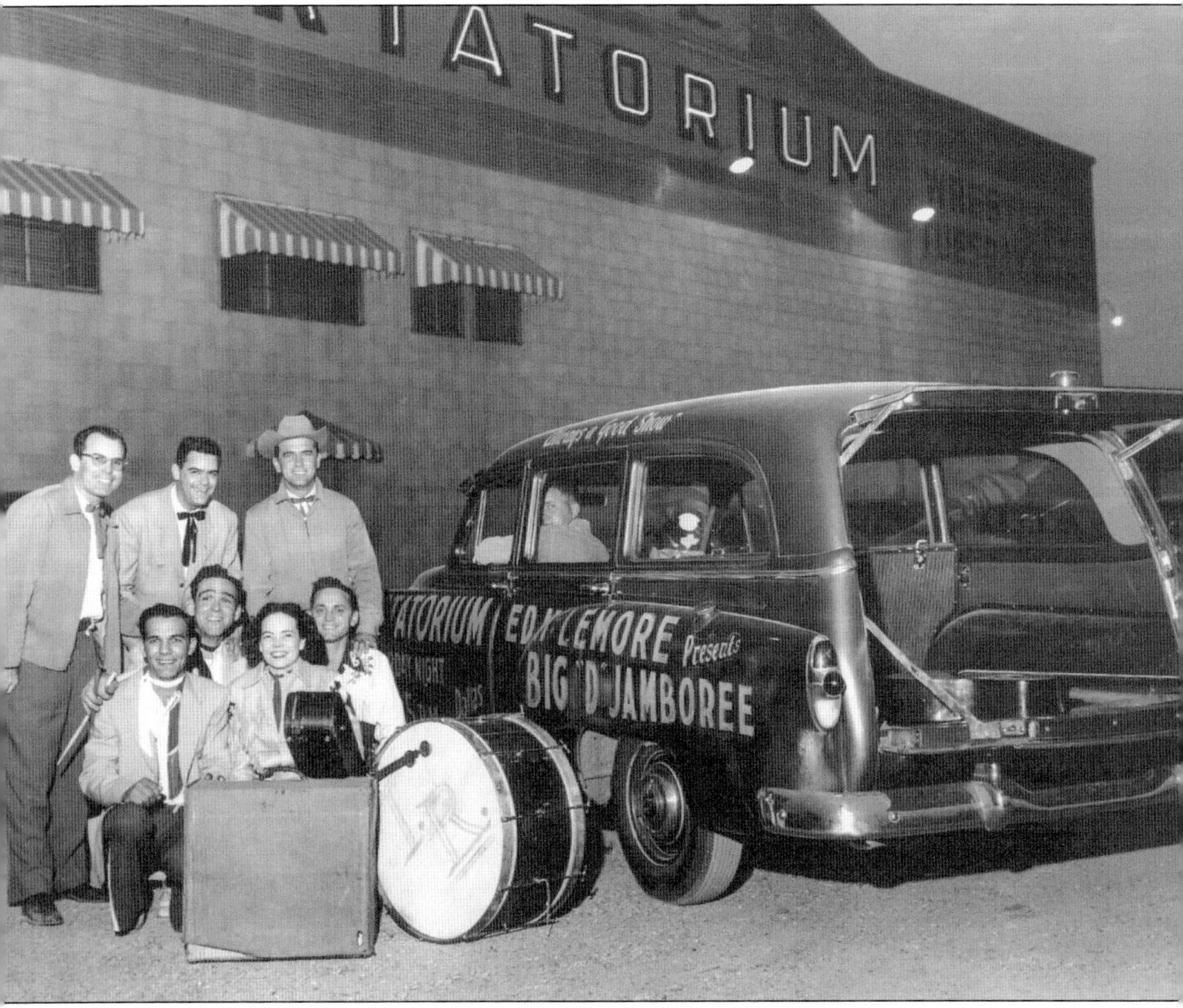


A 1955 photograph depicts participants in a *Jamboree* road show. Shown here are, from left to right, (kneeling) performers Douglas Bragg, Tex Raye, Charline Arthur, and Joe Bill; (standing) musical director Marvin "Smokey" Montgomery and performers Carroll Hubbard and Paul Blunt. At the wheel is Ed Watt, a key part of the show who handled advertising, booking, and promotion. (Courtesy of David Dennard.)

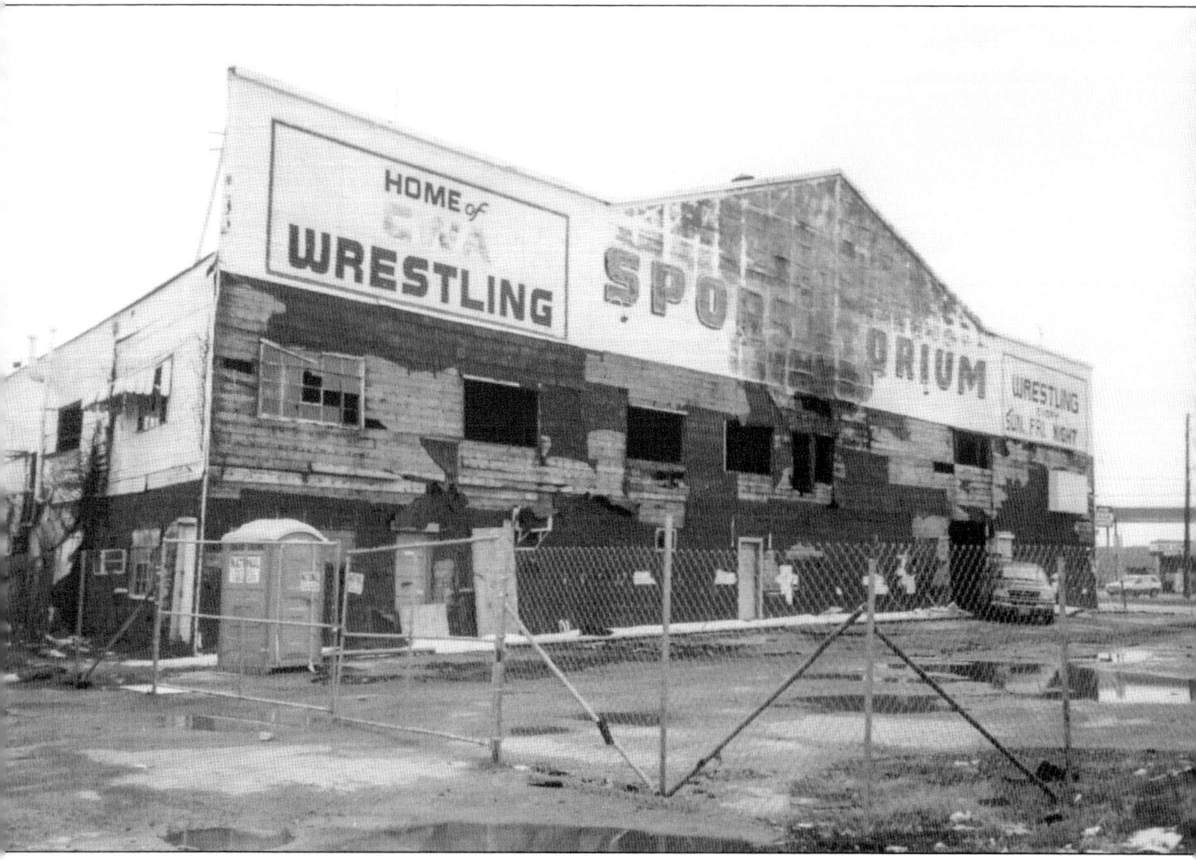


Despite efforts to save it, the Sportatorium's time had passed, and it was razed in 2003, long after its heyday as a venue for wrestling and music. The demise of the 50-year-old building marked the end of an era in Dallas. A decade later, the site still stood vacant in spite of extensive redevelopment of the south side of downtown Dallas. (Courtesy of David Dennard.)